T0301546

Developing Boundaries Knowledge for Innovation

Developing Boundaries Knowledge for Innovation

Edited by

Mitsuru Kodama

Professor of Innovation and Technology Management, College of Commerce and Graduate School of Business Administration, Nihon University, Tokyo, Japan

Edward Elgar
PUBLISHING

Cheltenham, UK • Northampton, MA, USA

Cover image: Joshua Sortino on Unsplash.

Published by
Edward Elgar Publishing Limited
The Lypiatts
15 Lansdown Road
Cheltenham
Glos GL50 2JA
UK

Edward Elgar Publishing, Inc.
William Pratt House
9 Dewey Court
Northampton
Massachusetts 01060
USA

A catalogue record for this book
is available from the British Library

Library of Congress Control Number: 2020942940

This book is available electronically in the **Elgar**online
Business subject collection
http://dx.doi.org/10.4337/9781789901931

ISBN 978 1 78990 192 4 (cased)
ISBN 978 1 78990 193 1 (eBook)

Printed and bound by CPI Group (UK) Ltd, Croydon, CR0 4YY

Contents

Figures

Tables

Boxes

Contributors

Masashi Kimura is a Dean and Professor of Art Design, Faculty of Arts at Nihon University. After graduating from Nihon University College of Art, he completed graduation school at Washington State University and then worked as an illustrator at National Geographic Society on an annual contract. In 1985, he studied scientific illustration with illustrator George L. Venable and the entomologist Dr. Terry Erwin at the Smithsonian National Museum of Natural History. After returning to Japan, he was greatly influenced by his meeting with entomologists Dr. Ryosuke Ishikawa and Dr. Kiyohiko Ikeda. Kimura also studied the interest and potential of science communications with underwater archaeologist Professor Torao Mozai, and became fascinated with communications design with Japanese scientists. In 1997 he encountered the impact of Mr. Claude Kuhn, Art Director of the Bern Natural History Museum of Switzerland, and in 2001 studied under Dr. George McGavin of the Oxford University Natural History Museum in the UK, resulting in an even deeper interest in entomology and science communication. Currently, he is researching the potentials of science design from the visualization of science communications, and has a great passion for the linkages of science and design in many industry–government–academia collaborations. Kimura has published a wide range of academic works and books on fields such as scientific illustration, communications and science design, both in Japan and internationally.

Mitsuru Kodama is Professor of Innovation and Technology Management in the College of Commerce at Nihon University. He has been in his current position since April 2003 after 21 years of business experience in the information and communications field (NTT, NTT East, NTT DOCOMO etc.). Kodama specializes in strategic management and innovation, and ICT strategies. His research has been published in international scholarly journals such as *Long Range Planning, Organization Studies, Journal of Management Studies, Systems Research and Behavioral Science, Technovation* and *Information Systems Management*, among others. He also has published 17 books in English such as *Developing Holistic Strategic Management in the Advanced ICT Era* (World Scientific Publishing Europe, 2019), Collaborative Dynamic Capabilities for Service Innovation (Palgrave Macmillan, 2018), *Sustainable Growth Through Strategic Innovation: Driving Congruence in Capabilities* (Edward Elgar, 2018), *Ma Theory and the Creative Management of Innovation* (Palgrave Macmillan, 2017), *Developing Holistic Leadership: A Source of Business Innovation* (Emerald Publishing Limited, 2017), *Collaborative Innovation: Developing Health Support Ecosystems* (Routledge, 2015), *Competing through ICT Capability* (Palgrave Macmillan, 2012), *Knowledge Integration Dynamics* (World Scientific, 2011), *Boundary Management* (Springer, 2009) and *Knowledge Innovation* (Edward Elgar, 2007), among others.

Yuji Mizukami is Professor of Nihon University College of Industrial Engineering as an incumbent from 2014. He worked at Philips Japan Ltd. and Bose International K.K., specializing in the areas of Education, Business Engineering and Statistical Science. At present he is working as an Executive Director/Editor-in-chief of Japan Management Systems Association and System Researcher of Japan Aerospace Exploration Agency (JAXA).

Takashi Oka is Vice Dean and Professor of Social Psychology in Department of Psychology, College of Humanities and Sciences at Nihon University. His research has been published in international journals such as *International Journal of Psychology*, *Journal of Cross-cultural Psychology*, *Progress in Asian Social Psychology* and also in books such as *Computers in Human Behavior* (Elsevier), *Food Quality and Preference* (Elsevier) and *Psychology of Stereotypes* (Nova), among others. He also has published several books in Japanese.

Yoshiki Takano is Associate Dean and Professor of Material Engineering in Department of Physics, College of Science and Technology at Nihon University. His research has been published in international journals such as *Physical Review B*, *Journal of Applied Physics* and *Solid State Communications*, among others. He also has published several books in Japanese.

Nobuyuki Tokoro is Professor of Environmental Management at the College of Commerce and the Graduate School of Business Administration at Nihon University. His research has been published in international journals such as *Asian Business and Management*, among others. He also has published several books in English (Springer, Palgrave Macmillan, Routledge).

Mana Yamamoto is Assistant Professor of Social Psychology in the College of Commerce at Nihon University. Her research has been published in *Japanese Journal of Psychology* and *Japanese Journal of Social Psychology*, among others.

Takehiko Yasuda is Professor of Industrial Policy and Strategy in the College of Commerce at Nihon University. He is the Former Vice President of Japan Academy for Consumption Economy (JACE) and an editor of *Economy of Consumption Research*. He is also a Director of Japan Economic Policy Association (JEPA). His research focuses on Service Innovation and Creative Cluster Policy in Asia. He has published several books and more than thirty academic articles.

Acknowledgments

This book could not have been brought to fruition without the exhaustive and robust interaction of the authors with many practitioners (innovators or creators). The authors would like to extend their gratitude to these practitioners that are of a number too great to name here. We would also like to express our gratitude for the support of Nihon University's College of Commerce and for the Nihon University Multidisciplinary Research Grant (2018–2019) which we received to undertake research for this book.

I am also deeply grateful for the valuable comments offered by the two reviewers of the proposal for this book. Concerning the publication of this book, I wish to extend my appreciation to Ms. Francine O'Sullivan, publisher for the business and management list at Edward Elgar, who provided tremendous support.

Mitsuru Kodama

Preface and introduction

Viewed in the context of business and management, creativity is the ability to bring about ideas and knowledge that have specific impacts on corporate activities not only to upgrade and improve products, but also to realize new product developments and build new business processes and business models, etc. (e.g., Amabile, 1983). The creativity of people and groups is an important research theme for generating ideas for new products and businesses, and attempts at exploration and exploitation of it have advanced around the world both in academic research (social psychology, I/O psychology, cognitive psychology, business administration, science and technology, education, linguistics, arts and social engineering, etc.) and practical application fields (creativity engineering, design engineering, etc.). To date, this is a theme for which much literature (from academic research through to practical documentation) has accumulated.

It has long been identified in academic research that creativity is difficult to clearly define because it entails complex concepts that combine various intellectual abilities (Sternberg and Lubart, 1996). What can be agreed upon to some extent in psychological research is a definition of creativity as "the abilities to create new and useful things" (e.g., Sternberg and Lubart, 1999; Runco and Jaeger, 2012). As abilities, creativity includes not only the ability to bring about more good ideas, but also the generational ability to achieve products and services from such ideas. Much research on creativity at the personal, team and organizational levels has also been accumulated in I/O psychology (e.g., Mumford et al., 2012; Reiter-Palmon et al., 1997; Reiter-Palmon, 2018a).

In business studies and psychology to date, the importance of "intrinsic motivation" has been identified as a factor in raising creativity (e.g., Amabile, 1988, 1995; Elsbach and Hargadon, 2006). It has been clearly identified that intrinsic motivation raises personal interests, curiosity and the desire to learn as well as knowledge flexibility and sustainability, and hence raises creativity (Ryan and Deci, 2000; Shalley et al., 2004). Amabile (1996) suggests that psychological effects come into play when novelty as ideas that have come about through intrinsic motivation shift to utility (usefulness) as the later subsequent stage. Crucially in this perspective, creativity is both "novelty" and "utility", and achieves new objects or events that broadly impact society (in other words innovation).

From existing research on creativity and innovation, the importance of not only intrinsic motivation of individuals (e.g., Frese et al., 1997; Mumford, 2012; Mumford and Hemlin, 2017) but also its expansion to the levels of teams and entire organizations has been identified (e.g., Hemlin et al., 2004; Kodama, 2007a, 2009b, 2014; Mumford, 2012; Sternberg, 1999; Tidd and Bessant, 2013). Generating creativity and innovation in organizations entails mutual linking of the organizational and personal levels. This results in many cases in which innovation processes occur in teams as projects (e.g., Kodama, 2007b; Reiter-Palmon, 2018b).

Also, from the perspective of knowledge creation theory (Nonaka and Takeuchi, 1995; Nonaka et al., 2014), creativity is also the capability to contribute to society by bringing about businesses with high ethical standards and new value by converging and converting the various knowledge and specializations of the human resources working in corporations, etc. Knowledge creation theory is not the same as organizational learning theory (e.g., Huber, 1991). In contrast to learning, creativity entails producing something that hasn't existed in the past, although it doesn't mean that something is born from nothing. Creativity also means creating new combinations of diverse knowledge such as that of existing objects or events. In terms of cognitive science, creativity is the process of newly linking existing and dissimilar knowledge networks, as opposed to learning, which is the process of enriching networks by incorporating new information into existing knowledge networks (Nonaka and Takeuchi, 1995; Kodama, 2009a, b, 2014).

Although both learning and creativity enrich knowledge networks, the processes to arrive at such an enriched state are not the same. Learning involves the provision from the outside of information that forms new relationships, whereas creativity spontaneously occurs at the personal or group level (in which the aforementioned intrinsic motivation is a factor). Thus, while learning comes from externalities such as teachers or teaching materials, creativity is rooted in spontaneous searching and new combinations for self-fulfillment by humans themselves. Although the triggers for creative processes come from the outside, the processes of discovery of solutions are spontaneous and generative. Knowledge creation theory emphasizes tacit knowledge that is both subjective and physical as an internal source of will and commitment (Nonaka and Takeuchi, 1995).

Such processes of forming new links between dissimilar networks have a significant relationship with creativity. In his insightful work "The Act of Creation" (Koestler, 1964), Arthur Koestler (a Hungarian-born thinker, writer and journalist) describes concepts about the creative process. Koestler devoted himself to clarifying human creativity, and provided significant knowledge on the subject. A representative example is the concept of "bisociation" (his coinage) central to Koestler's theory of creativity. Bisociation is the recognition of common conditions, theories or concepts in frameworks of two or more dissimilar recognitions (or pieces of knowledge) that have respective uniformities, and that have been stylized traditionally and historically as having no association with each other – conflicts between such dual or multiple frames of reference (matrices) are overcome, and dialectically fused and integrated in a new dimension. Koestler asserted that this bisociation was the essence of creativity.

In other words, creative ideas are born when two dissimilar concepts collide and two ideas that would at first glance seem unrelated are combined (converged and integrated). For example, this suggests the importance of thinking on two or more different straight lines or planes instead of thinking with existing (or path-dependent) methods of thinking with a single line or a two-dimensional plane. In practice, ideas rich in creativity have often emerged in cases in which previously unrelated ideas and things have been linked by independent methods.

For example, abilities such as the auditory ability in music, motor sense ability in dance, design ability in mechanical engineering or mathematical ability in physics dominate the activities of those different disciplines while using intellectual abilities from other fields at the same time (Robinson, 2017). Even in traditional psychology research, it has been reported that the more different the elements of new combinations, in other words the more dissimilar the concepts, the more creative the processes and their results (Mednick, 1962).

Koestler found that bisociation in the intellectual activities of humans and higher primates entails advanced intelligence functioning in a different dimension to the processes of ordinary object recognition and thinking with language, or the generally assumed (e.g., in experiments with mice) problem solving through trial and error. For example, this was demonstrated in experiments once conducted on a smart chimpanzee by Wolfgang Köhler, one of the founders of Gestalt psychology. Koestler (1981) further notes that such creative originality is ubiquitous not only in the minds of those with good humor, artists and scientists, but also in developmental processes in all kinds of evolution.

In recent years, the concept of bisociation has spread to human resource development in product development training and employee training in companies, etc. This book aims to pursue the theory and mechanism of creativity development and knowledge convergence (Kodama, 2014) with a view to nurturing creative human resources that will bring about innovation and hence greatly contribute to society in all fields and industries.

This book presents two concepts related to Koestler's bisociation concept, as a method of thinking to bring about innovative ideas. One is the concept of "boundaries vision", which entails the idea that as boundary vision increases, the ability to "see what cannot be seen" arises and results in innovative capability. The other concept is that of "boundaries knowledge (knowing)". This entails the idea that new value, products and services can be brought about by combining dissimilar objects and events through the creation of boundaries knowledge. This book shows that the concepts that express the concept of "bisociation" are those of boundaries vision and boundaries knowledge.

For example, there is a mobile phone (e.g., a smartphone) game to connect two different concepts that is now widely used worldwide. Twenty years ago, playing games on a mobile phone was unthinkable. iPhone's optical image stabilization function was introduced in Brian Merchant's "THE ONE DEVICE" (Merchant, 2017). This function was invented by Mitsuaki Oshima of the Japanese company Panasonic. This invention measures the rotational angle of the video camera with a vibrating gyroscope often used in car navigation systems to correct the image and eliminate camera shake. Oshima (2010) asserts that innovation is creating a new network that connects different ideas.

The book also discusses in detail case studies of new technologies, products and services that have been born through the convergence of the mobile phone with something else, for example the merging of cameras and mobile phones to produce the mobile phone with built-in camera (currently smartphones); devices which have greatly impacted on our leisure and daily living environments. Having become infused into our enjoyment of life, these can also be called groundbreaking innovations brought about by boundaries vision and boundaries knowledge (knowing).

The purpose of this book is to apply the concepts of boundaries vision and boundaries knowledge in the field of business and management both theoretically and practically. Specifically, while focusing on literature on strategy theory (in particular dynamic capabilities) and knowledge creation theory, the book presents a theoretical framework about how the concepts of boundaries vision and boundaries knowledge, which exist in the background of the concept of bisociation, can be applied to dynamic capabilities and knowledge creation. Then, the book observes and discusses the dynamic mechanisms of boundaries vision and boundaries knowledge through in-depth case studies.

REFERENCES

Amabile, T. M. (1983). Brilliant but cruel: Perceptions of negative evaluators. *Journal of Experimental Social Psychology*, *19*(2), 146–156.

Amabile, T. M. (1988). A model of creativity and innovation in organizations. *Research in Organizational Behavior*, *10*(1), 123–167.

Amabile, T. M. (1995). Attributions of creativity: What are the consequences? *Creativity Research Journal*, *8*(4), 423–426.

Amabile, T. M. (1996). *Creativity in Context: Update to the Social Psychology of Creativity*. Boulder, CO: Westview Press.

Elsbach, K. D., & Hargadon, A. B. (2006). Enhancing creativity through "mindless" work: A framework of workday design. *Organization Science*, *17*(4), 470–483.

Frese, M., Fay, D., Hilburger, T., Leng, K., & Tag, A. (1997). The concept of personal initiative: Operationalization, reliability and validity in two German samples. *Journal of Occupational and Organizational Psychology*, *70*, 139–161.

Hemlin, S., Allwood, C. M., & Martin, B. R. (Eds) (2004). *Creative Knowledge Environments:The Influences on Creativity in Research and Innovation*. Cheltenham, UK and Northampton, MA, USA: Edward Elgar Publishing.

Huber, G. P. (1991). Organizational learning: The contributing processes and the literatures. *Organization Science*, *2*(1), 88–115.

Kodama, M. (2007a). *The Strategic Community-Based Firm*. London, UK: Palgrave Macmillan.

Kodama, M. (2007b). *Knowledge Innovation: Strategic Management as Practice*. Cheltenham, UK and Northampton, MA, USA: Edward Elgar Publishing.

Kodama, M. (2009a). Boundaries innovation and knowledge integration in the Japanese firm. *Long Range Planning*, *42*(4), 463–494.

Kodama, M. (2009b). *Innovation Networks in Knowledge-Based Firms: Developing ICT-Based Integrative Competences*. Cheltenham, UK and Northampton, MA, USA: Edward Elgar Publishing.

Kodama, M. (2014). *Winning Through Boundaries Innovation: Communities of Boundaries Generate Convergence*. Oxford, UK: Peter Lang.

Koestler, A. (1964). *The Act of Creation*. New York: Penguin Books.

Koestler, A. (1981). The three domains of creativity. In *The Concept of Creativity in Science and Art* (pp. 1–17). Dordrecht: Springer.

Mednick, S. (1962). The associative basis of the creative process. *Psychological Review*, *69*(3), 220–232.

Merchant, S. (2017). The promise of creative/participatory mapping practices for sport and leisure research. *Leisure Studies*, *36*(2), 182–191.

Mumford, M. D. (Ed.) (2012). *Handbook of Organizational Creativity*. London: Academic Press.

Mumford, M. D., & Hemlin, S. (Eds) (2017). *Handbook of Research on Leadership and Creativity*. Cheltenham, UK and Northampton, MA, USA: Edward Elgar Publishing.

Mumford, M. D., Hester, K. S., & Robledo, I. C. (2012). Creativity in organizations: Importance and approaches. In *Handbook of Organizational Creativity* (pp. 3–16). London: Academic Press.

Nonaka, I., & Takeuchi, H. (1995). *The Knowledge-Creating Company*. New York, NY: Oxford University Press.

Nonaka, I., Kodama, M., Hirose, A., & Kohlbacher, F. (2014). Dynamic fractal organizations for promoting knowledge-based transformation: A new paradigm for organizational theory. *European Management Journal*, *32*(1), 137–146.

Oshima, M. (2010). *How to Bring Up Your Inspiration (in Japanese)*, Tokyo, Japan: Aki Shobou.

Reiter-Palmon, R. (2018a). Are the outcomes of creativity always positive? *Creativity: Theories–Research–Applications*, *5*(2), 177–181.

Reiter-Palmon, R. (Ed.) (2018b). *Team Creativity and Innovation*. New York, NY: Oxford University Press.

Reiter-Palmon, R., Mumford, M. D., O'Connor Boes, J., & Runco, M. A. (1997). Problem construction and creativity: The role of ability, cue consistency, and active processing. *Creativity Research Journal*, *10*(1), 9–23.

Robinson, J. (2017). *Economic Philosophy*. Abingdon: Routledge.

Runco, M. A., & Jaeger, G. J. (2012). The standard definition of creativity. *Creativity Research Journal, 24*(1), 92–96.

Ryan, R. M., & Deci, E. L. (2000). Intrinsic and extrinsic motivations: Classic definitions and new directions. *Contemporary Educational Psychology, 25*(1), 54–67.

Shalley, C. E., Zhou, J., & Oldham, G. R. (2004). The effects of personal and contextual characteristics on creativity: Where should we go from here? *Journal of Management, 30*(6), 933–958.

Sternberg, R. J. (Ed.) (1999). *Handbook of Creativity.* Cambridge, UK: Cambridge University Press.

Sternberg, R. J., & Lubart, T. I. (1996). Investing in creativity. *American Psychologist, 51*(7), 677–688.

Sternberg, R. J., & Lubart, T. I. (1999). The concept of creativity: Prospects and paradigms. In R. J. Sternberg (Ed.), *Handbook of Creativity*, (pp. 3–15). Cambridge, UK: Cambridge University Press.

Tidd, J., & Bessant, J. (2013). *Managing Innovation: Integrating Technological, Market and Organizational Change.* 5th ed. London: John Wiley & Sons.

1. Innovation through boundaries vision and dynamic capabilities: the strategic management perspective

Mitsuru Kodama

1. BACKGROUND AND OBJECTIVES OF THIS BOOK

It goes without saying that raising creativity across generations to contribute to wide-ranging social activities is important, not only for corporate organizations, but also in wider social organizations and individual people. In recent years in the business world, there has been heightened interest in new product and service developments brought about through "knowledge convergence" (or knowledge creation/knowledge integration) (Nonaka and Takeuchi, 1995; Kodama, 2011) that entails fusing dissimilar technologies and services as new product developments that differentiate from other companies or as novel business developments in different fields. This is because there are now many cases of never-before-seen and uniquely creative new products and services achieved through the merging of knowledge from one field with those of another (Kodama, 2007b).

For example, the necessity to develop business strategies to respond to convergence, such as that of differing technologies and services, or of product and service developments and new business model formation across dissimilar industries, is becoming more and more pronounced. There is also a strengthening of training and employment of personnel who think creatively at the corporate side. Against this backdrop, this book focuses on the thinking and actions of organizations and individuals for creative thinking and innovation, and is aimed at research on a theoretical framework for creating knowledge and developing creativity.

In business studies and psychology to date, the importance of "intrinsic motivation" has been identified as a factor in raising creativity (see Figure 1.1) (e.g., Elsbach and Hargadon, 2006). Intrinsic motivation raises personal interests, curiosity and the desire to learn as well as knowledge flexibility and sustainability, and further raises creativity (Ryan and Deci, 2000; Shalley et al., 2004). However, regarding thinking on creativity, intrinsic motivation has been reported in past empirical research as not necessarily raising creativity, depending on whether the focus is on novelty or utility (e.g., Amabile, 1996; George and Zhou, 2007). Conventional motivational information processing theory has the focus of intrinsic motivation on novelty, and not necessarily on utility.

Amabile (1996) asserts that psychological effects come into play in the shift from novelty born of ideas that have come about from intrinsic motivation to the subsequent stage – i.e., utility (usefulness). In this perspective, it is important that "creativity" includes both novelty and utility, and it should achieve new creations or events that impact broadly on society (in other words innovation). Centered on Amabile (e.g., 1988, 1995), there is an accumulation of academic research on creativity in the fields of psychology and business studies. However, much of this research presents only spot relationships regarding causality and relationships between factors, and does not fully clarify why such results occur, or the micro processes fundamental to the acquisition of creativity.

On the other hand, traditional organizational learning theory discusses development of individual and organizational capabilities and the related processes of practice (e.g., Cyert and March, 1963). However, learning is not the same as creativity. Creativity entails producing something that has not existed in the past, but does not mean something is created from nothing. Creativity is finding new combinations of existing knowledge and objects (e.g., Zhou and Shalley, 2007). Put in terms of cognitive science, as opposed to learning, which is the process of enriching networks by incorporating new information into existing knowledge networks, creativity is the process of forming new links between existing and dissimilar networks (e.g., Fauconnier and Turner, 1998). Although both learning and creativity enrich knowledge networks, the processes to arrive at that state are not the same. In other words, learning involves forming linkages with information from outside, while the spontaneous occurrence of information is creativity. Thus, learning comes from externalities such as teachers or teaching materials, while creativity requires spontaneously searching and newly combining knowledge for self-realization from within – opportunities come from the outside, but the discovery of solutions is a process that is spontaneous and generative.

There is hardly any existing creativity-based research on strategy in the field of strategic management. Currently, "sensing" (Teece, 2007), a sub-capability of the dynamic capabilities framework in focus in the field of strategy, is a crucial element consisting of capabilities required for scrutiny, creation, learning and interpretation, and investment of it in research and related activities is crucial. In particular, the capability to sense the emergence of threats or opportunities (sensing) is a fundamental factor of corporate responses to unstable markets, uncertain technologies and unpredictable competitors. Sensing requires constant alertness through scrutiny, investigation and searching by surveying latent customer needs, exploratory investments into related technologies and timely intelligence gathered from various parts of ecosystems.

Nevertheless, leading practitioners are even more aware of the fundamental importance of intuition (an aspect of creativity) in the sensing process, which results in their ability to react quickly to stimulation and recognize opportunities (Hodgkinson and Healey, 2011). While sensing is rooted in perception and attention capability, in contrast, perceptions and interpretations of unexpected new information are steered by previous knowledge (Helfat and Martin, 2015). However, not much has been clarified on the relationship between creativity and this kind of sensing. Also, although literature on organizational management presents a range of sensing processes, including March's (1981) distinction of exploration and exploitation through to the concept of the ambidextrous organization that balances creativity with efficiency, etc., not much detail has been clarified about the processes of bringing about creativity.

In addition, Nonaka and Takeuchi's (1995) knowledge creation theory focuses on subjective and corporeal tacit knowledge and Aristotle's "phronesis" as the sources of internal commitment. The fundamental differences of these are that the roots of learning theory lie in the behavioral theory of stimulation–reaction, whereas the roots of Nonaka's knowledge creation theory lie in the philosophies of ontology and epistemology. Organizational learning theory is how-to oriented, but is not based on any theoretical construction that searches for truth, goodness and beauty, such as human reasons for existence or self-realization as sources of knowledge. In comparing these two main theories (organizational learning and knowledge creation theories), organizational learning theory also advocates the concept of "double loop learning" in terms of supplementation of passive learning, although that process has so far not been clarified (e.g., Argyris, 2004).

On the other hand, Nonaka et al. propose knowledge creation processes through a triad structure of tacit knowledge, explicit knowledge and phronesis (Nonaka et al., 2014; Kodama, 2018c), but have not presented great detail on creative practical processes. Also, in traditional academic research on innovation management, the main focus is on industry policy and research and development (R&D) organizational management, but there is little perspective focusing on the micro creative processes of people and organizations.

While there is much research accumulated in the fields of business studies and psychology as described above, there has not been much clarification on the particular factors and practical processes that bring about creativity (novelty and utility) (see Figure 1.1). Against this academic backdrop, and with the aim of contributing to existing research, this book presents the new concept of "boundaries knowledge (knowing)" and "boundaries vision" in the thinking of individuals, which are both frameworks and processes to accelerate knowledge creation as dynamic creativity at the micro level.

This book will focus on the new concept of "knowledge differences" that arise between people, organizations, and various different objects and events, and names the new knowledge that comes about through the awareness, perception and discovery by people of such differences as "boundaries knowledge" (or "boundaries knowing"). In the past, this boundaries knowledge (knowing) has hardly been discussed (taken up) in the field of knowledge management or business management or in other academic fields (such as the social sciences or humanities). This book identifies that boundaries knowledge (knowing) through boundaries vision impacts on the creativity and innovation of people and organizations. In other words, the book shows that boundaries knowledge (knowing) brings about capabilities to achieve optimized solutions and processes for innovation activities entailed in the challenge of creating new knowledge taken up by people or organizations, or to find solutions to the problems and issues that they face.

2.   SYNERGIES BETWEEN CORPORATIONS AND EXTERNAL ENVIRONMENTS

In the view of strategic management as a dynamic process, corporate systems (capability factors in a company such as strategies, organizations, technologies, operations and leadership) must change dynamically to adapt to dynamically changing environments surrounding corporations (markets, technologies, competition and cooperation, structures) (Kodama, 2010a). The boarders or corporate boundaries between environments and corporate systems define the relationships with environments and company business models (Kodama, 2009b, 2018a, b). Changes in environments bring about changes in corporate boundaries and simultaneously affect individual elements of capabilities in corporate systems. Conversely, changes to

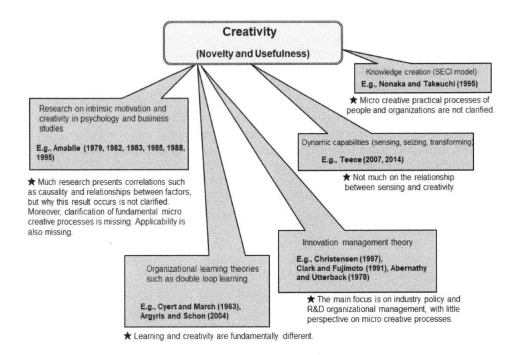

Figure 1.1   The creativity-themed field of existing research

the individual capabilities in corporate systems (either active or passive) bring about changes to the corporate boundaries of a company, and in turn also affect the environment.

Teece (2007) argues that the activities of coordination and resource allocation by managers form markets (environments, ecosystems) in the same way markets (environments, ecosystems) form corporations. In other words, companies and markets are in co-evolution relationships (see Figure 1.2). Thus, good asset orchestration by managers with technical fitness (DC, dynamic capabilities) enable a company to create favorable external environments, which as a result ties in with raising "evolutionary fitness" (Helfat et al., 2007).

Also, Teece (2007) states that in a multinational enterprise, one of the core functions of management is to develop and implement the company's unique strategies, which means they must "fit" assets, structures and processes globally (and their individual internal elements), and the company management team must also decide or uncover the technological opportunities and customer needs the company is facing while securing the resources and assets needed to execute strategy. Hence, the capabilities to proactively adapt, redeploy, and reconfigure in an entrepreneurial fashion gives meaning to "orchestration" and thus to "dynamic capabilities".

Interpreted differently, this could be a company establishing and executing an "environment adaption strategy" to adapt to environmental changes, or could mean a company establishing and executing an "environment creation strategy" to create new environments by acting dynamically on environments (ecosystems). Thus, practitioners in companies have to intentionally change business factors related to capabilities of strategy, organizations, technologies, operations and leadership in corporate systems to bring congruence to the boundaries between capabilities elements. This means that both the capabilities congruence between corporate systems and markets (ecosystems) (dynamic external congruence) [Insight-1] and capabilities congruence between capabilities in corporate systems (dynamic internal congruence (congruence between subsystems)) [Insight-2] are required (Kodama, 2018a, b). The function that achieves capabilities congruence both in and outside of companies is asset orchestration through dynamic capabilities (DC) (see Figure 1.2).

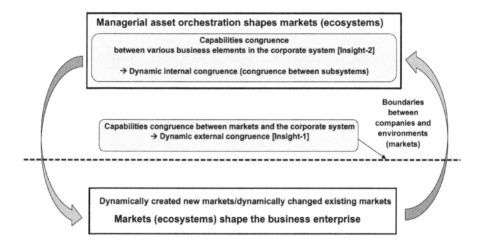

Figure 1.2   Capabilities congruence inside and outside of companies

Firstly, this chapter discusses elements of dynamic capabilities for capabilities congruence between corporate systems and markets (ecosystems) (dynamic external congruence) [Insight-1]. The three crucial elements of sensing, seizing and transforming required for successful organizational adaption are identified in the dynamic capabilities framework (Teece, 2007, 2014). Companies equipped with dynamic capabilities enact organizational transformation required to maintain superiority by sensing business opportunities ahead of the competition and utilizing them more effectively. Dynamic capabilities directed through a clear strategic vision enable companies to adapt to fluid and uncertain situations.

Day and Schoemaker (2016) deductively extracted the six sub-capabilities that comprise dynamic capabilities from existing theories on best practices. Figure 1.3 shows the comprehensive cluster relationship between sensing, seizing and transforming advocated by Teece (2007) and the six sub-capabilities. The chapter outlines the DC sub-capabilities of Day and Schoemaker (2016), and then presents the three new sub-capability elements proposed in this book.

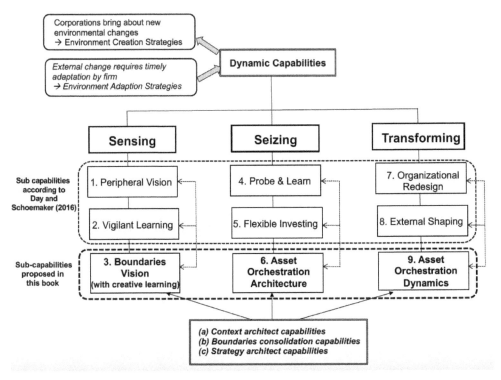

Figure 1.3   *The framework of this chapter in contrast to Teece (2007) and Day and*
                Schoemaker (2016)

3.   DC SUB-CAPABILITIES

3.1   Sensing in Fast-Changing Environments

According to research by Day and Schoemaker (2016), sensing leading to success can be
understood through two mutually related learning processes that function as DC. These two
processes are peripheral vision (sensing faint signals from business boundaries) (Day and
Schoemaker, 2005) and vigilant learning (correctly interpreting the meaning of the faint
signals that arise).

3.1.1   Peripheral vision
There are greater requirements on this sub-capability than analysis of the influence of trends
identifiable through the foresight activities often undertaken by companies. The purpose of
peripheral vision is to distinguish the early signs of latent opportunities or threats ahead of
the competition. Just like human vision, there is a fuzzy zone in the periphery away from the
focal point. In this area, it is difficult for companies to see and scrutinize peripheries due to
the adverse effects of the signal-to-noise ratio. Information overload, intelligence dispersal
and confusion are major impediments to improving peripheral vision. The two important steps

of setting a scope and scrutiny are required to overcome these difficulties and acquire strong peripheral vision.

3.1.2   Vigilant learning

The process of sensing changes in the external environment begins with scrutinizing faint signals. The second sub-capability of sensing requires exploratory and vigilant interpretation of signals. In this context, vigilance refers to a state of heightened awareness and curiosity, and is characterized by alertness, curiosity and proactive reactions to fragmented information. Rapid learning requires a strong market-oriented attitude, attention on people for filtering, suppression of biases, and a triangulated perspective on complex issues.

3.2   Seizing: Developing Opportunities

Once a company senses initial changes occurring in the environment and understands some of its profound implications, the next question is what to do with the new knowledge gained. Then, at the same time as action and commitment arrive on the scene, the very real risks of pursuing reckless strategies based on incomplete or biased information must be dealt with.

3.2.1   Probe-and-learn experimentation

Small, well-designed experiments to investigate new strategic initiatives enable continuous investment that is most likely to lead to positive results. For example, rapid prototyping with quasi-experimental designs can be very useful for complex design decision-making. Leading companies raise the level of these practices to DC implementable across many fields.

In trial and error learning, leaders need to actively nurture and support cultures that tolerate, and in some cases encourage, failure. Although failure due to carelessness or neglect should be avoided, no organization can learn by pursuing a policy of zero tolerance for failure. It is important to allow and learn from failure and to develop a culture in which experimentation is the norm.

3.2.2   Deploying real options

Trying out different approaches, exploring incomprehensible challenges in detail, and staying alert to unexpected situations are all great ways to learn quickly. Companies devise a range of real options to respond to various degrees of technology and market uncertainty. Crucially, successful companies need to develop a portfolio of different options (for protection and conservation, procurement and exploration) because the objectives are different for each type of option.

3.3   Transforming: Internal and External

Although sensing and seizing create business opportunities for a company, for a company to properly implement a new strategy, it must be able to steer the external environment as well as have the ability to form environments in addition to the ability to adjust its internal organizational design. A transformative organization is an organization that actively nurtures agile and entrepreneurial thinking and has a broad approach to building networks outside of itself.

3.3.1 Organizational redesign

New strategic initiatives may or may not succeed depending on how organizations are separated. The degree of their independence required in each case depends on the magnitude of the technology discontinuity, the speed of change and whether the value of the competencies in core businesses is reviewed with new strategies.

3.3.2 External shaping

Transformative power includes not only internal redesign, but also renegotiation with the environment to form a corporate ecosystem, which can be done through joint lobbying, development of new industry standards, and redevelopment of corporate business ecologies. Business ecology redevelopment can result in particularly powerful changes because it relies extensively on external networks.

The corporate ecosystem can act as a strategic radar system, and using these networks at multiple touchpoints can catch faint signals and speed up the sensing process.

3.4 The New DC Sub-Capabilities Proposed in This Book

In contrast to the six DC sub-capabilities of Day and Schoemaker (2016) outlined above, this book presents the elements of "boundaries vision", a new peripheral vision, "asset orchestration dynamics" and "asset orchestration architecture" as further sub-capabilities.

3.4.1 Boundaries vision

(a)   Knowledge boundaries

In the knowledge economy, diverse human knowledge (of which technology is one element) is the source of valuable products, services and business models that can give a company new competitiveness. New value chains are formed as new strategic models by converging diverse technologies and different industries to bring about new products, services and business models that transcend various boundaries (Kodama, 2014). Accordingly, for companies to build new businesses, they must refresh their perspectives on business across the boundaries between the knowledge of individuals, groups and organizations.

Technical convergence, in other words "knowledge convergence", has become crucial for successful new innovation across different areas of specialization (e.g., Klein, 1990; Porter and Teisberg, 2006). New innovation happens by bringing together the unique knowledge of different types of specializations and the technical convergence process (e.g., Kodama, 2005a, b, 2009a, b; Hacklin et al., 2009; Rafols and Meyer, 2010), in other words, the knowledge convergence process can be thought of as operating on a level straddling different specialist fields. Convergence of knowledge that once belonged to separate areas of technical expertise is essentially the precondition for technical convergence. Therefore, to make technical convergence occur, it stands to reason that knowledge convergence across different areas of technical expertise is required.

However, knowledge boundaries (Carlile, 2002) generally exist between dissimilar types of knowledge. This means unique differences with dissimilar characteristics and details exist between different types of knowledge. For example, a corporation is divided into various functional organizations and specialist fields, and various business types and functions are separated from each other between corporations and industries, and among all these, from the macro to the micro levels, many visible and invisible boundaries exist. In corporations, practitioners do not only face the organizational boundaries as sectionalism, but also the knowledge boundaries that exist at the micro levels as a result of their values, backgrounds and areas of specialization (see Figure 1.4). These various knowledge boundaries isolate the unique mental models and path dependent knowledge of practitioners, and are a hindrance to new innovation (e.g., Spender, 1990; Kogut and Zander, 1992; Leonard-Barton, 1995; Nonaka and Takeuchi, 1995; Brown and Duguid, 2001; Carlile, 2002).

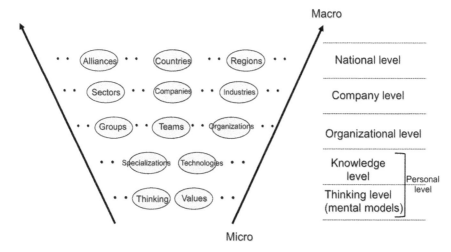

Figure 1.4   Existing various boundaries

Furthermore, as the novelty in circumstances surrounding individuals, organizations or companies or knowledge boundaries between different types of knowledge become more pronounced, both quality and quantity of knowledge boundaries also expands (or rises) (Carlile, 2004). However, to date, most of the new knowledge creation that has come about with innovation has been shown to have occurred on the boundaries between different specializations (e.g., Leonard-Barton, 1995; Nonaka and Takeuchi, 1995; Kodama, 2007a, b). This suggests that the thinking and ideas between people and the actions of organizations straddling different fields of specialization are major factors in bringing about innovation success, and therefore factors that contribute to competitive excellence.

In contrast, existing research also clarifies why it is difficult to generate and maintain innovation (Leonard-Barton, 1995; Carlile, 2004). Also, it has been reported that the ideas of people and actions of organizations straddling different fields of specialization are constrained by knowledge path dependency (March, 1972; Rosenkopf and Nerkar, 2001). For example, traditionally it was recognized as easier to concentrate exploration for innovation in closely related specialized fields. However, deep communication and collaboration processes between different fields of specialization have also been reported to contribute greatly to new innovations (e.g., van Rijnsoever and Hessels, 2011). Thus, to encourage this kind of communication and collaboration, the way the knowledge boundaries perceived by individuals and organizations are uncovered and tied to hints that will lead to new innovation is critical. In short, this is the capability required for practitioners to grasp whether the dissimilarities and differences on diverse boundaries will be a source of new knowledge convergence (Kodama, 2014) (or new knowledge creation). Generally, most people feel uncomfortable when facing unfamiliar boundaries (boundaries of different contents to which they are unaccustomed), and different people have different perception and recognition capabilities at the boundaries where such discomforts occur.

Moreover, many practitioners recognize that there are "unseen walls" in complicated business settings that straddle businesses and areas of specialization in companies, and between organizations including customers. The problems and issues that relate to new business in relationships with external partners and customers are further complicated by the far greater degrees of tension that exist in the contexts inside a company. So, how can we manage the knowledge possessed by various practitioners to create new knowledge by transcending organizational and knowledge boundaries? The capability that drives recognition and perception of these various boundaries, and triggers the convergence of dissimilar knowledge is "sensing through boundaries vision", as described as follows.

(b)   Sensing through boundaries vision
As discussed earlier, sensing is the ability to seek out business opportunities and filter and analyze them, and is dependent on the cognitive capabilities of individual practitioners such as leading organizational members mainly in managerial layers. In the process of selecting new technologies and R&D with innovation, the cognitive capabilities of management layers are of extreme importance for appropriately responding to dynamic external environments or business opportunities.

In recent years, Helfat and Peteraf (2015) have discussed how differences (heterogeneity) in the cognitive capabilities of top manager teams bring about disparities in organizational performance in changing situations. According to their reviews of the theories of cognitive psychology, cognitive science, social psychology, cognitive neuroscience and behavioral decision theory, cognitive capabilities entail important aspects that are fixed to certain contexts or areas. They argue that existing research (e.g., Ericsson and Lehmann, 1996) suggests that these aspects can affect heterogeneity in cognitive capabilities.

Helfat and Peteraf (2015) assert that cognitive capabilities, the foundation for these mental processes (or mental models), has been considered as an important attribute in managers at the top of organizations in many years of research into management, and present a number of cases of evidence such as research by Rosenbloom (2000) into NCR, and research by Tripsas and Gavetti (2000) into Polaroid. Furthermore, they also suggest that top managers should strengthen "paradoxical cognition" (Smith and Tushman, 2005) to be able to pursue exploration and exploitation (March, 1991) simultaneously, and at the same time they warn that empirical knowledge of the past may bring about hindrance by unwittingly and inappropriately relying on specialist knowledge of the past when companies search for new technologies and strategies (Miller and Ireland, 2005). As confirmed by existing research into the field of management, heterogeneity in the cognition of top management teams affects the heterogeneity of approaches to strategic change and their outcomes.

However, the role played by the cognitive capability of the intuition of leading practitioners is large, and gives them awareness and flashes of insight brought about by interactions with a wide range of stakeholders (including customers and partners). To demonstrate the cognitive capability of intuition, practitioners must have the capability of boundaries vision (Kodama, 2011; Kodama and Shibata, 2016) to be able to acquire new insights from complex and diverse boundaries. The concept of boundaries vision is a new proposition that entails dissimilar knowledge integration capability – the ability to orchestrate dissimilar intangible assets (see Box 1.1), boundaries architecture – the corporate design to achieve new business models by defining new corporate boundaries by integrating dissimilar boundaries, and boundaries innovation – the process of innovation across the boundaries between companies and even industries (Kodama, 2009a) and so forth (Kodama, 2011).

"Peripheral vision" is what is required for dynamic vision and sensitivity to stay ahead of speedy environmental changes. Driving peripheral vision enables risk management and acquisition of opportunities without missing signs to survive in an era of change. Boundaries vision in Figure 1.3 encapsulates the concept of "peripheral vision".

Boundaries vision is not only the engagement of peripheral vision limited to the periphery of a company's main business domain, but also includes the business domains of different industries across diverse boundaries previously unrelated to the company (or in which the company had no interest). Figure 1.5 shows the differences between peripheral vision and boundaries vision.

Boundaries vision does not only mean a view of the fuzzy zone of the peripheral area that cannot be easily exposed by the light of a flashlight or laser. Boundaries vision is more like an omnidirectional camera. An omnidirectional camera has two lenses, one at the front and one at the rear. Each lens covers those respective views, and the images of the two lenses are combined to give a 360° view from the ground to the sky. Omnidirectional cameras are able to capture 360° panorama images in all directions, up down, right and left, or even 360° video, and are also called 360° cameras, VR cameras, or full dome cameras.

As discussed, it is necessary to engage in "vigilant learning" to demonstrate peripheral vision, although to demonstrate boundaries vision, creative learning is also a crucial element, as discussed later (see Figure 1.3). However, boundaries vision and peripheral vision are in a complementary relationship with each other and must be used accordingly to respond to the environments and situations, etc. facing companies.

In his fieldwork to date, the author has recognized patterns of action based on network thinking characterized by boundaries vision, which practitioners use to bridge the diverse boundaries both in and between companies, to share knowledge, and to create new knowledge. Boundaries vision is the insights and thinking that practitioners have and use to design new business and corporate strategies through asset orchestration by recognizing and bridging diverse boundaries.

Put differently, boundaries vision means the capability of practitioners to seek out various differences and discomforts on boundaries and from them uncover whatever new knowledge, such as hints or ideas, are available. Boundaries vision is also the capability to figure out what types of boundaries are discovered and how to link them together to trigger new knowledge as new ways of perceiving or discovery of new things ("boundaries knowledge" discussed in detail in Chapter 2). Boundaries vision is not static, but is a dynamic, constantly changing capability. For individual practitioners and organizations, training and demonstration of boundaries vision is an essential source of new knowledge convergence, and similarly, boundaries vision is the most fundamental element for convergence of dissimilar knowledge.

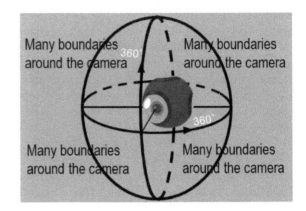

Flashlight/laser   **Omnidirectional camera**

Source: Day and Schoemaker (2004, Figure 1).

Figure 1.5   Difference between boundaries vision and peripheral vision

To achieve knowledge convergence dynamically on diverse and multiple boundaries, practitioners must demonstrate boundaries vision, and bring about external knowledge convergence capabilities: the cognitive capabilities to converge dissimilar knowledge (see Box 1.1) to achieve new products, services and business models. In practice, managers have to focus on various boundaries and use their "external knowledge convergence capabilities" to bring about new innovation through the convergence of dissimilar knowledge.

External knowledge convergence capabilities through boundaries vision are capabilities beyond peripheral vision for detecting dissimilar knowledge that is only loosely related or entirely unrelated, and uncovering relationships with one's own knowledge and converging it with that knowledge. Much of the existing research to date has already reported that the crossing or fusing of dissimilar knowledge is a source of new innovation (e.g., Johansson, 2004). Accordingly, for practitioners, being able to uncover relationships between a variety of dissimilar or existing knowledge, and discovering new meaning in those relationships, is an important initial trigger to demonstrate external knowledge convergence capabilities.

When practitioners have little experience (for example when joining a company in their younger years), as their mental models, their thinking frameworks are restricted to specific tasks and routines in the workplace. Then, as they accumulate empirical knowledge and work in various specialties or job functions, they come to know and understand various thinking frameworks and relationships between dissimilar knowledge. The author describes these concepts as "shared thought worlds" and "harmonized knowledge" respectively (Kodama, 2007b; Kodama and Shibata, 2014). However, the deeper practitioners in certain specialist jobs (for example, researchers or specialist engineers) go into the area of specialty, the higher the probability that they will be unable to escape from the thinking framework they have built on such particular knowledge (e.g., Kodama, 2007a).

In contrast, innovative and humble practitioners tend to have a strong tendency to perceive things beyond the framework of their own specializations, professions, organizations, companies or industries. These people understand mental models and thinking frameworks different to their own, and constantly learn to absorb dissimilar knowledge (e.g., Kodama, 2007b). It is the core human abilities of innovative practitioners that enable them to subjectively bring about new knowledge. In particular, to converge knowledge by external knowledge convergence capabilities through the demonstration of boundaries vision, "creative learning" (e.g., Kodama, 2007a, b) and collaboration is required among practitioners by forming human networks that span in and between organizations (and between companies) (e.g., Tushman, 1977; Owen-Smith and Powell, 2004; Lin and Kulatilaka, 2006). The organizational platforms required to form networks to bring about this creative learning are called "strategic communities" (SC hereinafter) (see Box 1.2) (e.g., Kodama, 2002, 2005a, 2009a).

BOX 1.1   EXTERNAL KNOWLEDGE CONVERGENCE CAPABILITIES THROUGH BOUNDARIES VISION

As Herbert Simon (1996, 1997) pointed out, human cognitive faculties have their limitations. Hence, humans built the world of multilayered organizations and functionally separated management. Simon described "limited rationality" to illustrate the limits of human cognitive and information processing capabilities which include the limits of rationality and cognition. In other words, there is a limit to how much information humans can process, and human beings can never be completely rational. In answering the question of why human beings form organizations, Simon argued that within a certain limited scope, objective and rational judgments can be made, and the organization is a social device that enables shrinking of the complexities of the world by restricting such scope to within the limits of human cognition. Thus, by forming the layer structures of organizations, the complexity of decision-making can be distributed across subsystems (or modularized). In this way, Simon asserts that high-level decision-making can be performed that would otherwise be impossible for individuals.

Certainly, corporate activity consists of a wide range of business processes (basic research through to applied research, marketing, product development, manufacture, sales, distribution and after sales services, etc.), and there are many diverse contexts in which businesses operate. There really is not any one person in any company who has all the basic skills needed to perform every task from R&D for new product and services through to sales and support (or even if there are, they are very few).

To create concepts for excellent new products, services and business models, and implement these, strategic communities (SC) and networked SC as multilayered SC formations are indispensable, and in these SC there must be such mechanisms with which practitioners in core departments in new product development such as marketing, R&D and production create and share dynamic contexts across the boundaries of organizations. This enables practitioners to create and put into practice new knowledge (business concepts for new products and services, etc.).

Individual practitioners in departments have diverse and unique world views and values.

Patterns of behavior and thinking as certain paradigms based on past experiences (with jobs or specialist technologies in various departments such as marketing, R&D and production) lie at the root of the way an individual lives. For example, practitioners in charge of marketing engage in "dialectical synthesis" (Kodama, 2007a) through the synergy of their own subjective perceptions (a viewpoint to uncover latent demand by assimilating with customers) and objective perceptions (analysis of competing products and customer data) to unceasingly create new recognition such as "we have to plan products that will provide customers with new value", or "how do we grasp the latent needs of customers to plan such products?" However, that does not mean that they have absolutely no technical perspective. These practitioners are always keeping an eye on technical trends both in and outside of their companies, and making efforts to verify concepts of latent usage systems that customers themselves would probably not notice, while always bearing in mind that although there are many uncertainties, if they can bring about a particular technology it will be possible to provide customers with new functions and services.

In contrast, practitioners in R&D and production departments engage in dialectical synthesis through the synergy of their own subjective perceptions (thoughts and beliefs about what they want to develop) and objective perceptions (concentration and selection based on analysis of technical trends and benchmarks of other companies' technologies) to unceasingly create new recognition such as "we have to develop technologies that will satisfy customers", or "we have to develop core technologies that competing companies can't imitate". Nevertheless, that does not mean that engineers have no idea about markets. Certainly, engineers can make proposals to customers from their own seed-oriented ideas about what is possible.

Thus, practitioners in various departments proactively form multilayered SC in their companies, and as their subjectivities clash from market and technology contexts and perspectives they collide with these paradigms, bring about new energy and create contexts with a higher dimension. Practitioners come to understand each other's diverse world views and values, and bring about mutual recognition and new rules through creative and dialectical dialogue, and creative learning between different organizations. However, as practitioners mutually understand and share their thoughts and feelings, they combine both assertiveness and humility, and question how to create new knowledge. This enables individuals to develop in the dimension of higher thoughts and ideas. These are "external knowledge convergence capabilities" – abilities to generate and achieve new business concepts by synthesis of dissimilar knowledge through "abduction" (Peirce, 1998) (see Figure 1.6). Practitioners' external knowledge convergence capabilities are the driving force behind the achievement of knowledge convergence.

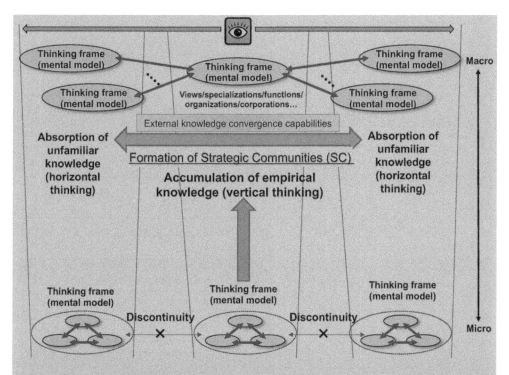

Figure 1.6   External knowledge convergence capabilities through boundaries vision, demonstration of boundaries vision

BOX 1.2   FORMING STRATEGIC COMMUNITIES (SC) TO BRING ABOUT EXTERNAL KNOWLEDGE CONVERGENCE CAPABILITIES

(1)   The Characteristics of "ba" and "Small-World Networks" (swn)

SC have the quality of "ba" (Nonaka and Takeuchi, 1995; Nonaka and Konno, 1998), and are defined as follows (Kodama, 2005a, p. 28):

> Strategic communities are based on the concept of "ba" as shared spaces for emerging relationships that serve as a foundation for knowledge creation. Participating in a ba means transcending one's own limited perspective or boundaries and contributing to the dynamic process of knowledge creation. In a strategic community, members (including customers) with different values and knowledge consciously and strategically create a ba in a shared yet constantly changing context. New knowledge and competencies are formed by the organic merging and integrating of communities to form new ba to address multiple new eventualities. From the practical aspect, we see the strategic communities as informal organizations possessing elements coherent with both the resource-based view of emergent shared-context learning and the planned strategic-based view of planning for a targeted market position.

Furthermore, Kodama (2009a, p. 469) asserts that SC have the characteristics of the "small-world structures" of network theory, described as follows:

> SC are groups forming small-world structures where practitioners in diverse specialisations realize innovations to solve the issues facing them and implement problem-solving and creative strategies. Short connections between nodes (people are the first unit nodes) and local clustering are features of small-world structures. For example, short paths among nodes of practitioners belonging to different organisations enable easier access to other practitioners within a firm or based in other firms, including customers. Each node in a small-world structure is embedded in a local cluster. This clustering then enhances the possibility of fostering reliable accessibility. A small-world structure can be formed by either randomly rewiring a portion of an existing regular network or attaching each new node to a "neighbourhood" that already exists.

In this way, SC have the small-world structure characteristics of ba or networks.

(2)   SC Driving Collaborative Activities through Creative Learning

In practice, SC have the characteristics of "pragmatic boundaries" (Carlile, 2004). For example, Kodama (2005b, p. 40) asserts that SC plays the following role in real business activities:

> Boundaries. The third principle is that the SC provides pragmatic boundaries, allowing actors with different contexts to transform existing knowledge. A variety of problems or issues are posed in the pragmatic boundary, and actors face the challenge of solving these problems and issues by creating new knowledge. The actors of an organization thus have to engage in practical yet creative confrontations or conflicts and also political negotiating practice. Innovation and creativity emerge on the boundaries between the disciplines and specializations of different organizations.

In other words, to bring about creativity, creative learning by dialogue and practice through creative confrontations and discord among members is necessary.

In addition, Taifi and Passiante (2012, p. 2125), who discussed "new products and service development through strategic community creation", stated the following about the importance of SC formation.

> The case study provides and analyzes the structuring characteristics and success factors of an SC of after-sales services firms in the automotive sector. The study shows that it is important to have entities – more precisely SC – dedicated to the after-sales services firms for the integration of their technical knowledge in the innovation process. The SC plays the key role of contributing to the development of both the products and the services of the automaker. The paper contributes to the literature on the SC, which is one of the most important entities of inter-organizational collaboration and innovation.

In other words, integration (convergence) of knowledge through collaboration between companies is crucial for service innovations.

Looking at this existing research, SC can be called "organizational platforms" for evolving core knowledge both in and out of companies while actively searching for the best knowledge from around the world and converging it with the core knowledge in the company. How do practitioners form SC and create new business concepts in companies that bring about a competitive edge through such knowledge convergence?

(3)   Forming Strategic Communities with Boundaries Vision

Through boundaries vision, practitioners must leverage their external knowledge convergence capabilities and build SC in and out of the companies. Boundaries vision, the foresight of practitioners to achieve asset orchestration, is also the capability to obtain new insights into the complicated and diverse boundaries that exist both within and outside of companies and organizations. Boundaries vision is the ability to create assets (knowledge) through external knowledge convergence capabilities, redefine corporate boundaries and promote radical innovation to achieve new products and business models, as well as drive incremental innovation for existing business. The process of dynamically changing corporate boundaries and combining incremental and radical innovation by exploration and exploitation activities through the building of asset orchestration architecture (described in section 3.4.2) is "asset orchestration dynamics", the "transforming" sub-capability (described in section 3.4.3).

It is important that practitioners in companies have a perspective on creating new assets (knowledge) by the boundaries vision of individuals, groups and organizations to achieve asset orchestration dynamics to simultaneously grow existing business and create new markets through incremental and radical innovation. For this reason, it is necessary to embed the spiral dynamic process of demonstration of external knowledge convergence capabilities through boundaries vision (sensing) → building asset orchestration architecture (seizing) → and achieving asset orchestration dynamics (transforming). Through the synergies between external knowledge convergence capabilities by boundaries vision and asset orchestration architecture, practitioners converge (orchestrate) different and diverse knowledge needed to achieve their corporate visions and strategic objectives, and through recursive processes, continually bring about new assets (knowledge). This is also the "dynamic capabilities framework" triggered by boundaries vision (see Figure 1.7).

Strategic communities (SC) play the role of dynamically achieving asset orchestration dynamics both in and out of companies across the company internal (people, organizations, different specializations, etc.) and external boundaries (between companies, between companies and customers, and between different industries, etc.).

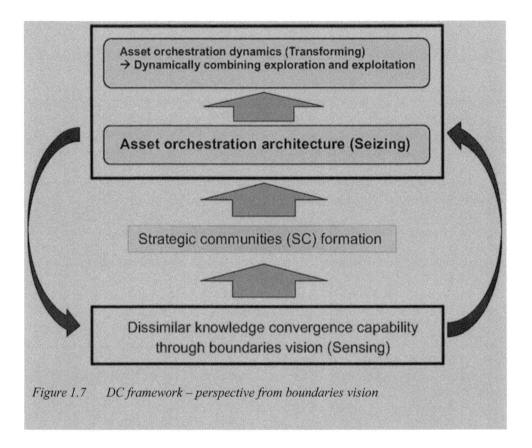

Figure 1.7   DC framework – perspective from boundaries vision

3.4.2   Asset orchestration architecture

(a)   Seizing through asset orchestration architecture

Recently in many countries, it has become necessary to design open innovation (Chesbrough, 2003) to expand the scope of searches for business opportunities through joint research systems between industry, government and academia that transcend the boundaries between corporate organizations and enable leading middle managers and top management teams to cooperate with suppliers to grasp customer needs and bring in the best technologies from the outside or hybrid innovation, an intermediate between open and closed innovation (Kodama, 2011), to bring in the best technologies from the outside. In the aforementioned era of convergence, important managerial considerations include new knowledge about the dynamic strategic processes of configuring new business models with practitioners using their boundaries vision to draw up grand designs for new asset orchestration architecture (see Box 1.3).

Managers have to face these issues in their strategic thinking and actions as they focus on diverse boundaries to orchestrate different intangible assets (and co-specialized assets) (Teece, 2014) to bring about innovations. Recently, the best core technologies of the world's cutting-edge businesses are becoming dispersed and diffuse across the globe. Accordingly, going forward in this era of convergence, in which valuable co-specialized assets bring about wealth, management that can integrate the best intangible assets spread within and outside of organizations including customers (assets orchestration by DC) from multiple perspectives in open systems will become increasingly important. Thus, in the knowledge economy, the concepts of open and hybrid innovation are of major importance to create new products, services and business models through the orchestration of the company's intangible assets (and co-specialized assets) with those of other companies by developing and accumulating competitive intangible assets in a company at the same time as incorporating intangible assets outside of the company.

As discussed earlier, in the sensing process, the demonstration of boundaries vision, which is also the cognitive capability of intuition, is extremely important for leading practitioners to uncover the best intangible assets (and co-specialized assets). Thus, asset orchestration architecture, which is the architecture thinking to analyze and evaluate excellent intangible and tangible assets (tacit and explicit knowledge) and combine these through boundaries vision, a sub-capability of sensing, is required (see Figure 1.3). For example, Apple's foray into the music distribution and smartphone businesses (Kodama, 2011, 2017c, 2018a), and Fujifilm of Japan's foray into the cosmetics business (Kodama and Shibata, 2016) are also the results of the demonstration of (1) boundaries vision and (2) asset orchestration architecture (see Figure 1.3).

(b)   Developing opportunities by building asset orchestration architecture
In sluggish (or extremely slow) environmental changes observed at the initial stage of radical innovation, moreover, in highly uncertain environments, a creative process stage for new technology through new ideas, business concepts, discoveries and inventions is crucial. As shown in Figure 1.3, the exploration process is driven by the seizing sub-capability of "probe-and-learn experimentation". There are a wide range of patterns for asset orchestration architecture in such exploration processes (see Box 1.3).

There are many cases of traditional large corporations that have mainly driven closed innovation with in-house research laboratories and development departments under conventional hierarchical systems. Closed innovation is an important process for incremental innovation with path-dependent assets built up over years. In traditional high-tech fields such as the heavy electrical, nuclear power generation, aviation, vehicle equipment, machine tool, medical equipment, semiconductor processing equipment and R&D machinery industries, closed innovation plays a critical role.

In contrast, in industries such as IT, technologies are rapidly advancing, and the best technical achievements and know-how are becoming increasingly spread out across the globe. In environments which are changing rapidly, asset orchestration through hybrid innovation (Kodama, 2011) to converge and integrate knowledge both inside and outside of companies by adopting open innovation or partially incorporating external core assets is an effective method.

Should a company adopt a vertically integrated model with "vertical integrated architecture" or concentrate on a particular area of specialization with "horizontal integrated architecture" or "linkage relationship architecture"? Should a company look to form partnerships with other companies (with strong or weak ties) to supplement the company's technology, and converge and integrate the strengths of other companies with the strength of the company through collaboration across different business types to build new value chains? Thinking about how to uncover such business models is necessary in the exploration process of this creative stage. Accordingly, practitioners have to concentrate on experiments through trial and error, and trial activities while considering the seizing sub-capability of "deploying real options" as shown in Figure 1.3, while allowing for higher diversity of asset orchestration architecture as asset architectural thinking (vertical integrated architecture, horizontal integrated architecture, linkage relationship architecture) (see Box 1.3).

In whatever case, in environments of high risk and uncertainty, companies have to hypo-thetically test their corporate boundaries in response to strategic objectives or business environments and make attempts at various asset orchestration architecture through these processes of trial and error. If it is advantageous to develop or manufacture in-house, then it is better to engage the company's creativity and configure a vertical value chain model. In contrast, if another company has achieved more with its developments than those in-house, often a company must take the risk of abandoning its development efforts and focus on effi-ciency through partnerships or mergers and acquisitions (M&A) to acquire and access external intangible assets. Accordingly, practitioners have to pursue hypothesis testing according to strategic objectives and asset orchestration through diverse asset architectural thinking in asset orchestration architecture in the process of such creative exploration.

Through the subsequent processes of invention, trial experimentation and verification in R&D, companies have to set down and execute plans to acquire human resources in-house (or sometimes from outside the company), and streamline and upgrade organizations to incubate the new business of core technologies or business concepts. As such environments surround-ing companies shift to more variable environments inside and outside the company, the uncer-tainty will remain. Asset orchestration architecture in such rapidly changing environments (the speed of external environment such as markets or in-house activities) entails selection of diverse asset orchestration architecture invented, trialed and tested in R&D, which is then raised to a higher level of asset orchestration completion as products, services or business models.

On the other hand, the diversity of factors of asset orchestration architecture – vertical integrated architecture, horizontal integrated architecture and linkage relationship architec-ture – is lowered with repeated testing and verification processes. Moreover, depending on the situation, sometimes companies review their structural architecture of vertical integrated architecture or horizontal integrated architecture, or review their relationships with other partner companies by changing their linkage relationship architecture.

Thus, through selection by various processes of incubation, and elimination of a certain degree of uncertainty, new businesses with future prospects (including new products, services) shift to business environments with relatively low uncertainty despite changes ongoing outside the company (in the environment) or in-house. In such a business environment for commer-cialization (business creation), a company determines the management elements (strategy, organizations, technologies, operations, etc.) inside the corporate system by asset orches-tration towards the completion of a firm value chain. As a result, the degree of perfection of products and services will be improved. At the stage of commercialization, changes to the factors of "vertical integrated architecture", "horizontal integrated architecture" and "linkage relationship architecture" are lower, and the overall optimization of asset orchestration archi-tecture and related adjustments become the most important issues.

On the other hand, in such commercialization stages, companies must strategically and con-tinually review their business models and raise the level of their technologies to raise the value of their products and services to respond to fast and competitive environments. Therefore, as existing products and services are constantly given major upgrades (due to new technical developments or new business models), the need to review asset orchestration architecture arises.

The commercialization stage also includes the original concept of DC to drive incremental innovation, which can be interpreted as the capabilities to generate high performance by the evolution and diversification of operating routines (ordinary capabilities: OC) through high-level learning to generate profits in response to internal and external changes.

In contrast, for many stable existing businesses with their low levels of change and uncertainty and sluggish market environments, companies drive incremental innovation for the thorough efficiency of the business through processes of upgrading and improving existing business (exploitation) with existing organizations (main streams). Asset orchestration with such existing business pursues existing routines and operational efficiency in the framework of fixed and established vertical integrated architecture, horizontal integrated architecture and linkage relationship architecture under continually maintained and precise strategic planning.

As described above, the significance of asset orchestration architecture as seizing is the role it plays in the design of the future when constructing a new business through the orchestration of various assets (knowledge) generated from a boundaries vision that is sensing. In particular, to create new assets by co-specialization, a company needs a unique integration mechanism (difficult for other companies to imitate). This is also asset orchestration architecture.

BOX 1.3   ASSET ORCHESTRATION ARCHITECTURE – ASSET ORCHESTRATION THINKING

How are SC and networked SC formed, and how are different assets orchestrated through SC and networked SC? The author would like to systemize this based on empirical cases of existing research. This is because the network structures of SC are small-world structures, which determine the patterns of asset orchestration processes. The author would like to present this proposition from design thinking on human networks and organizational networks – in other words, from an architecture perspective, for example, what mechanisms form SC or networked SC in and out of companies? Or, what kind of patterns do practitioners use to form networks? As processes executed through the asset architectural thinking of practitioners, asset orchestration in the cases experienced by the author and other contributors have so far consisted of three general types (vertical integrated architecture, horizontal integrated architecture, linkage relationship architecture) which are divided into two individual models.

In the following, the author describes the research process leading to the derivation of the framework for the architecture of asset orchestration. Regarding the vertical value chain model and linkage relationship architecture, the author analyzed synergies between business activities (the level of vertical integration), the relationship between the transactional relationships between businesses (contract details, contract periods of validity, power relationships, etc.) and the level of knowledge sharing (levels of information sharing, knowledge transfer and collaboration), and value networks in which business models are created. Regarding the multilayered model, the author conducted structural analysis of project organizations in companies. In addition, regarding the horizontal value chain and complementary model, the author analyzed the level of knowledge sharing and processes that lead to the formation of business models through joint development and strategic alliances among companies.

(1)   Vertical Integrated Architecture

Vertical integrated architecture means vertically integrated forms of SC, which are divided into the multilayered model and the vertical value chain model (see Figure 1.8).

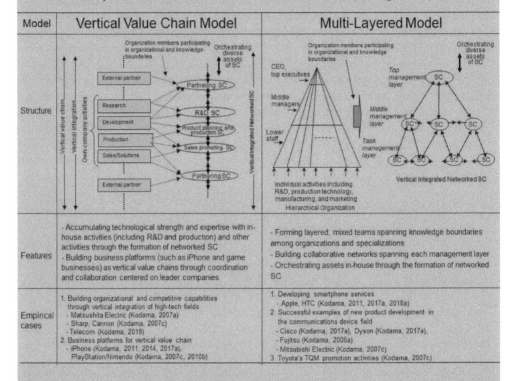

Model	Vertical Value Chain Model	Multi-Layered Model
Structure		
Features	- Accumulating technological strength and expertise with in-house activities (including R&D and production) and other activities through the formation of networked SC - Building business platforms (such as iPhone and game businesses) as vertical value chains through coordination and collaboration centered on leader companies	- Forming layered, mixed teams spanning knowledge boundaries among organizations and specializations - Building collaborative networks spanning each management layer - Orchestrating assets in-house through the formation of networked SC
Empirical cases	1. Building organizational and competitive capabilities through vertical integration of high-tech fields - Matsushita Electric (Kodama, 2007a) - Sharp, Cannon (Kodama, 2007c) - Telecom (Kodama, 2019) 2. Business platforms for vertical value chain - iPhone (Kodama, 2011, 2014, 2017a), PlayStation/Nintendo (Kodama, 2007c, 2010b)	1. Developing smartphone services - Apple, HTC (Kodama, 2011, 2017a, 2018a) 2. Successful examples of new product development in the communications device field - Cisco (Kodama, 2017a), Dyson (Kodama, 2017a), - Fujitsu (Kodama, 2005a) - Mitsubishi Electric (Kodama, 2007c) 3. Toyota's TQM promotion activities (Kodama, 2007c)

Figure 1.8   Vertical integrated architecture

(a)   Multi-layered model

In the multilayered model, SC have hierarchy and are structured through the cross-functional formation of multiple SC by practitioners working in various functional sections of a company at the same time as the formation of hierarchical networks at management levels. The multilayered model is often observed in large-scale cases of new product development (NPD) or large-scale projects (Kodama, 2005a, 2007c, 2009a). For example, in the NPD multilayered model, professionals in various divisions and specialist areas collaborate and form SC at all management levels to design overall architecture for the target developmental product, various subsystems design, software development, hardware development, and production technologies, etc. Moreover, these SC are hierarchical. The reason for this is product architecture is dependent on product functions and product structure (whether its components are integral or modular, or a mix of the two), and because the entire systems can be broken down into a hierarchical structure of many subsystems (e.g., Baldwin and Clark, 2000; Clark, 1985; Simon, 1996). Specific empirical cases have been reported for corporations in the IT field (e.g., Kodama, 2005a).

The multilayered model has been observed in product development processes requiring convergence and integration of a wide range of technologies. For example, this was an effective organizational architecture for achieving large-scale business model development or NPD such as Apple's iPod or iPhone (Kodama, 2011, 2017a, 2018a). In this multilayered model, individual and autonomous SC consisting of groups of professionals secure creativity and flexibility when turning missions to achieve new product developments and business models into specific tasks. SC hierarchy has the advantage of securing efficiency and speed of decision-making in executing tasks.

(b)   Vertical value chain model
The vertical value chain model means the formation of SC, and networked SC consisting of these as vertical integration for coordination and collaboration among various tasks to achieve vertical integration in all tasks in a company such as R&D, product technologies, manufacturing and sales. Empirical cases of networked SC that achieve in-house vertical integration in Japanese manufacturers have been reported (e.g., Kodama, 2007a, c, d, e, 2017a). As discussed in existing research, networks of SC between different organizations and specialist areas in appliance and communications equipment manufacturers, or telecommunications carriers, orchestrate internal assets and bring about vertical integration-type business models unique to their companies.

Also, these vertical value chain models function to network companies with strong ties in the mobile telephone industry involved in smartphones, etc. and the automotive industry. In networked SC, creating these vertical value chain models in these industries in which the level of knowledge and information sharing is high, leader companies (for example, Apple, Google, GM, Toyota etc.) have bargaining power and leadership in technologies and markets (Kodama, 2011, 2014, 2017a, 2018a). For example, these are typified by the inter-company networks of automotive manufacturers (Toyota, etc.) and components manufacturers (e.g., Amasaka, 2004; Dyer and Hatch, 2004).

Smartphone business models also consist of vertical integration-type value chains of component manufacturers (hardware/software), smartphone manufacturers, application providers (AP) (SNS, etc.) and content providers (CP). In Apple's iPhone development, the mobile phone function details and technical architecture and detailed specifications needed to achieve these functions are decided, and then design and development takes place in-house based on these details (software such as the operating systems, and some hardware parts such as semiconductors). In contrast, electronic manufacturing services (EMS) deliver completed products to Apple. This entails deep sharing of information and knowledge between Apple and the main partner companies brought together through strongly networked SC. Moreover, Apple exercises its authority to control many AP and CP to determine what applications and content from which AP or CP will be included with or adopted for the iPhone. Hence, for Apple, coordinating huge numbers of AP and CP through vertical integration is an important task (Kodama, 2011, 2017a, 2018a). Game businesses such as Sony Computer Entertainment's PlayStation, Nintendo's Wii and Switch also entail coordination of many game software producers, components manufacturers and EMS through vertical integration (Kodama, 2011, 2017a).

Behind the success of the smartphone businesses such as Apple (Kodama, 2011, 2017a), not only small-world networked SC between the entrepreneurial organizations and traditional organizations within Apple but also numerous small-world networked SC consisting of parts manufacturers, EMS, AP and CP are formed. Thus, for Apple, the way clusters as small-world networked SC are formed by linking certain external partners is key. The birth of the iPhone business model entailed the formation of numerous small-world networks in-house at Apple and between parts manufacturers, EMS, AP and CP to enable the co-creation of new business models as Apple collaborated with its external partners. Hence, this vertical value chain model accelerated the asset orchestration process by the formation of networks of small-world structures (networked SC) both inside and outside of Apple, and was an important factor in driving the co-evolution of the new business model in the smartphone industry (business ecosystem).[1]

(c)   The vertical integrated architecture and the "creativity view"

The unique creativity view of companies (Kodama, 2009a, b) promotes the building of a vertical integrated architecture. In particular, innovative companies like Apple drive asset orchestration by mobilizing the assets of individuals in various locations through the formation of networked SC to achieve creative technological innovation under a multilayered model. In addition, the level of creativity is raised to respond to new technical changes and develop new technologies by accumulating the intangible assets (tacit knowledge) of know-how and experience between tasks through a vertical value chain model. As well as that, the vertical value chain model enabled through networked SC transcending companies is a factor in the formation of unique business platforms such as creative smartphone businesses (e.g., iPhone, iPad, iCloud, etc.).

(2)   Horizontal Integrated Architecture

Horizontal integrated architecture means horizontally integrated forms of SC, which are divided into the horizontal value chain model and the complementary model (see Figure 1.9).

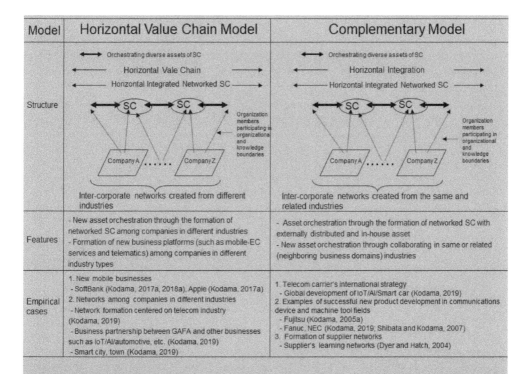

Model	Horizontal Value Chain Model	Complementary Model
Structure	Inter-corporate networks created from different industries	Inter-corporate networks created from the same and related industries
Features	- New asset orchestration through the formation of networked SC among companies in different industries - Formation of new business platforms (such as mobile-EC services and telematics) among companies in different industry types	- Asset orchestration through the formation of networked SC with externally distributed and in-house asset - New asset orchestration through collaborating in same or related (neighboring business domains) industries
Empirical cases	1. New mobile businesses - SoftBank (Kodama, 2017a, 2018a), Apple (Kodama, 2017a) 2. Networks among companies in different industries - Network formation centered on telecom industry (Kodama, 2019) - Business partnership between GAFA and other businesses such as IoT/AI/automotive, etc. (Kodama, 2019) - Smart city, town (Kodama, 2019)	1. Telecom carrier's international strategy - Global development of IoT/AI/Smart car (Kodama, 2019) 2. Examples of successful new product development in communications device and machine tool fields - Fujitsu (Kodama, 2005a) - Fanuc, NEC (Kodama, 2019; Shibata and Kodama, 2007) 3. Formation of supplier networks - Supplier's learning networks (Dyer and Hatch, 2004)

Figure 1.9   Horizontal integrated architecture

(a)   Horizontal value chain model

The horizontal value chain model entails the construction of networked SC to expand business to new areas from existing business domains, and build new value chains. In other words, to answer questions such as what kind of products and services a company should keep or what kind of business diversification a company should achieve to bring about value, a horizonal value chain model is a factor that determines the horizontal boundaries of a company. In particular, small-world networks between different industries and businesses drive access to dissimilar assets (knowledge), and drive dialogue on knowledge boundaries. Creative learning (see Figure 1.3) through creative abrasion and productive friction on knowledge boundaries inspires new assets, and raises the creativity needed to achieve new business models. Apple's strategy transformation from its PC business to music distribution and smartphone businesses in recent years is a good example of this (Kodama, 2011, 2017a, 2018a).

As observed in collaborations with multiple players in various industries and the so-called GAFA (Google, Apple, Facebook, Amazon) business leaders in the Internet field, new business models such as electronic money using smartphones, credit card businesses, convergence of communications and broadcasting (merging of Internet businesses with TV broadcasting for mobile phones), convergence of mobile phones and automobiles (Telematics), self driving vehicles, IoT/AI/big data, various sharing services and e-healthcare, are enabled by building horizontal value chains through the formation of networked SC across dissimilar types of businesses (Kodama, 2018b, 2019). Such asset orchestration architecture entails proactively forming strategic alliances, or alliances through capital participation and M&A in the finance, credit card, broadcasting, railroad, distribution, tourism, healthcare, education, advertising and automobile industries to achieve Internet businesses with new added value.

Asset orchestration architecture through the formation of business networks covering different types of business is an important factor in building horizontal value chains to generate new business models.

(b)   Complementary model
Complementary models entail collaborative SC and networked SC on an equal footing with external partners in the same industry (or in adjacent business areas), and do not have many of the hierarchical elements seen in vertical integrated architecture. This model entails cases of disseminating common knowledge with external partners, and engaging in joint development of new products and services, etc. on an equal footing. Joint developments with competing or partner companies are also examples of this complementary model. With NPD in the high-tech field, there are many cases of successful NPD through collaboration enabled by the formation of networked SC with numerous external partners. Automotive, appliance, communications equipment and machine tool manufacturers execute horizontal integration of external assets by absorbing the assets of external partners (specialist partners in business layers of horizontal divisions of labor) by the formation of external networked SC with external partners, while orchestrating assets through vertical integration by the formation of networked SC internally. In the case of Fanuc of Japan (e.g., Kodama, 2019), networked SC are fundamental to the asset orchestration architecture to orchestrate external assets with those in-house. Also, as a case in the automotive industry, the learning networks that are continually formed among suppliers to Toyota are also examples of this complementary model.

(c)   Horizontal integrated architecture and the "dialectic view"
The unique dialectic view of companies (Kodama, 2009a, b) promotes the building of a horizontal integrated architecture. To build win–win relationships in business models, innovative companies drive the orchestration of diverse assets through the formation of networked SC with partners including companies in different industries. Also, the dialectic view drives coordination and collaboration among partners (including competitive companies) through complementary model constructions, and achieves NPD and joint business. In addition, co-creation between dissimilar businesses through the formation of the horizontal value chain model generates new business models and drives co-evolution across entire new industries.

(3)   Linkage Relationship Architecture

Boundaries are asset platforms that entail practitioners sharing dynamic contexts (time, location, relationships with people) to generate new knowledge. "SC as boundaries" are equivalent to space–time that generates and changes through the synergies between individuals sharing and changing contexts with each other – an SC is space–time for sharing intangible assets (tacit knowledge), dialogizing and practicing.

"Organizations" and "individuals" are in dialectic relationships with each other, hence the humanity of individual practitioners changes organizations through recursive relationships between organizations and "here and now" space–time as an SC and "practical consciousness" – tacit knowledge in dynamic contexts. While human beings have to accept the limitations of the organizations that they have created, they also have the practical power to transform those organizations (Giddens, 1984; Giddens and Pierson, 1998). SC are platforms that bridge individuals with organizations (companies), and through their micro-existence, human beings form (or eliminate) SC or link them together, and in doing so, have influence on macro structures such as organizations, companies, industries or even entire societies.

Accordingly, SC are important not only as macro–micro linkages in social networks, but also as units for analysis from the perspective that how they influence company performance through the generation and accumulation of social capital (Coleman, 1988; Burt, 1997; Nahapiet and Ghoshal, 1998; Cohen and Prusak, 2000) as individuals form and link SC in relationships between individuals, organizations, SC, companies and industries, and how they conversely influence individuals.

On the other hand, in the flow of knowledge management, SC are also important to the clarification of processes in which social capital as knowledge capital is born centered on SC, and various knowledge transcending SC boundaries are integrated. Also, there is practical significance for practitioners on the perspective of how new knowledge is born through the formation and linking of SC (see Figure 1.10).

The new perspective obtained from the case of the aforementioned iPhone business model (Kodama, 2011, 2014, 2017b, 2018a) is the fact that diverse, different and multilayered SC whose contexts are always different and networked structures of these exist. These are formed and linked together as practitioners proactively work on others in their environment (customers, etc.) or in their organizations. Practitioners intentionally (or emergently) form and link SC. In particular, as observed in the case of Apple, new product development in the high-tech fields in recent years have led to the necessity to converge and integrate dissimilar technologies. Historically, technological innovation was developed through the pursuit of specialized knowledge in a particular field, but there are now many cases of new products and services that have been developed with new and unconventional ideas that converge technologies from one area with those of another (Kodama, 2014).

An important issue is how to integrate different and dispersed assets. From a technical perspective, this means what kind of technology integration to engage in and co-specialize (e.g., Teece, 2007) with assets in different technological fields. Dispersed assets are embedded in SC dispersed in space–time. To orchestrate assets, individual assets must transcend the boundaries of SC and be networked together. Put differently, distributed SC must be joined in networks, and the knowledge dispersed throughout those SC must be deeply embedded in the networks. In terms of social network theory, SC can be interpreted as cliques of practitioners (collections of actors with close mutual ties), and the network connections between SC and SC are equivalent to ties.

Practitioners committed to multiple SC play a central role in tying together SC with SC for asset orchestration. For dissimilar knowledge to be integrated, practitioners must deeply understand and share dissimilar assets (tacit knowledge and explicit knowledge) in respective SC, and also must deeply embed shared knowledge in networks that transcend the borders of SC (the factor of deep embeddedness is crucial) (Kodama, 2005a, 2005b). In particular, for intangible asset (tacit knowledge) sharing, it is necessary to deeply share contexts on networks, and strongly tie together SC with each other.

In the iPhone value chain, SC are strongly tied together and dissimilar assets are shared through deep embeddedness to generate new knowledge as technical convergence for new products and services. In this way, "building SC networks with strong ties" is an important proposition in integrating dissimilar assets (knowledge), and practitioners must intentionally consider SC relationships as these strong ties.

On the other hand, according to the teachings of social network theory, it is also possible to bridge new dissimilar information with weak ties (Granovetter, 1973). Also, Burt (1992) identified the high possibility of acquiring new business opportunities by actors accessing new information through weak ties with "structural holes". Hence, corporations need to focus on cases where the building of SC networks with weak ties is an effective measure (see Figure 1.9).

Also, while there is not much case research in the field of business, smartphone businesses such as the iPhone could be one of these. The iPhone business model consists of the integration of various assets (knowledge) such as components (hard and soft), smartphone development, technical platform development, manufacturing, applications and contents development. Among these, the smartphone development and technical platform development were produced in various strongly tied SC formed in and out of Apple's organizations.

On the other hand, regarding the development of various applications and contents (a variety including text content, games, location information, music distribution, movie distribution, various SNS services, electronic money services with QR codes, etc., healthcare, welfare and educational services), Apple does not have close network relationships with particular application and contents providers. Instead, the company builds SC networks with weak ties to application and contents providers (AP and CP) to access new application and content information, and hence access opportunities for new application and content business.

As described above, in "asset architecture" to achieve asset orchestration, not only are strongly tied SC networks built, but also weakly tied SC networks are an important proposition in the promotion of new business development, and hence practitioners must intentionally consider both these strongly tied and weakly tied SC relationships and their ongoing combination (or proper usage). This is called "linkage relationship architecture" in asset orchestration. Maintaining or building SC networks with strong ties at the same time as SC networks with weak ties and bridging structural holes in a timely manner enables absorption and integration of dissimilar assets. The iPhone business model can be said to be an example of skillfully using the linkage relationship architecture of SC (Figure 1.11).

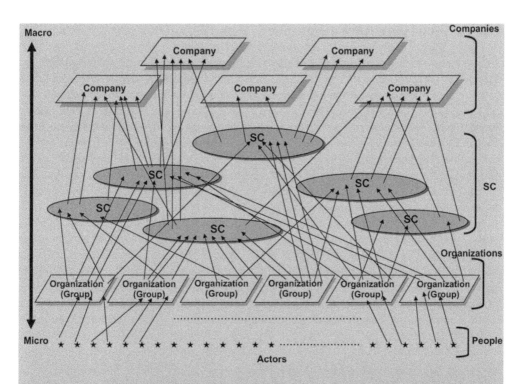

Figure 1.10   Relationship of individuals, organizations and corporations with SC

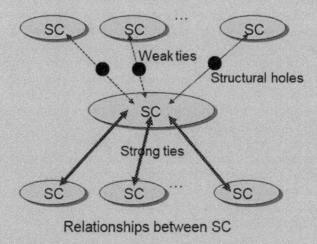

Figure 1.11   Linkage relationship architecture

3.4.3   Transforming internal and external through asset orchestration dynamics
(a)   Dynamically combining new and existing business

As sensing, boundaries vision is that ability to gain insight to design the most suitable vertical or horizontal boundaries using asset orchestration architecture, architecture thinking as seizing. Not only does that mean dynamically changing the boundaries of a company to suit changing environments (or markets), but also means dynamically changing the company's boundaries to create new environments (markets) and bring out new boundaries innovation (Kodama, 2009a), and is a way of thinking that should not be limited to top management, but acquired by managers at all levels. Asset orchestration dynamics that build and drive the aforementioned boundaries vision and asset orchestration architecture as architecture thinking, and continually and dynamically execute transformation and innovation, are the sub-capability of "transforming" (see Figure 1.3).

The first characteristic of asset orchestration dynamics is its driving ability to dynamically execute the optimization of value chains for a company's core business by changing the vertical boundaries inside and outside of the company. The second characteristic of asset orchestration dynamics is its ability to search out business not only in the periphery of the company's core business but also in different (completely unrelated) business domains, stimulate new business, radically alter the company's horizontal boundaries, uncover the relationships between completely dissimilar knowledge and the company's own knowledge, and demonstrate dissimilar knowledge convergence capability. Asset orchestration dynamics is an enabler that not only promotes growth and development of existing business by refining existing assets, but also creates new business by converging dissimilar assets (knowledge).

The string of innovation research of recent years on radical innovation (e.g., Leifer et al., 2000), breakthrough innovation (e.g., Hargadon, 2003), discontinuous innovation (e.g., Kaplan et al., 2003) and disruptive innovation (Christensen, 1997) has offered both theoretical and practical guidelines of strategy transformation that companies can use to pioneer new markets or create new technologies. The important implication of these innovation strategies is not just to be able to respond quickly to environmental changes, but also to acquire capabilities to drive business development to create new environments (markets). As described by Figure 1.3, this suggests that changing external environments require a company to execute "environment adaption strategies" to adapt to them, and simultaneously, it is necessary for the company to execute "environment creation strategies" to bring about changes in the environment. These are the core elements of dynamic capabilities.

To swiftly respond to changing circumstances, companies have to continually polish their existing core competencies to fortify their main businesses. Here, incremental innovation by advancing ordinary capabilities (OC) through successive and regular improvement and reform activities is important. In contrast, radical innovation that can acquire new and never-before-seen core competencies through the convergence of differing assets, is needed to acquire the dynamic capabilities (DC) required to drive the development of business for the creation of new environments (markets). Of these two innovation processes – incremental (exploitation) and radical (exploration) – the former pursues the efficiency of existing business (or main businesses) assets (knowledge) in the company, while the latter pursues the creation of assets (knowledge) to pioneer the businesses of the future. However, corporations have to simultaneously manage both of these disparate innovation processes (or properly apply them to suit certain situations), and build them into the core of their corporate strategy. This is the crucial function of asset orchestration dynamics.

There is a dynamic relationship between the creation and use of assets (knowledge). Technical know-how and personnel skills are trained through the use of knowledge, thus, in turn, the accumulation of knowledge is the fuel for new asset orchestration. Accordingly, it is important that companies understand how to balance the creation and use of knowledge, and they must be proactive in its management. How can knowledge creativity and efficiency be combined? Put differently, creating knowledge to bring about groundbreaking radical innovation at the same time as using knowledge for incremental innovation of existing core businesses is the proposition of "combined exploration and exploitation" to maintain competitiveness (March, 1991).

For this reason, business leaders and managers need new perspectives to pioneer businesses for new markets, while at the same time accumulating and advancing core assets to reinforce their core businesses. The process of asset orchestration dynamics, which simultaneously executes and combines (or probably applies them to suit the situation) these two substantially different innovation processes to pioneer new and highly individualized strategic positions, is a superior corporate strategy that also leads to the achievement of sustainable competitiveness (e.g., Markides, 1999; see Figure 1.12). Asset orchestration dynamics is a core framework of strategic innovation (Kodama, 2018a) to achieve sustainable corporate growth. Asset orchestration dynamics drive organizational redesign and external shaping, the sub-capabilities of transforming, and entail mutually complementary relationships with these sub-capabilities in Figure 1.3.

The cases of Fujifilm's new business development (Kodama, 2014, 2018a; Kodama and Shibata, 2016), Apple's transformation from its PC business to the music distribution and mobile phone businesses (Kodama, 2011, 2014, 2017b, 2018a), and Japan's 711 and NTT DOCOMO forays into the financial sector (e.g., Kodama, 2007a), are examples of companies that massively altered their horizontal boundaries through asset orchestration dynamics. These companies do not only maintain growth of their existing businesses, but also engage in strategic change for new business. Japanese general trading companies such as Mitsubishi and Mitsui also skillfully combine growth of their existing businesses with R&D through asset orchestration dynamics (see Box 1.4).

Traditional innovation in mature industries mainly involves companies carrying out research in closed, hierarchical and autonomous systems within themselves in which all processes are controlled by the company, and most or all intellectual properties are held by the company. In closed innovation systems like these, the governance mechanisms bring about the company's unique core competences, and are the source of the company's competitiveness. However, based on transactional cost theory, companies were able to raise business efficiency across the board by changing the vertical boundaries that determine their corporate value chains through outsourcing to other companies for resources and knowledge that they did not have. When circumstantial and environmental change is soft, it is advantageous for a company to configure value chains with vertical integration within the company or group of companies through coordination between related business units and close interdependency of technical resources. The traditional automobile industry, etc. are good examples of this. However, while it may be a strength of path dependency with close internal integration, if the environment changes and a serious problem arises, weaknesses can surface in such close interdependencies

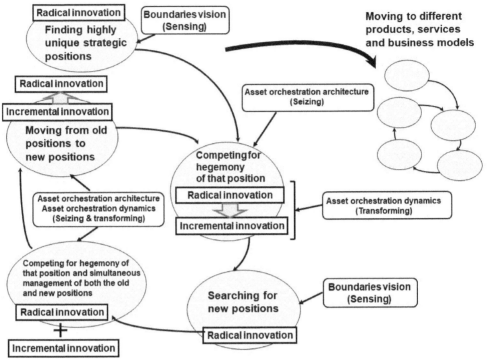

Source: Markides (1999), partially modified.

Figure 1.12   Dynamically combining new and existing business through asset orchestration dynamics

(e.g., Henderson and Clark, 1990; Hargadon and Sutton, 1997; Siggelkow, 2001). Also, fixed technologies or value chains that are a company's strengths can be weakened by changes in the market or destructive technologies (Christensen, 1997; e.g., Levitt and March, 1988; Leonard-Barton 1992, 1995; Martines and Kambil, 1999).

Nevertheless, it will be necessary to dynamically change the corporate boundaries of a company (vertical and horizontal boundaries) while maintaining existing business to shift to the completely different businesses of the future such as environmental vehicle and self driving vehicle developments with AI technologies at their core, and mobility as a service (MaaS). In rapidly changing market circumstances and in the technological environment of convergence, dynamic capabilities as dynamic asset orchestration are required to further strengthen and maintain existing core competencies with selection and concentration, while at the same time proactively bring in knowledge and resources from outside the company and flexibly reassemble accumulated knowledge and resources to respond to the changing circumstances (Teece et al., 1997; Teece, 2007, 2014). This means the processes of boundaries innovation (Kodama, 2009a, 2014) to create new products, services and business models by improving and developing the company's own knowledge, dynamically taking up knowledge from outside the company through the processes of open innovation (Chesbrough, 2003) or hybrid innovation (Kodama, 2011), and through the convergence of knowledge within and outside the company.

For this to happen, companies need to engage in the dynamic processes of converging knowledge dispersed within and outside the company and reconfiguring it as necessary. This means that companies have to constantly reconfigure the vertical or horizontal boundaries of the company's business models to respond to circumstantial change (or intentionally create new circumstantial change as convergence). As in the Fujifilm case, horizontal boundaries are a driver that determines the strategic domain for businesses related to a company's core business or new business (Kodama, 2018a).

To achieve new business models, it is important to dynamically integrate internal assets (knowledge) by integrating internal corporate boundaries (between people, organizations and different areas of technical specialty) through internal convergence networks with external assets (knowledge), and integrating external corporate boundaries (between companies, between companies and customers, and between different industries, etc.) through external convergence networks using the practice of asset orchestration dynamics. Through the asset convergence process entailing asset orchestration dynamics via convergence networks both within and outside companies on these vertical and horizontal boundaries, new assets (knowledge) transcending diverse boundaries are created. In this book, companies that achieve boundaries innovation through asset orchestration dynamics in this way are referred to as "asset orchestration firms" (see Figure 1.13).

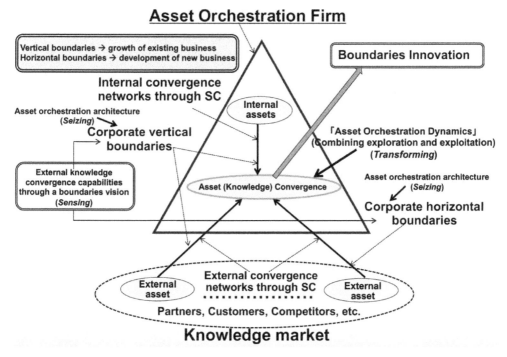

Figure 1.13   Asset orchestration firm

In order to not only grow their core businesses but also to acquire new business opportunities, asset orchestration firms use their dissimilar knowledge integration capabilities through boundaries vision (sensing) of vertical or horizontal boundaries. They cleverly combine assets inside the company, in group companies, in the same industries, in different industries and in customers through strategic alliances, strategic outsourcing, joint developments, ventures and M&A etc., and demonstrate capabilities (asset orchestration dynamics) (transforming) to keenly and prudently acquire new assets by building and establishing asset orchestration architecture (seizing). These asset orchestration dynamics activities are factors in the formation of healthy business ecosystems with all stakeholders such as the company and its partner group companies.

For example, fabless companies like Apple, Nintendo and Qualcomm use selection and concentration to clearly define their vertical boundaries, concentrate resources on R&D and product planning, and build ecosystems to provide end-users with final products through collaboration strategies with leading global partners (components manufacturers, manufacturers, distributors and sales enterprises, etc.; e.g., Kodama, 2011). Also, telecommunications carriers such as the Japanese company SoftBank and Taiwan's Chunghwa Telecom concentrate resources on product planning as well as telecommunications infrastructure and facilities businesses, while engaging in collaboration strategies with their best global partners (mobile telephone device manufacturers, communications equipment manufacturers, software vendors, semiconductor manufacturers, contents providers application vendors and other corporations) to build and advance their smartphone business value chains and ecosystems (e.g., Kodama, 2009b, 2011).

Boundaries innovation is generally divided into incremental innovation for changing a company's core business and radical/breakthrough innovation for bringing about new business. As described earlier, the formation of internal convergence networks (internal asset convergence) and external convergence networks (external asset convergence) through building asset orchestration architecture (seizing) is crucial in processes for achieving these two types of innovation.

To achieve incremental innovation, value chains must be optimized through the formation of internal convergence networks and external convergence networks to respond to changing environments (or markets). On the other hand, to achieve radical innovation, it is necessary to configure new value chains for the creation of new environments (or markets). For this reason, the boundaries where dissimilar assets (knowledge) intersect must be uncovered, external convergence networks built, and these many assets (knowledge) converged. Companies dynamically form these internal convergence networks and external convergence networks through external knowledge convergence capabilities using boundaries vision and the building of asset orchestration architecture (seizing). Thus, through the practice of asset architecture dynamics (transforming), companies dynamically change their horizontal and vertical boundaries to combine exploration and exploitation (see Figure 1.13).

It is the aforementioned SC that form the basis of these network configurations. This means that from the micro perspective, networks are made up of people or knowledge, whereas from the macro perspective, networks can be seen as collections of linked groups, organizations and companies (e.g., Kodama, 2005b). These can span different job functions and diverse layers of management, and exist both within and outside companies, and include customers. To date, the relationship between networks of companies and innovation has been reported in much academic research (e.g., Powell and Brantley, 1992; Powell et al., 1996; Rosenkopf and Tushman, 1998). In the concept of driving boundaries innovation in this way, SC as networks (and networked SC) dynamically formed by practitioners tie together multi-layered dissimilar SC assets (knowledge) to build ecosystems within and between companies and across industries, and raise the potential to bring about boundaries innovation.

(b)   Building strategic communities brings about organizational transformation and speeds up corporate transforming

According to our research to date, to demonstrate DC and create new markets or new value in dynamically changing markets, practitioners have to demonstrate: (a) context architect capabilities, (b) boundaries consolidation capabilities, and (c) strategy architect capabilities (Kodama, 2011, 2014, 2018a).

"Context architect capabilities" are also the capabilities of innovators to generate new meaning between different contexts. Differences arise on the boundaries between different contexts (Carlile, 2002, 2004). These differences give rise to further diversity and contradictions in various contexts, and are factors that drive boundaries vision. Overcoming contradictions originating in contextual diversity dynamically gives rise to new contexts, which enables sharing of "specific contexts" (Kodama, 2006). To overcome these contradictions, the execution of creative learning through dialectical and creative dialogue (Kodama, 2007b), creative confrontations or abrasion (Leonard-Barton, 1995), productive friction (Hagel and Brown, 2005) and political negotiating practice (Brown and Duguid, 2001) and so forth among practitioners is an important factor.

To achieve their business visions or missions, the context architect capabilities of practitioners to bring about specific contexts enables the creation and practice of new concepts though productive and creative dialogue and learning on questions such as why, how things should be and how to achieve certain things. As a result, the quality of these specific contexts in turn determines the quality of the knowledge produced. In the Apple case mentioned earlier, creating new markets is the vision for the future in which collaborating partners as professionals with a range of backgrounds and skills question themselves and each other to dynamically bring about and share specific contexts.

Next, regarding boundaries consolidation capabilities, the aforementioned specific contexts are rooted in specific practitioners building and rebuilding SC (Kodama, 2005a). Practitioners does not mean simply anybody, but importantly means a number of certain people (Kodama, 2006) who have the human capability of constantly pursuing self improvement. Expressed in the contexts of engineers, this also means specific practitioners who have common knowledge (shared language and knowledge; see, for example, Star, 1989). These people proactively bring about specific contexts based on their beliefs and thoughts, and build and rebuild strategic communities. "Specific practitioners" means executives and managers in managerial layers in organizations, executives and managers in partner companies, and leading customers.

Thus, specific practitioners build "specific strategic communities" to generate valuable new knowledge with the human network systems that they have. The author calls this behavior, and the capability of specific practitioners to link specific organizational and knowledge boundaries together and network them, "boundaries consolidation capabilities". Furthermore, these specific strategic communities are reconfigured over time by practitioners in response to strategic objectives. Accordingly, these can more precisely be called "specific strategic communities that change".

Finally, "strategy architect capabilities" are practitioners' capabilities to formulate and implement strategy by dynamically forming strategic communities to bring about new business models through context architect capabilities and boundaries consolidation capabilities. These capabilities include the know-how and skills to draw a grand design of strategy as asset orchestration architecture (seizing) and bring it to reality. A factor of strategy architect capabilities is the practice of asset orchestration dynamics (transforming) to skillfully use and integrate different strategy-making processes to combine exploration and exploitation (see Box 1.4).

The above three capabilities lead to the promotion of the three processes of sensing (boundaries vision), seizing (asset orchestration architecture) and transforming (asset orchestration dynamics) (see Figure 1.3). Because the nine sub-capabilities shown in Figure 1.3 are interconnected in a system, with interactions or synergies in response to environmental changes, the weight of each sub-capability element is a contingent in responses to situations.

Also, the dynamic capabilities framework shown in Figure 1.3 focuses on the situation-adaptive nature of capabilities for handling external change (adaptive or active). There are also critical contingencies in relation to strategy, organizational design and culture within corporations (Day and Schoemaker, 2016). In response to these situations-adaptive changes, subsystem elements (sub-capabilities) within corporate systems must be specified and their characteristics must be scrutinized. This is because the inherently hardened nature of a company's ordinary capabilities (OC) due to the strength of dependency of a corporation's development path, or bureaucracy and dullness of decision-making capabilities caused by organizational inertia limit the speed and scale of change of a company's dynamic capabilities (DC). To avoid this, the "capabilities congruence (dynamic internal congruence)" between the capabilities in a corporate system mentioned at the beginning (congruence between subsystems) [Insight-2] is required. This is discussed in detail in Chapter 9.

BOX 1.4 STRATEGY-MAKING PROCESSES THROUGH DYNAMIC FORMATION OF STRATEGIC COMMUNITIES

To innovate in uncertain environments, practitioners continuously create concepts for new business models (new products, services and business frameworks, etc.) based on imagination and creativity, and execute emergent strategies (Mintzberg and Walters, 1985) through the formation of multiple emergent external strategic communities (ESC) with strategic partners outside the company, including customers. Emergent strategies are strategies created by practitioners through the process of trial and error at the workplace level (there may be various cases, for example, at the divisions close to customers or middle management) as they recognize changes in the environment that they did not predict. However, in reality, strategy-making processes in corporations are generally intended or deliberate, whereas the details of strategy are emergent. Through the author's long practical experience, it was found that strategy-making processes in corporations have characteristics that are simultaneously planned and emergent (for example, entrepreneurial strategies; Mintzberg, 1978; Kodama, 2007a).

The two types of organizational forms (emergent organizations that promote exploration for new business, and traditional organizations that drive exploitation for existing business) in "strategic community-based firms" discussed in Kodama (2007a) are broadly defined as emergent organizations pursuing creativity and autonomy, and traditional organizations pursuing efficiency and control. Therefore, they are paradoxical. Thus, there is always a tug of war and conflict occurring between these organizations, and this hinders the integration of the knowledge of formal organizations, internal strategic communities (ISC) within companies and external strategic communities (ESC) outside companies. Nevertheless, "leadership teams" promote this synthesis and achieve transformation of corporate culture (Kodama, 2005b).

These leadership teams are formed from leaders (the CEO, executives, division managers, department managers, project leaders and managers, etc.) at all management levels (top management layer, middle management layer, management teams consisting of top and middle management layers, cross-functional teams, and task forces). As SC and networked SC, leadership teams bring about dynamic (DC) and ordinary (OC) capabilities across entire corporations through the integration and synthesis of knowledge in the two types of formal organizations (emergent and traditional organizations) and/or internal and external strategic communities.

To achieve a strategic community-based firm it is important that leadership teams simultaneously combine the apparently contradictory creative and planned strategic processes (exploration and exploitation) and synthesize them (asset orchestration dynamics (transforming)). Leadership teams at Apple are characterized by their combination of both creativity and efficiency (Kodama, 2017a). Existing research identifies the importance placed on building "ambidextrous organizations" in innovative American corporations by combining organizations driving new business (equivalent to emerging organizations) and organizations driving existing business (equivalent to traditional organizations). However, through our research (e.g., Kodama, 2019), we found it necessary to build leadership teams that have multilayered and "invisible" SC structures for asset orchestration dynamics (transforming) to succeed.

Managers in leader teams engage in deep dialogue and discussion to select strategies and plans that will genuinely enable innovation to flourish, which are then executed through the leadership of those managers. The synergy of leadership enabled by collaboration among managers at all management levels including the CEO and executives focuses creative learning through dialectical dialogue, and promotes carefully selected deliberate strategies to achieve synthesis of the knowledge and strategies of different organizations. At the root of asset orchestration dynamics (transforming) centered on leadership teams lies strategic dynamics of knowledge through abduction to build asset orchestration architecture (seizing) (e.g., Kodama, 2007a). Strategy architect capabilities are also capabilities to execute the abduction process of strategy formulation and implementation through the building and rebuilding of internal and external strategic communities (ISC and ESC). This is the strategy view in the "strategic community-based firm".

BOX 1.5   JAPANESE GENERAL TRADING COMPANIES' ASSET ORCHESTRATION DYNAMICS (SEE FIGURE 1.14)

The asset orchestration of Japanese general trading companies is deeply related to formation of their value chains. General trading companies use their multiple functions upstream and downstream in the value chain (finance, investment, consulting, distribution, etc.), and make efforts to optimize their vertical value chain models (see Box 1.3) through collaboration with both internal and external leading partners, and at the same time drive the co-evolution model to build win–win relationships with partners.

The architecture on which value chains are built are the diverse strategic communities spread widely around the world. Thus, the source of the configuring of these strategic communities are the people and human resource networks that can sense, converge, integrate and use diverse, global-scale assets through DC functions (sensing, seizing, transforming). In short, the dynamic configuring of SC and networked SC is an important factor for general trading companies. The specializations required for innovation in general trading companies are indicated by the 3-axis matrix of "the axis of goods and industry, the axis of region and the axis of function" and "people × goods × services × know-how as information", and entrepreneurial persons ideally having goods, region and function orchestrate assets on the global scale.

New business development in general trading companies are R&D-type business commercialization processes, and differ from the closed innovation of traditional manufacturers, in that asset orchestration through the convergence and integration of multiple assets via open innovation (Chesbrough, 2003) with leading internal and external partners is dominant.

With vertical integrated architecture as asset orchestration architecture (see Box 1.3), how should the vertical value chain model and the co-evolution model committed from the upstream, midstream through to the downstream be configured? In industries structured with the horizontal specialization business model such as the IT industry, how should a company collaborate with other companies to concentrate business resources into the certain functions of value chains, and configure the overall target value chain (vertical value chain model and co-evolution model)? Or should resources be concentrated into certain specialist areas only with horizontal integrated architecture or linkage relationship architecture to maximize profits? Or, how should new value chains be configured by converging and integrating the strength of a company with that of another by finding partnerships (with strong or weak ties) with other companies to compensate for the weaknesses of a company or through strategic collaboration across different business types, etc.? In any case, when general trading companies pioneer new businesses, considering how to uncover business models and value chains is required in these R&D processes.

Accordingly, based on open innovation thinking, managers of general trading companies allow expanded diversity of asset orchestration architecture (vertical integrated architecture, horizontal integrated architecture, leadership relationship architecture: see Box 1.3), and concentrate on the core businesses selection process through experiments and trials to build optimized value chains (the vertical value chain model and co-evolution model). Furthermore, they pursue the process of hypothesis verification and selection to suit strategic objectives with their diverse "asset architectural thinking".

In contrast, "value chain development-type" businesses entail developmental review of vertical integrated architecture and, depending on the situation, horizontal integrated architecture and linkage relationship architecture to uncover new partners or rethink partnerships in the horizontal direction to build new vertical value chain models. Thus, asset orchestration in this domain entails developmental review of strategic objectives.

In "domain horizontal expansion-type business", as an applied asset model, existing vertical integrated architecture is adopted, strategic objectives remain almost unchanged, and partners are selected by geographical considerations. Or, successful models are applied and adopted by adjacent areas, horizontal boundaries are extended, and existing vertical value chain models are adapted and applied to horizontal boundaries. On the other hand, in the shift from R&D-type business to commercialization, strategy objectives and plans are determined and concentrated, and the asset orchestration architecture selected as a result of hypothesis testing is further optimized in its entirety.

In existing businesses, continual maintenance of strategic planning is crucial. Hence, asset orchestration architecture is pursued for efficiency to strengthen and maintain the value chains of such existing businesses. As discussed above, general trading companies execute asset orchestration dynamics by flexibly selecting and properly using the company's asset orchestration architecture and configuring vertical value chain models and co-evolution models, to dynamically combine the growth and development of existing business and the pioneering of new businesses (and properly apply these to suit the situation), by using their capabilities to achieve their strategies in the target business domains and value chains.

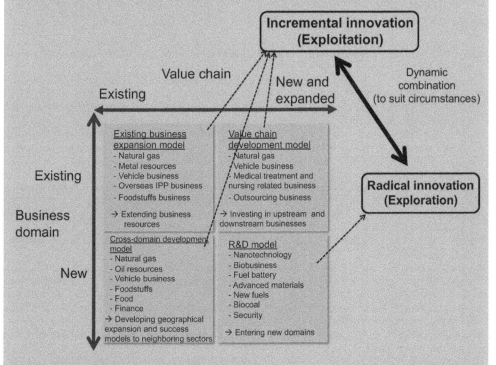

Figure 1.14   Japanese general trading companies' asset orchestration dynamics

4.   CONCLUSION OF THIS CHAPTER

This chapter has presented the new concept of "boundaries vision", and new perspectives from a theoretical, empirical and practical viewpoint on the relationship between boundaries vision and "sensing" in "dynamic capabilities" (e.g., Teece, 2007, 2014), the core framework of strategic management. Then, the chapter proposed that "sensing through boundaries vision" raises the creativity of practitioners, organizations and corporations. Moreover, the chapter has presented how the three DC framework sub-capabilities of sensing (boundaries vision), seizing (asset orchestration architecture) and transforming (asset orchestration dynamics) achieve dynamic combination of exploration and exploitation through the dynamic reconfiguration of corporate and organizational boundaries, and hence promote boundaries innovation.

NOTE

1. The Apple-centered "Small-World Network" (SW) consists of hubs and a network structure resembling a scale-free network (Barabasi, 2002) with a huge number of links. Barabasi (2002) also observes a similar trend, in which 80 percent of all World Wide Web connections are "occupied" by only 20 percent of "hub" websites. Realistically, however, the number of business-related partners is limited. At the same time, a company comprised of micro-practitioners who think subjectively must discuss the pros and cons as well as transaction costs of building relationships with partners. This is why the networked SC formation differs somewhat (Watts, 2003) from the highly centralized, scale-free network (Cole and Cole, 1973; Barabasi and Albert, 1999).

REFERENCES

Abernathy, W.J. and Utterback, J.M. (1978), 'Patterns of industrial innovation', *Technology Review*, 80(7), 40–47.

Amabile, T.M. (1979), 'Effects of external evaluation on artistic creativity', *Journal of Personality and Social Psychology*, 37(2), 221–233.

Amabile, T.M. (1982), 'Social psychology of creativity: A consensual assessment technique', *Journal of Personality and Social Psychology*, 43(5), 997–1013.

Amabile, T.M. (1983), 'Brilliant but cruel: Perceptions of negative evaluators', *Journal of Experimental Social Psychology*, 19(2), 146–156.

Amabile, T.M. (1985), 'Motivation and creativity: Effects of motivational orientation on creative writers', *Journal of Personality and Social Psychology*, 48(2), 393–399.

Amabile, T.M. (1988), 'A model of creativity and innovation in organizations', *Research in Organizational Behavior*, 10(1), 123–167.

Amabile, T.M. (1995), 'Attributions of creativity: What are the consequences?', *Creativity Research Journal*, 8(4), 423–426.

Amabile, T.M. (1996), *Creativity in Context: Update to the Social Psychology of Creativity*, Boulder, CO: Westview Press.

Amasaka, K. (2004), 'Applying new JIT–A management technology strategy model at Toyota: strategic QCD studies with affiliated and non-affiliated suppliers', *Proceedings of the Production and Operations Management Society*, Cancun, Mexico, 1–11.

Argyris, C. (2004), 'Double-loop learning and implementable validity', in Tsoukas, H. and Mylonopoulos, N. (eds), *Organizations as Knowledge Systems*, London: Palgrave Macmillan, pp. 29–45.

Argyris, C. and Schon, D. (2004), *Theory in Practice: Increasing Professional Effectiveness*, San Francisco: Jossey Bass.

Baldwin, C.Y. and Clark, K.B. (2000), *Design Rules, Vol. 1: The Power of Modularity*, Cambridge, MA: MIT Press.

Barabasi, A.-L. (2002), *Linked: The New Science of Networks*, Boston: Perseus.

Barabasi, A.-L. and Albert, R. (1999), 'Emergence of scaling in random networks', *Science*, 286, October, 509–512.

Brown, J.S. and Duguid, P. (2001), 'Knowledge and organization: A social-practice perspective', *Organization Science*, 12(6), 198–213.

Burt, R. (1992), *Structural Holes: The Social Structure of Competition*, Cambridge, MA and London: Harvard University Press.

Burt, R. (1997), 'The contingent value of social capital', *Administrative Science Quarterly*, 42(2), 339–365.

Carlile, P. (2002), 'A pragmatic view of knowledge and boundaries: Boundary objects in new product development', *Organization Science*, 13(4), 442–455.

Carlile, P. (2004), 'Transferring, translating, and transforming: An integrative framework for managing knowledge across boundaries', *Organization Science*, 15(5), 555–568.

Chesbrough, H. (2003), *Open Innovation*, Boston, MA: Harvard Business School Press.

Christensen, C.M. (1997), *The Innovator's Dilemma: When New Technologies Cause Great Firms to Fail*, Boston, MA: Harvard Business School Press.

Clark, K.B. (1985), 'The interaction of design hierarchies and market concepts in technological evolution', *Research Policy*, 14(2), 235–251.

Clark, K.B. and Fujimoto, T. (1991), *Product Development Performance: Strategy, Organization, and Management in the World Auto Industry*, Boston, MA: Harvard Business School Press.

Cohen, D. and Prusak, L. (2000), *In Good Company: How Social Capital Makes Organizations Work*, Boston, MA: Harvard Business School Press.

Cole, R. and Cole, S. (1973), *Social Stratification in Science*, Chicago: University of Chicago Press.

Coleman, J. (1988), 'Social capital in the creation of human capital', *American Journal of Sociology*, 94, 95–120.

Cyert, R.M. and March, J.G. (1963), *A Behavioral Theory of the Firm*, Englewood Cliffs, NJ: Prentice Hall.

Day, G.S. and Schoemaker, P. (2004), 'Peripheral vision: Sensing and acting on weak signals', *Long Range Planning*, 2(37), 117–121.

Day, G. and Schoemaker, P.J. (2005), 'Scanning the periphery', *Harvard Business Review*, 83(11), 135–148.

Day, G.S. and Schoemaker, P.J. (2016), 'Adapting to fast-changing markets and technologies', *California Management Review*, 58(4), 59–77.

Dyer, J.H. and Hatch, N.W. (2004), 'Using supplier networks to learn faster', *MIT Sloan Management Review*, 45(3), 57–63.

Elsbach, K.D. and Hargadon, A.B. (2006), 'Enhancing creativity through "mindless" work: A framework of workday design', *Organization Science*, 17(4), 470–483.

Ericsson, K.A. and Lehmann, A.C. (1996), 'Expert and exceptional performance: Evidence of maximal adaptation to task constraints', *Annual Review of Psychology*, 47(1), 273–305.

Fauconnier, G. and Turner, M. (1998), 'Conceptual integration networks', *Cognitive Science*, 22(2), 133–187.

George, J.M. and Zhou, J. (2007), 'Dual tuning in a supportive context: Joint contributions of positive mood, negative mood, and supervisory behaviors to employee creativity', *Academy of Management Journal*, 50(3), 605–622.

Giddens, A. (1984), *The Constitution of Society*, Berkeley, CA: University of California Press.

Giddens, A. and Pierson, C. (1998), *Conversation with Anthony Giddens: Making Sense of Modernity*, Oxford: Blackwell Publishers Ltd.

Granovetter, M. (1973), 'The strength of weak ties', *American Journal of Sociology*, 78(6), 1360–1380.

Hacklin, F., Marxt, C. and Fahrni, F. (2009), 'Coevolutionary cycles of convergence: An extrapolation from the ICT industry', *Technological Forecasting and Social Change*, 76(6), 723–736.

Hagel III, J. and Brown, J.S. (2005), 'Productive friction', *Harvard Business Review*, 83(2), 139–145.

Hargadon, A. (2003), *How Breakthroughs Happen: The Surprising Truth about How Companies Innovate*, Boston, MA: Harvard Business School Press.

Hargadon, A. and Sutton, R. (1997), 'Technology brokering and innovation in a product development firm', *Administration Science Quarterly*, 42, 716–749.

Helfat, C. and Martin, J. (2015), 'Dynamic managerial capabilities: A perspective on the relationship between managers, creativity and innovation', in Shalley, C.E., Hitt, M.A. and Zhou, J. (eds), *The Oxford Handbook of Creativity, Innovation and Entrepreneurship*, Oxford: Oxford University Press, pp. 421–433.

Helfat, C.E. and Peteraf, M.A. (2015), 'Managerial cognitive capabilities and the microfoundations of dynamic capabilities', *Strategic Management Journal*, 36(6), 831–850.

Helfat, C.E., Finkelstein, S., Mitchell, W., Peteraf, M.A., Singh, H., Teece, D. J. and Winter, S.G. (2007), *Dynamic Capabilities: Understanding Strategic Change in Organizations*, Oxford: Blackwell.

Henderson, R.M. and Clark, K.B. (1990), 'Architectural innovation: The reconfiguration of existing product technologies and the failure of established firms', *Administrative Science Quarterly*, 35(1), 9–30.

Hodgkinson, G.P. and Healey, M.P. (2011), 'Psychological foundations of dynamic capabilities: Reflexion and reflection in strategic management', *Strategic Management Journal*, 32(13), 1500–1516.

Johansson, F. (2004), *The Medici Effect*, Boston, MA: Harvard Business School Press.

Kaplan, S., Murray, F. and Henderson, R. (2003), 'Discontinuities and senior management: Assessing the role of recognition in pharmaceutical firm response to biotechnology', *Industrial and Corporate Change*, 12(4), 203–233.

Klein, J.T. (1990), *Interdisciplinarity: History, Theory, and Practice*, Detroit, MI: Wayne State University Press.

Kodama, M. (2002), 'Transforming an old economy company through strategic communities', *Long Range Planning*, 35(4), 349–365.

Kodama, M. (2005a), 'Knowledge creation through networked strategic communities: Case studies on new product development in Japanese companies', *Long Range Planning*, 38(1), 27–49.

Kodama, M. (2005b), 'How two Japanese high-tech companies achieved rapid innovation via strategic community networks', *Strategy & Leadership*, 33(6), 39–47.

Kodama, M. (2006), 'Knowledge-based view of corporate strategy', *Technovation*, 26(12), 1390–1406.

Kodama, M. (2007a), *The Strategic Community-Based Firm*, Basingstoke, UK: Palgrave Macmillan.

Kodama, M. (2007b), *Knowledge Innovation: Strategic Management as Practice*, Cheltenham, UK and Northampton, MA, USA: Edward Elgar Publishing.

Kodama, M. (2007c), *Project-Based Organization in the Knowledge-Based Society*, London, UK: Imperial College Press.

Kodama, M. (2007d), 'Innovation and knowledge creation through leadership-based strategic community: Case study on high-tech company in Japan', *Technovation*, 27(3), 115–132.

Kodama, M. (2007e), 'Innovation through boundary management: A case study in reforms at Matsushita Electric', *Technovation*, 27(1–2), 15–29.

Kodama, M. (2009a), 'Boundaries innovation and knowledge integration in the Japanese firm', *Long Range Planning*, 42(4), 463–494.

Kodama, M. (2009b), *Innovation Networks in Knowledge-Based Firm: Developing ICT-Based Integrative Competences*, Cheltenham, UK and Northampton, MA, USA: Edward Elgar Publishing.

Kodama, M. (2010a), 'Theoretical framework of dynamic strategic management through boundary management', in *Boundary Management*, Berlin, Heidelberg: Springer, pp. 15–35.

Kodama, M. (2010b), Developing new business models through dynamic boundary management: Case studies of Sony and NTT-DATA', in *Boundary Management*, Berlin, Heidelberg: Springer, pp. 37–62.

Kodama, M. (2011), *Knowledge Integration Dynamics: Developing Strategic Innovation Capability*, Singapore: World Scientific Publishing.

Kodama, M. (2014), *Winning Through Boundaries Innovation: Communities of Boundaries Generate Convergence*, New York: Peter Lang.

Kodama, M. (2017a), *Developing Holistic Leadership: A Source of Business Innovation*, Bingley, UK: Emerald Group Publishing.

Kodama, M. (2017b), 'Developing strategic innovation in large corporations: The dynamic capability view of the firm', *Knowledge and Process Management*, 24(4), 221–246.

Kodama, M. (ed.) (2017c), *Ma Theory and the Creative Management of Innovation*. Palgrave Macmillan, USA.

Kodama, M. (2018a), *Sustainable Growth Through Strategic Innovation: Driving Congruence in Capabilities*, Cheltenham, UK and Northampton, MA, USA: Edward Elgar Publishing.

Kodama, M. (ed.) (2018b), *Collaborative Dynamic Capabilities for Service Innovation*, London: Palgrave Macmillan.

Kodama, M. (2018c), 'Boundaries innovation through knowledge convergence: Developing triad strategic communities', *Technology Analysis & Strategic Management*, 30(5), 609–624.

Kodama, M. (2019), *Developing Holistic Strategic Management in the Advanced ICT Era* (Vol. 35), Singapore: World Scientific Publishing.

Kodama, M. and Shibata, T. (2014), 'Strategy transformation through strategic innovation capability: A case study of Fanuc', *R&D Management*, 44(1), 75–103.

Kodama, M. and Shibata, T. (2016), 'Developing knowledge convergence through a boundaries vision: A case study of Fujifilm in Japan', *Knowledge and Process Management*, 23(4), 274–292.

Kogut, B. and Zander, U. (1992), 'Knowledge of the firm, combinative capabilities and the replication of technology', *Organization Science*, 5(2), 383–397.

Leifer, R., McDermott, M., O'Connor, C., Peters, S., Rice, M. and Veryzer, W. (2000), *Radical Innovation: How Mature Companies Can Outsmart Upstarts*, Cambridge, MA: Harvard Business School Press.

Leonard-Barton, D. (1992), 'Core capabilities and core rigidities: A paradox in managing new product development', *Strategic Management Journal*, 13(2), 111–125.

Leonard-Barton, D. (1995), *Wellsprings of Knowledge: Building and Sustaining the Source of Innovation*, Cambridge, MA: Harvard Business School Press.

Levitt, B. and March, J.B. (1988), 'Organization learning', in Scott, W.R. and Blake, J. (eds), *Annual Review of Sociology*, 14, Palo Alto, CA: Annual Reviews, pp. 319–340.

Lin, L. and Kulatilaka, N. (2006), 'Network effects and technology licensing with fixed fee, royalty, and hybrid contracts', *Journal of Management Information Systems*, 23(2), 91–118.

March, J.G. (1972), 'Model bias in social action', *Review of Educational Research*, 42(4), 413–429.

March, J.G. (1981), 'Footnotes to organizational change', *Administrative Science Quarterly*, 26(4), 563–577.

March, J. (1991), 'Exploration and exploitation in organizational learning', *Organization Science*, 2(1), 71–87.

Markides, C. (1999), *All the Right Moves: A Guide to Crafting Breakthrough Strategy*, Boston, MA: Harvard Business School Publishing.

Martines, L. and Kambil, A. (1999), 'Looking back and thinking ahead: Effects of prior success on managers' interpretations of new information technologies', *Academy of Management Journal*, 42(3), 652–661.

Miller, C.C. and Ireland, R.D. (2005), 'Intuition in strategic decision making: Friend or foe in the fast-paced 21st century?', *The Academy of Management Executive*, 19(1), 19–30.

Mintzberg, H. (1978), 'Patterns in strategy formation', *Management Science*, 24, 934–948.

Mintzberg, H. and Walters, J. (1985), 'Of strategies deliberate and emergent', *Strategic Management Journal*, 6, 257–272.

Nahapiet, J. and Ghoshal, S. (1998), 'Social capital, intellectual capital, and the creation of value in firms', *Academy of Management Review*, 23(2), 242–266.

Nonaka, I. and Konno, N. (1998), 'The concept of "ba": Building a foundation for knowledge creation', *California Management Review*, 40(1), 40–54.

Nonaka, I. and Takeuchi, H. (1995), *The Knowledge-Creating Company*, New York: Oxford University Press.

Nonaka, I., Kodama, M., Hirose, A. and Kohlbacher, F. (2014), 'Dynamic fractal organizations for promoting knowledge-based transformation: A new paradigm for organizational theory', *European Management Journal*, 32(1), 137–146.

Owen-Smith, J. and Powell, W.W. (2004), 'Knowledge networks as channels and conduits: The effects of spillovers in the Boston biotechnology community', *Organization Science*, 15(1), 5–22.

Peirce, C.S. (1998), *Chance, love, and logic: Philisophical essays.* University of Nebraska Press.

Porter, M.E. and Teisberg, E.O. (2006), *Redefining Health Care: Creating Value-Based Competition on Results*, Boston, MA: Harvard Business Press.

Powell, W. and Brantley, P. (1992), 'Competitive cooperation in biotechnology: Learning through networks?' in Noria, N. and Eccles, R.G. (eds), *Network and Organizations: Structure, Form and Action*, Boston, MA: Harvard Business School, pp. 366–394.

Powell, W., Koput, K. and Smith-Doerr, L. (1996), 'Inter-organizational collaboration and the locus of innovation: Networks of learning in biotechnology', *Administrative Science Quarterly*, 41, 116–146.

Rafols, I. and Meyer, M. (2010), 'Diversity and network coherence as indicators of interdisciplinarity: Case studies in bionanoscience', *Scientometrics*, 82(2), 263–287.

Rosenbloom, N. (2000), 'Leadership, capabilities and technological change', *Strategic Management Journal*, 21, 1083–1103.

Rosenkopf, L. and Nerkar, A. (2001), 'Beyond local search: Boundary-spanning, exploration, and impact in the optical disk industry', *Strategic Management Journal*, 22(4), 287–306.

Rosenkopf, L. and Tushman, M. (1998), 'The coevolution of community networks and technology: Lessons from the flight simulation industry', *Industrial and Corporate Change*, 7(6), 311–346.

Ryan, R.M. and Deci, E.L. (2000), 'Self-determination theory and the facilitation of intrinsic motivation, social development, and well-being', *American Psychologist*, 55(1), 68–78.

Shalley, C.E., Zhou, J. and Oldham, G.R. (2004), 'The effects of personal and contextual characteristics on creativity: Where should we go from here?', *Journal of Management*, 30(6), 933–958.

Shibata, T., and Kodama, M. (2007), Knowledge integration through networked strategic communities: two case studies in Japan. *Business Strategy Series*.

Siggelkow, N. (2001), 'Change in the presence of fit: The rise, the fall, and the renaissance of Liz Claiborne', *Academy of Management Journal*, 44(4), 838–857.

Simon, H.A. (1996), *The Science of the Artificial*, 3rd edn, Cambridge, MA: MIT Press.

Simon, H.A. (1997), *Models of Bounded Rationality: Empirically Grounded Economic Reason* (Vol. 3), Cambridge, MA: MIT Press.

Smith, S. and Tushman, M. (2005), 'Managing strategic contradictions: A top management model for managing innovation streams', *Organization Science*, 16(5), 522–536.

Spender, J.C. (1990), *Industry Recipes: An Enquiry into the Nature and Sources of Managerial Judgement*, Oxford: Basil Blackwell.

Star, S.L. (1989), 'The structure of ill-structured solutions: Boundary objects and heterogeneous distributed problem solving', in Huhns, M. and Gasser, I.L. (eds), *Readings in Distributed Artificial Intelligence*, Menlo Park, CA: Morgan Kaufman, pp. 37–54.

Taifi, N. and Passiante, G. (2012), 'Speeding up NPSD through strategic community creation: Case of automaker after-sales services partners', *The Service Industries Journal*, 32(13), 2115–2127.

Teece, D.J. (2007), 'Explicating dynamic capabilities: The nature and microfoundations of (sustainable) enterprise performance', *Strategic Management Journal*, 28(13), 1319–1350.

Teece, D.J. (2014), 'The foundations of enterprise performance: Dynamic and ordinary capabilities in an (economic) theory of firms', *The Academy of Management Perspectives*, 28(4), 328–352.

Teece, D.J., Pisano, G. and Shuen, A. (1997), 'Dynamic capabilities and strategic management', *Strategic Management Journal*, 18(3), 509–533.

Tripsas, M. and Gavetti, G. (2000), 'Capabilities, cognition, and inertia: Evidence from digital imaging', *Strategic Management Journal*, 21(10/11), 1147–1161.

Tushman, M.L. (1977), 'Special boundary roles in the innovation process', *Administrative Science Quarterly*, 22, 587–605.

van Rijnsoever, F.J. and Hessels, L.K. (2011), 'Factors associated with disciplinary and interdisciplinary research collaboration', *Research Policy*, 40(3), 463–472.

Watts, J. (2003), *Six Degrees: The Science of a Connected Age*, New York: W.W. Norton and Company.

Zhou, J. and Shalley, C.E. (2007), *Handbook of Organizational Creativity*, Hove, UK: Psychology Press Limited.

2. Developing boundaries knowledge (knowing): the knowledge creation perspective

Mitsuru Kodama

1. KNOWLEDGE CONVERGENCE AND BOUNDARIES KNOWLEDGE (KNOWING)

The first section, "Background and objectives of this book", in Chapter 1 presented the importance of the concept and framework of creativity development from the perspective of corporate strategy, which has not been deeply explored in psychology, organizational learning theory, knowledge creation theory or innovation management. The chapter presents new propositions on the boundaries vision of practitioners, which is also a cognitive capability as intuition to uncover the best intangible assets (and co-specialized assets). One of the required factors of dynamic capabilities (Teece, 2007, 2014) is the "sensing" ability of practitioners. Sensing is the ability to seek out business opportunities, filter, and analyze, and is dependent on the cognitive capabilities of individual practitioners such as leading organizational members mainly in managerial layers. The appropriate cognitive capabilities in managerial layers to respond to dynamic external environments or business opportunities are crucial in the processes of R&D through innovation and selection of new technologies (e.g., Helfat and Peteraf, 2015).

However, the role played by the cognitive capability of the intuition of leading practitioners is large, and gives them awareness and flashes of insight which are brought about through the deep interactions with a wide range of stakeholders (including customers and partners). Practitioners require boundaries vision, a capability to acquire new insight into multiple and diverse boundaries, to demonstrate the cognitive capability of intuition. To demonstrate boundaries vision, Chapter 1 identified the importance of the micro strategy elements of dynamic capabilities (DC) practiced to optimize asset orchestration processes ("seizing" through the configuration of "asset orchestration architecture" → "transforming" through the execution of "asset orchestration dynamics").

This chapter presents the concept of "boundaries knowledge (knowing)", a new kind of knowledge. Then, the chapter describes how the creation of boundaries knowledge is indispensable at the source of knowledge creation through new knowledge convergence (Nonaka and Takeuchi, 1995). Hence, boundaries knowledge is the most fundamental element of converging different kinds of knowledge to create "convergence knowledge" (tacit or explicit knowledge).

Also discussed later, boundaries knowledge entails the capabilities of practitioners to seek out the discomforts and differences of these dissimilarities on various boundaries, and from them uncover new knowledge. Such boundaries knowledge is also the capability to figure out what types of boundaries exist, link them together and inspire knowledge as new ways of seeing and perceiving. This means that boundaries knowledge is not static, but also entails dynamic and constantly changing capabilities. It is essential to create boundaries knowledge at the source of knowledge creation through new knowledge convergence; thus, boundaries knowledge is the most basic element in the creation of convergence knowledge by combining different types of knowledge (see Figure 2.1).

To succeed with knowledge convergence, the most important factor is the creation of the boundaries knowledge. The capability to uncover (or create) new boundaries and integrate different boundaries when required (in response to conditions) to create new convergence knowledge is a crucial capability. To create convergence knowledge as the final knowledge achievement as an intended or strategic objective, practitioners use boundaries knowledge that they created, and integrate (or converge) different and diverse knowledge (existing convergence knowledge). The author calls the capability of practitioners to converge and integrate different knowledge "convergence knowledge". In the same way as boundaries knowledge mentioned earlier, convergence knowledge is not static, but entails constantly and dynamically changing capabilities.

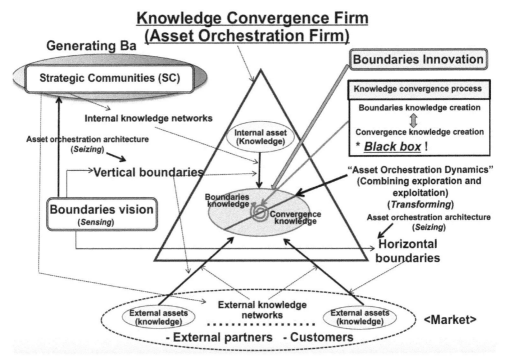

Figure 2.1   A corporate model for knowledge convergence

As identified also in Chapter 1, strategic communities (e.g., Kodama, 2005, 2007) based on "ba" (Nonaka and Takeuchi, 1995) are dynamically formed by the boundaries vision of practitioners. Seen from the perspective of the knowledge-based view, the boundaries vision of practitioners drives the spiral of the knowledge convergence process (the synergies between boundaries knowledge and convergence knowledge: see Figure 2.1). These processes are the source of boundaries innovation (Kodama, 2009), and lead to the acquisition of dynamic capabilities (DC) to bring about sustainable competitiveness in a corporation (performing the sub-capabilities; the demonstration of boundaries vision through sensing, the building of asset orchestration architecture through seizing, and the practice of asset orchestration dynamics through transforming) (see Figure 2.1). As shown in Figure 2.1 the definitions of "knowledge" and "assets" are similar, while the "asset orchestration firm" described in Figure 1.13 in Chapter 1 is equivalent to a "knowledge convergence firm".

However, the spiral knowledge convergence process (the synergies between boundaries knowledge and convergence knowledge) remains in a black-boxed form. Accordingly, there is even more need for future research on the micro core framework of the knowledge convergence process. Thus, as a research approach, this chapter delves deeper into theoretical, empirical and practical aspects through comparative analysis with the SECI model (Nonaka and Takeuchi, 1995).

2. THE CONCEPT AND FRAMEWORK OF BOUNDARIES KNOWLEDGE (KNOWING)

2.1 The Necessity of Boundaries Knowledge (Knowing) and Boundaries Vision from Existing Research

In the knowledge economy, in addition to the necessity for individuals living in corporate society to create diverse knowledge across differing values and areas of specialization in organizations, it is also important to form global networks of the best people and organizations around the world to converge the best knowledge dispersed across the globe with the knowledge of individuals and organizations. As a proposition, this paper presents the concept of boundaries knowledge (knowing) and boundaries vision (Kodama and Shibata, 2016) in the thinking of individual people, which is a driver that accelerates the knowledge creation process.

The acquisition of creativity to generate new knowledge is indispensable for practitioners in modern society. In the knowledge economy, diverse human knowledge (of which technology is one element) is the source of valuable products, services and business models that can give a company new competitiveness. New value chains are formed as new strategic models by merging diverse technologies of different industries to bring about new products, services and business models that transcend various boundaries. Accordingly, for a company to build new business, the company must refresh its perspectives on management to span the boundaries between the knowledge of individuals, groups and organizations (e.g., Kodama, 2007, 2011).

Boundaries knowledge (knowing) is crucial for knowledge creation spanning different fields of specialization for successful new innovation. New innovation occurs through the process of converging diverse knowledge of dissimilar and unique areas of specialization (e.g., Kodama, 2005, 2009; Hacklin et al., 2009; Rafols and Meyer, 2010). In other words, the knowledge creation process through boundaries vision can be thought of as occurring at the level that spans different areas of expertise. By its nature, bringing together knowledge that once belonged to separate areas of technical expertise is the precondition for convergence. Therefore, to make convergence occur, boundaries knowledge spanning different areas of specialist expertise is required.

In general, knowledge boundaries exist between dissimilar types of knowledge (Carlile, 2002). This means that details of dissimilar characteristics and unique knowledge differences essentially exist between different types of knowledge. For example, various functional organizations and specialist fields are separated from each other in a company, and various business types and functions are separated from each other between corporations and industries, and among all these, many boundaries from the visible to the invisible exist from the macro level down to the micro level (Kodama and Shibata, 2014). Also, in companies, individual practitioners do not only face the organizational boundaries of sectionalism, but also face knowledge boundaries that exist at the micro level as a result of their values, backgrounds and areas of specialization. These knowledge differences that arise due to various knowledge boundaries isolate the unique mental models and path-dependent knowledge of practitioners, and are a hindrance to new innovation (e.g., Kogut and Zander, 1992; Leonard-Barton, 1995; Nonaka and Takeuchi, 1995; Spender, 1996; Brown and Duguid, 2001; Carlile, 2002). Hence, the way practitioners perceive and interpret knowledge differences and their resulting actions is an important theme.

In the fieldwork to date by the author and collaborators, the author has confirmed patterns of action through network thinking enabled with boundaries vision, which practitioners use to discover (or create) diverse boundaries knowledge (knowing) and bridge the diverse boundaries both in and outside companies (both in and outside the organization and between people), to share knowledge, and to create new knowledge (Kodama and Shibata, 2016). Thinking about boundaries vision from the context of business, it is practitioners' thinking and discernment to design new business and corporate strategies through the knowledge creation process by recognizing various boundaries, discovering (or creating) boundaries knowledge (knowing) on those boundaries and forming bridges between the boundaries.

Put differently, boundaries vision is the capability of practitioners to discover boundaries knowledge (knowing) and seek out new knowledge such as new hints or ideas from the various discomforts and differences in the dissimilarities on boundaries. Boundaries vision is also the capability to figure out what types of boundaries are discovered and how to link them together to trigger new knowledge for new ways of perceiving or discovery of new things.

Boundaries vision is not static, but is a dynamic, constantly changing capability. For individual business practitioners and organizations, the training and demonstration of boundaries vision an essential source of new knowledge creation, and the most fundamental element of the convergence of dissimilar knowledge is the process of boundaries knowledge through boundaries vision, discussed as follows. To achieve knowledge creation dynamically on diverse and multiple boundaries, practitioners must demonstrate boundaries vision to bring about external knowledge conversions capabilities – the cognitive capabilities to converge dissimilar knowledge (Kodama and Shibata, 2016) and achieve new products, services and business models. In practice, management executives and managers have to use boundaries knowledge (knowing) and boundaries vision to focus on various boundaries to bring about new innovation through the convergence of dissimilar knowledge.

Boundaries knowledge (knowing) and boundaries vision are capabilities for detecting dissimilar knowledge that is only loosely related or entirely unrelated, and uncovering relationships with one's own knowledge and converging (integrating) it with that knowledge. Much of the existing research to date has already reported that the crossing or fusing of dissimilar knowledge is a source of new innovation (e.g., Johansson, 2004; Kodama, 2007). Accordingly, for practitioners, the discovery of relationships between multiple types of dissimilar knowledge, or between existing knowledge and dissimilar knowledge, and finding new meaning or new knowledge in those relationships, is an important trigger for knowledge creation.

2.2 The Concept of Boundaries Knowledge (Knowing)

This section presents the concept of boundaries knowledge (knowing), and discusses the relationship with the SECI model of existing research (Nonaka and Takeuchi, 1995). Then, the section presents the adaptive and intentional processes in boundaries knowledge (knowing), and illustrates that boundaries knowledge (knowing) and boundaries vision are important factors driving the spiral loop of the SECI model (see Figure 2.2).

An important proposition for a corporate strategy to adapt to, or create the convergence world view is the creation of boundaries knowledge. Knowledge boundaries exist between dissimilar knowledge. This means that details of dissimilar characteristics and unique knowledge differences essentially exist between different types of knowledge.

Practitioners recognize various organizational boundaries in their daily business activities. Here, organizational boundaries mean the boundaries between professional areas in official organizations such as research, development, production or sales, the boundaries between management layers in organizations, and the boundaries between customers, external partners, and businesses in different businesses and industries. Boundaries exist between actors with different backgrounds and knowledge, and between stakeholders and environments.

Carlile (2004) described three characteristics of knowledge on these boundaries as deference, dependency and novelty (Carlile and Rebentisch, 2003), and described that the correlative characteristics of these types of knowledge can be expressed by considering boundaries as vectors between two or more actors. These vectors start out from the origin where deference and dependency are known, which means that as knowledge differences broaden with increased novelty, the efforts required for knowledge creation for innovation also increase with increased complexity. This vector model can be extended not only to the interactive relationships between actors, i.e., stakeholders, but also to the interactive relationships in the environments that actors directly face (markets and technologies etc.) (see Figure 2.2).

Giddens' structuration theory (1984) lies at the background of this vector model extension. Giddens questioned how the actions of actors and social forces dialectically interact to form a society. His assertion was that actors are the agents of change that continually reproduce social structures (environments). Hence, in this perspective, actors have close-knit mutual relationships with social structures (environments), while humans proactively change environments while also accepting the impacts of environments. Hence, as novelty increases, the level of actors' interactions with the environment (the structure) and knowledge differences also increases, which means the level of efforts needed for knowledge creation for innovation in an environment also increases.

Carlile (2004) incorporated Shannon and Weaver's (1949) communications theory and adopted three levels of boundaries to this vector model to develop the "3T model" (Transfer [Syntactic boundary] → Translation [Semantic boundary] → Transformation [Pragmatic boundary]). Figure 2.2 describes the aforementioned Giddens' (1984) structuration theory considered in terms of this model. In environments where individuals, organizations or companies face the necessity to innovate or such significant challenges, novelty and uncertainty increase at once, and the quality and quantity of the "knowledge differences" – broadening vectors – also increase on the knowledge boundaries between actors and the environment (the structure), and between actors including stakeholders. In such situations with higher novelty (transformation level [pragmatic boundary]), actors and stakeholders achieve new knowledge creation by transforming existing knowledge (paraphrasing Giddens, actors proactively transform environments through practice and "knowledgeability" based on their own knowledge; Carlile, 2004).

However, most of the new knowledge creation that has come about with innovation to date has occurred on the boundaries between specializations (Leonard-Barton, 1995). This suggests that the thinking and ideas between people and the actions of organizations straddling different fields of specialization are major factors in bringing about innovation success, and are therefore factors that contribute to competitive excellence. Leading research also clarifies why it is difficult to generate and maintain innovation (Carlile, 2004; Kodama, 2007).

It has also been reported that the ideas of people and actions of organizations straddling different fields of specialization are constrained by knowledge path dependency (March, 1972; Rosenkopf and Nerkar, 2001). For example, just as past exploratory activities have been easier to carry out with concentration in close relationships between fields of specialization, the deep communication and collaboration processes between fields of specialization have also been reported to contribute greatly to new innovations (Kodama, 2011; van Rijnsoever and Hessels, 2011).

However, to encourage this kind of communication and collaboration, the way the knowledge boundaries perceived by individuals and organizations are uncovered and managed effectively is critical, and capabilities to determine whether boundaries knowledge acquired through dissimilarities and knowledge differences on diverse boundaries will be a source of new knowledge creation are required. Generally, most people feel uncomfortable when facing unfamiliar boundaries (boundaries with contents to which they are unaccustomed), and different people have different perceptive capabilities and awareness on boundaries where such discomforts occur.

Boundaries knowledge is the capability of practitioners to seek out the discomforts and differences of these dissimilarities on various boundaries (with people, organizations, customers, environments), and from them uncover whatever new knowledge is available. Boundaries knowledge is also the capability to figure out what types of boundaries exist, link them together and inspire knowledge as new ways of viewing and new ways of perceiving. Thus, practitioners are required to have building capabilities for making hypothetical settings as real targets (purposes) by questioning why differences occur, how contradictions can be eliminated or combined, or what sort of common targets should be set among stakeholders, etc. For this, the specific thinking and action of practitioners is called "abduction" (e.g., Anderson, 1986). Through abduction, the knowledge differences that arise between hypothetically set targets and verified results inspire awareness and discovery through the boundaries vision of practitioners, and raise the possibility of bringing about new meaning as boundaries knowledge – the "fourth knowledge" (see Figure 2.2).

Abduction begins with actual awareness, and more than anything requires practitioners to be conscious of objectives. New hypotheses are born by setting focal points based on one's own beliefs and thoughts, observing details (parts) and integrating them with the whole. In abduction, practitioners detect faint signs or changes in real individual events, create leaping hypotheses that combine all relevant knowledge, then with trial and error test the hypothesis and further refine and renew the hypothesis, which leads to new discoveries. This process of abduction is not the same as ordinary inductive or deductive methods.

Boundaries knowledge that comes about through testing of hypotheses set through abduction is not static, but is dynamic and constantly changing. It is essential to create boundaries knowledge as a source of new knowledge creation. This boundaries knowledge integrates and transforms dissimilar knowledge in the SECI model, and is the most fundamental factor in creating new knowledge (see Figure 2.2).

This dynamic boundaries knowledge (boundaries knowing) interlocks with boundaries vision (Kodama and Shibata, 2016), and brings about discomfort and differences or dissimilarities on boundaries as practitioners work to uncover any new awareness, discoveries and knowledge therein. The process of boundaries knowledge through boundaries vision is equivalent to the capabilities to uncover boundaries and link them together to inspire knowledge as new ways of viewing and new ways of perceiving (see Figure 2.2).

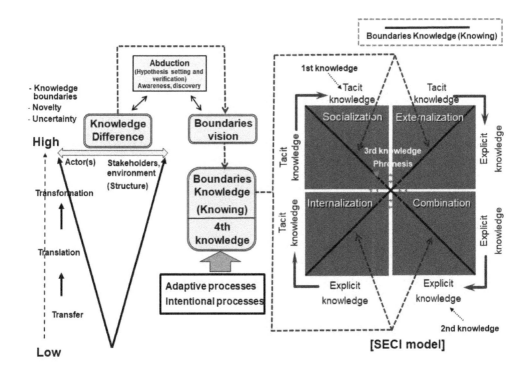

Source: Modeled on Carlile (2004); 3T model based on Shannon and Weaver (1949) and Giddens' (1984) structuration theory.

Figure 2.2   *Knowledge difference, boundaries knowledge, SECI model*

There are two general processes (modes) for boundaries knowledge (knowing). The first is the adaptive process for boundaries knowledge (knowing), which entails capabilities to adapt to changes in knowledge differences on diverse knowledge boundaries, discover or become aware of, and create boundaries knowledge, integrate and transform dissimilar (tacit or explicit) knowledge, and create new (tacit or explicit) knowledge, as described above. The second is the intentional processes for boundaries knowledge (knowing), which entail capabilities to actively incorporate dissimilar (tacit or message) knowledge into existing (tacit or explicit) knowledge, and to actively generate knowledge differences and then integrate and transform that dissimilar (tacit or explicit) knowledge to create new (tacit or explicit) knowledge.

In the SECI process, this means boundaries knowledge exists in the boundary areas in the phases of "Socialization" (tacit knowledge → tacit knowledge: knowledge integration), "Externalization" (tacit knowledge → explicit knowledge: knowledge transformation), "Combination" (explicit knowledge → explicit knowledge: knowledge integration), "Internalization" (explicit knowledge → tacit knowledge: knowledge transformation) (see Figure 2.2). Thus, the existence of boundaries knowledge (knowing) leads to the achievement of knowledge integration or knowledge transformation.

2.3   Boundaries Knowledge (Knowing) as the Fourth Knowledge – the Knowledge Creation Framework

"Dynamic fractal organizations for promoting knowledge-based transformation: A new paradigm for organizational theory" (Nonaka et al., 2014) presents tacit knowledge as the first knowledge, explicit knowledge as the second knowledge and practical knowledge (phronesis) as the third knowledge driving the spiral loop in the core model of the knowledge creation process of leading companies and organizations (the SECI process) (Nonaka and Takeuchi, 1995). However, there has not been any deep discussion on the details of the process of "knowledge integration" (tacit knowledge → tacit knowledge, explicit knowledge → explicit knowledge) or "knowledge transformation" (tacit knowledge → explicit knowledge, explicit knowledge → tacit knowledge) in the boundary areas in the four phases of the SECI process in Nonaka's Theory (Nonaka and Takeuchi, 1995; Nonaka et al., 2008).

Nonaka (2016) said the following about the relationship between tacit knowledge and explicit knowledge:

> The relationship between tacit knowledge and explicit knowledge has been described as the two sides of the same coin, but those boundaries are dynamic and cannot be clearly separated, and only have differences in shade, like gradation. Expressing the relationship between tacit knowledge and explicit knowledge using the metaphor of an iceberg, the part rising above the water that can be seen is the explicit knowledge, whereas the huge, many times bigger lump hiding below the surface of the water is the tacit knowledge, with a boundary constantly changing due to the movement of waves and the iceberg itself"

Thus, boundaries knowledge is knowledge that comes about on the border between tacit knowledge and explicit knowledge which is constantly changing similar to the movement of the iceberg and the waves described by Nonaka (2016, p.70).

Also, in tacit knowledge integration (tacit knowledge → tacit knowledge) to generate comprehensive new meaning by linking distributed tacit knowledge elements and inferring a consistent, comprehensive whole bottom-up and inductively, described by Polanyi (1962), boundaries knowledge exists between dissimilar elements of tacit knowledge. It is also clear that in explicit knowledge integration (explicit knowledge → explicit knowledge) to clarify knowledge and put it into words compared to tacit knowledge, boundaries knowledge exists between dissimilar elements of explicit knowledge. The existence of this boundaries knowledge (knowing) leads to the achievement of tacit knowledge integration and explicit knowledge integration, and the achievement of knowledge transformation (tacit knowledge → explicit knowledge, explicit knowledge → tacit knowledge).

This chapter identifies boundaries knowledge (boundaries knowing) as the fourth knowledge in the boundary areas of knowledge integration and knowledge transformation of the Socialization, Externalization, Combination, Internalization in Figure 2.2, and describes its positioning in the SECI model in detail as follows (see Figure 2.2).

2.3.1 Characteristics of boundaries knowledge in tacit and explicit knowledge domains – synthesis of images and substance

The SECI model entails dynamic processes to raise the level of quality and quantity of personal and organizational knowledge through the creation of knowledge in the interactions of transforming the tacit knowledge rooted in the different experiences of individuals, to shareable explicit knowledge and explicit knowledge to tacit knowledge, and their spiral circulation. SECI consists of four phases, beginning with "Socialization" (Figure 2.2). This involves the practitioner's body and five senses to detect knowledge embedded in the environment through direct experience in workplaces in-house such as sales and manufacturing, or through external exchange with customers and clients. However, knowledge must be put into words to be shared organizationally. Changing this knowledge by accumulating analogies, metaphors, inferences and dialogue into language, concepts and iconography is the next stage of "Externalization".

To crystallize (materialize) the concept, the knowledge must be combined with other explicit knowledge, analyzed and systemized, and processed into a form that anybody can use such as documentation, databases and theoretical models etc. through "Combination". This phase corresponds to the work of designing specific technologies, products, software and services by deploying IT. Finally, in "Internalization", the specific products, services and technologies are launched on to the market through actions based on the new designs. In this process, individuals master new tacit knowledge. At the same time as that, with products as the media, knowledge and values are inspired with customers, which lead back again to "Socialization".

To put it briefly in relation to innovation, this entails sharing tacit knowledge of customers who physically comprise living markets (Socialization), sublimating market knowledge as concepts through essential dialogue transcending the boundaries of organizations (Externalization), systemization transcending space–time deploying IT (Combination), and crystallizing technologies, products, software, services, business models and one's own know-how (Internalization) at the same time as inspiring new knowledge in market customers to lead to Socialization once again.

A core framework of this chapter is the existence of boundaries knowledge (knowing) on the boundaries of knowledge integration and knowledge transformation in these four phases. The following describes the characteristics of boundaries knowledge (knowing).

*(a)   The socialization domain (tacit knowledge → tacit knowledge: the knowledge inte-
            gration process)*

As shown in the socialization domains of Figures 2.2 and 2.3, practitioners in marketing have to experience and perceive social contexts such as trends in market structures or latent needs of customers that cannot be clarified as explicit knowledge in the life world domain. In such cases, marketers must perceive and recognize knowledge differences between their target product image and real social contexts at the macro and micro levels. On the other hand, through direct experience in the workplace or through close dialogue with marketers, practitioners in engineering and development fields have to sense and recognize new knowledge differences that are macro (overall) and micro (partial) technical contexts (for example, "foresee" as an engineer whether it's possible to cover the product image within the scope expected from the tacit knowledge built up through time) to conform to (adapt to) tacit social contexts (images and feelings of target products, etc.).

In the Abstract Space (Life World) [Socialization] domain in Figure 2.3, diverse tacit knowledge is interacted, exchanged and shared with oneself and others through the spiraling interactions (the abduction process) between social and technological contexts (and between social and technological contexts at the macro (overall) and micro (partial) levels). This abduction process, hypothesis setting and verification through trial and error leads to knowledge differences sensing and recognition by practitioners between the new intended hypothesis setting, and verification results at the macro (overall) and micro (partial) levels, and new boundaries knowledge is created from adaptive (or intentional) processes.

In particular, to achieve target (intended) tacit knowledge, it is important that practitioners correctly recognize the knowledge differences to determine whether they can achieve the target tacit knowledge through the knowledge integration process to integrate diverse tacit knowledge as tacit knowledge → tacit knowledge based on the accumulated experience and know-how of practitioners, and further bring about boundaries knowledge. In other words, boundaries knowledge is a factor that drives new (tacit) knowledge integration processes. This newly generated boundaries knowledge is embedded in newly set hypotheses, and leads to the discovery and generation of new tacit knowledge through the reconfiguration and reintegration of diverse tacit knowledge through dramatic refinement and renewal of hypotheses (see Figure 2.3).

Polanyi (1962) described the process of generating comprehensive new meaning by relating distributed tacit knowledge elements, and inductively inferring a consistent and comprehensive whole from bottom up as tacit knowledge integration. In contrast, Nonaka (2016) described the behavioral method of "knowing" of practitioners as being brought about through the capabilities of tacit knowledge integration, and tacit knowledge integration as the skill of invention, discovery and creation.

For this tacit knowledge integration, as described above, the generation of new meaning through the creation of boundaries knowledge by recognizing the knowledge differences is crucial. The generation of boundaries knowledge enables the integration of diverse tacit knowledge (tacit knowledge → tacit knowledge) and thus plays the role of new tacit knowledge creation (see "Socialization" in Figure 2.3).

On the other hand, the capabilities to discover, sense, recognize and create new boundaries knowledge from the spiraling interactions through abduction between these social and technological contexts (moreover, between social and technological contexts at the macro and micro levels) is also "boundaries vision" (Kodama and Shibata, 2016) (see Figures 2.3 and 2.4). Through their direct experiences in the abstract spaces (in the life world domain), marketers and engineers (sometimes customers as well) question whether the image of the product is exactly what the customers want, notice differences to what was originally sensed, and wonder whether doing things a certain way will go well, and hold creative dialectic dialogue (Kodama, 2007), and in the time and space abstracted as the image, practitioners' beliefs and thoughts clash.

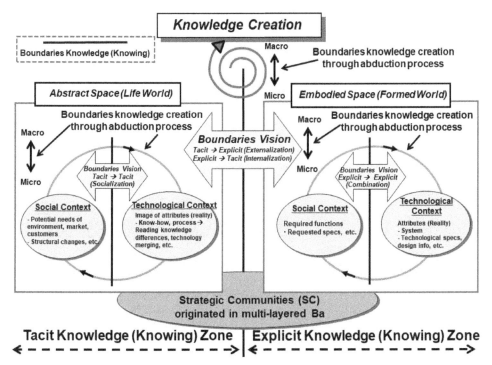

Figure 2.3   *Knowledge creation through boundaries knowledge (knowing) – positioning of boundaries knowledge (knowing) in the SECI model*

(b)   *Externalization domain (tacit knowledge → explicit knowledge: the knowledge transformation process)*

It is not always possible to achieve concrete concepts and prototypes while closed off in abstract space. As customer requirements, marketers have to embody more realistic explicit knowledge using the social contexts obtained through the dialectic dialog with engineers in the life world domain. To do this, practitioners must transform the image as tacit knowledge in the abstract space between marketers and engineers into substance. This is the embodied space (in the formed world domain), where metaphors and analogies are the media through which

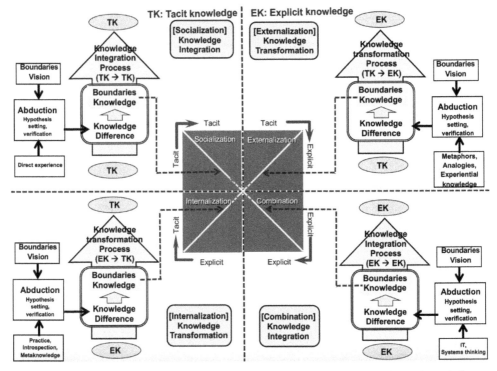

Figure 2.4   Knowledge integration, knowledge transformation, boundaries knowledge

images are converted into explicit knowledge (putting latent customer needs and requirements clearly into words) for analysis and design (see Figure 2.3).

An often-used method for generating concepts is a combination of deduction and induction. This could entail a deductive approach to generating concepts from such things as business philosophy or strategy, or inductively being guided by target customers or market research, etc. However, there are cases in which it is not possible to generate appropriate concepts from deductive or inductive approaches, and so a non-analytical approach is required. This could entail the use of metaphors or analogies.

Metaphors have been described as a method of sensing or intuitively understanding something different by painting a picture in the mind as a symbol of a thing. Through metaphors, people create new interpretations of experiences by appealing to listeners to see a thing as something different. Essentially, a metaphor entails understanding and experiencing something by relating it to something else (Lakoff and Johnson, 1980). In this way, a metaphor is a communication mechanism that functions to harmonize mismatches in meaning (Donnellon et al., 1986). Using metaphors effectively enables thinking about similarities between concepts, and enables awareness of knowledge differences such as imbalances and contradictions between concepts. This contributes to the generation of new meaning. Association through metaphors is more intuitive and image-based, and leads to the discovery of relationships to the object.

On the other hand, analogies focus on common points between different objects, and enable reduction of parts that cannot be understood. Association by analogy is done with logical thinking, and enables clarification of knowledge differences by focusing on similarities of the structure and function of the objects. The use of the aforementioned abduction and non-analytical metaphors and analogies enables practitioners to generate boundaries knowledge from knowledge differences, and effectively generate explicit knowledge as concepts from tacit knowledge.

Specifically, using metaphors and analogies prompts practitioners to become aware and discover, and at the same time forces them to recognize knowledge differences. Then, by generating new meaning from these knowledge differences, practitioners bring about boundaries knowledge through the abduction process of setting and verifying hypotheses through trial and error. In particular, to achieve target (intended) explicit knowledge, it is important that practitioners correctly recognize knowledge differences to determine whether they can achieve the target explicit knowledge through the knowledge transformation process as tacit knowledge → explicit knowledge based on experiential knowledge such as their accumulated experience and know-how, and further bring about boundaries knowledge. In other words, boundaries knowledge born from "foreseeing" the technical potential – target explicit knowledge (for example, differences between the potentials and the product development processes to date: also knowledge differences) – is a factor that drives new knowledge transformation processes (see Externalization in Figure 2.4).

Practically, in the Externalization phase, there are demands to complete product planning documentation etc. in-house, and with high-tech products engineers are required to "foresee" the potential of whether a new product can be technically achieved (differences between the potential and the product development processes to date: grasping the knowledge differences). There are many cases in innovation where commercialization has proven difficult using only the accumulated path-dependent technologies of the engineers themselves. To establish explicit knowledge as content with planning and documentation for the objective, engineers themselves must understand knowledge differences between their own technical capabilities and the target technical development, and conceptualize the technical development process. There are three patterns of conceptualization of this process.

Pattern A in Figure 2.5 describes the case of achieving a technical development through in-house internal knowledge integration, in which the corporation has full control over the innovation process. Closed innovation-type corporate systems are generally applied to industries and businesses where major merits can be found through configuration of value chains through vertical integration. The second pattern, Pattern B, is crucial for knowledge integration of internal (in-house) and external (outside the company) knowledge through the formation of internal and external integration networks through collaboration strategies both in and out of a company (Kodama, 2011, 2015) (see Figure 2.5, Pattern B). This innovation system can also be thought of as "hybrid innovation" (half-open innovation). Hybrid innovation simultaneously combines elements of both closed and open innovation, and is also called half-open innovation. In the third pattern, Pattern C, a company must adopt open innovation (Chesbrough, 2003) to respond to the technical environment. Open innovation is a concept that raises the value of innovation by effectively including external ideas and technologies and having other companies use the ideas of one's own company (see Figure 2.5, Pattern C). "Foreseeing" the above technical contexts of technical development processes with innovation

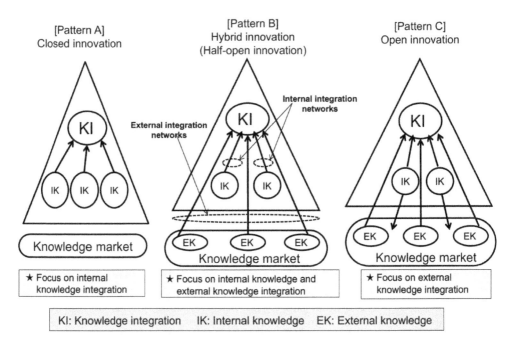

Figure 2.5   Innovation processes for knowledge transformation (tacit knowledge →
explicit knowledge)

systems (differences between the potential and the product development processes to date: grasping the knowledge differences) is a factor of boundaries knowledge to achieve knowledge transformation as tacit knowledge → explicit knowledge.

On the other hand, in the aforementioned Socialization phase and this Externalization phase, interaction as "dialectical dialogue" gives practitioners recognition of knowledge differences for awareness and discovery in hypothesis setting and verification, and plays the role of prompting the creation of boundaries knowledge to raise the level of supplementation and completion of the target knowledge integration and knowledge transformation processes.

In the knowledge transformation process, shifting from the abstract space (the life world domain) to the embodied space (formed world domain) (tacit knowledge → explicit knowledge), the aforementioned boundaries vision is the capability that enables discovery, sensing and recognition of new knowledge differences and boundaries knowledge through the abduction process via the spiraling interactions between social and technical contexts. Through their experience in the abstract spaces (the life world domain) and embodied spaces (the formed world domain), marketers and engineers question whether it is okay to think that such products and services are absolutely what the customer wants, whether such products and services are achievable, and whether it is possible to achieve them in certain ways and hold creative dialectic dialogue, and in the time and space abstracted as the image, practitioners' beliefs and thoughts clash.

However, it is not enough to simply shift once with the knowledge transformation process (tacit knowledge → explicit knowledge) from the abstract space (life world domain) to the embodied space (formed world domain). In real business activities, this process entails going back and forth between these spaces over and over again through abduction between micro and macro contexts until the image and reality become one. Finally, explicit knowledge comes to completion with actual concepts and prototypes. The quality of knowledge differences and boundaries knowledge brought about through such recursion between the macro and micro in social and technological contexts determines the quality of the creativity of concepts.

(c)   The combination domain (explicit knowledge → explicit knowledge: the knowledge integration process)

Combination is the process of creating one type of knowledge system by combining concepts that are fragmented pieces of explicit knowledge. This is also the process of creating new explicit knowledge by combining dissimilar explicit knowledge making full use of high-tech technologies such as IT and digital technologies. For this, engineers require "systems thinking" (e.g., Jackson, 2003).

In systems thinking, when considering matters we use the concept of a system to uniformly and comprehensively give meaning to the entirety of the matter we are considering, and we understand systems by thinking about them as indicative of some kind of work or activity, in which groups of structural elements are mutually linked to bring about a function or functions. These interactions and interdependencies in which collections of elements behave as some ordered whole is called a "system". Systems have boundaries, and it is impossible to understand the function or action that the whole provides just by removing some part of its internal structure or mechanism. Therefore, systems thinking is a method of thinking that focuses on the relationships between the parts of a system in order to understand the whole, rather than just focusing on the individual parts themselves.

A system is an independent organization in which multiple parts organically link together with its own boundary and is distinguished from the outside world by that boundary. In actual fact, all of the products, services and business models that surround us are systems. Similarly, the organic linking of multiple business processes that form independent organizations or companies can also be understood as systems. What this means is our everyday lives are full of systems and, hence, perceiving them as such is helpful.

Thus, one of the factors that determines the characteristics of a system is its relationships. There are two types of relationship, one being the relationships between parts inside the system and the other being the relationships between the system and the external world. These internal and external relationships have a major impact on the character of the system. In product development and design, systems are formed from the mutually interdependent close-knit and complex relationships between the parts (integral systems) and systems that have simple interdependent relationships based on rules (modular systems). These two types of systems are vastly different in character. In the former, changing one part can bring about unexpected effects on the whole system due to the chain of interdependencies in the system. But in the latter, even if a part is changed, the effects on the entire system can be controlled, because its interdependent relationships have rules. Therefore, in addition to the character of the parts of a system, an entire system can be greatly affected depending on the types of relationships on which it is built (e.g., Baldwin and Clark, 2000).

Systems are numerous elements assembled according to certain rules to achieve an objective, and a system needs certain functions to achieve its objectives. To achieve a function, a number of elements must be brought together according to certain rules, which determines the domain of the system. This domain is then regulated by boundaries, called the "system" internally and "the environment" externally. There is always some relationship between the objectives of a system and its boundaries. If a system is large, it is usually separated into partial systems which are each given a purpose, and efforts made to achieve those purposes, and thus the objectives of the overall system as a collection of its parts working effectively. The partial systems are also called subsystems. In this way, systems thinking gives rise to boundaries knowledge to design boundaries (see Figure 2.6).

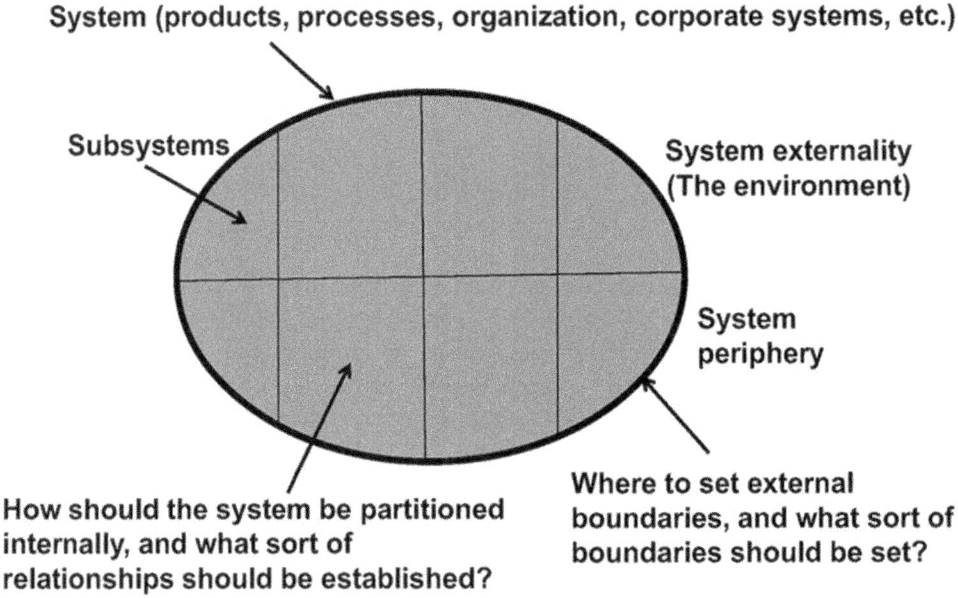

System (products, processes, organization, corporate systems, etc.)

Subsystems

System externality
(The environment)

System
periphery

How should the system be partitioned internally, and what sort of relationships should be established?

Where to set external boundaries, and what sort of boundaries should be set?

Figure 2.6   Boundaries knowledge creation through systems thinking in the combination phase

Systems thinking entails analyzing customer requirements and creating specifications for functions, and designing systems for prototyping and the achievement of products (a whole range of design and analysis methods including total and subsystem design, function and structure design, integral and modular, open or closed, hardware and software coordination, total and partial optimization) and bring about technical contexts as explicit knowledge. Marketers and engineers engage in dialectical dialogue in embodied space to raise the level of completion of explicit knowledge.

In the Combination domain, knowledge differences from the technical context, for example in new product development, are clarified through breaking down and reusing existing knowledge assets, and improvement of existing knowledge assets and new developmental elements. Engineers require the ability to break down, analyze and reconfigure development elements of the objective product as new elements (including improvements to existing knowledge) and existing elements (knowledge) based on the existing tacit knowledge (the experience and know-how of engineers and engineering groups) and existing explicit knowledge. Thus, knowledge differences capabilities entail the ability to recognize the three categories of: (1) the reuse of existing knowledge, (2) the improvement of existing knowledge, and (3) elements of new development to achieve new products through thorough discussions among engineers. This recognition capability is one factor that brings about boundaries knowledge.

An important point for engineers is that they require the capability to quickly and precisely determine the level of elements required for new development (developmental difficulty and scale etc.) because they determine development costs and timescales. Reuse and improvement of existing technology is greatly affected by the so-called historic accumulation of technologies – high levels of path dependency. With new development, path dependency is relatively low, and entails capabilities that engineers must acquire anew. These capabilities must be built in-house from scratch, or acquired through mutual learning in strategic partnership with other companies. Also, with the high necessity for complex technical convergence and large weight on new developmental elements in dramatic environmental changes, all new developments can be achieved by making the most use of the core technologies of one's own company while quickly accessing the core technologies of other companies and integrating them (e.g., Kodama, 2005, 2006).

However, to determine how explicit knowledge should be combined to achieve new technological elements, the discovery and creation of boundaries knowledge from knowledge differences between different types of explicit knowledge is required. To uncover such new technological elements, the process of setting hypotheses and testing them through abduction with systems thinking is important, and the knowledge differences resulting from hypothesizing and verification should refine the classification and division in the aforementioned three different categories. As a result of this process, engineers are able to drive the (explicit) knowledge integration process through the creation of boundaries knowledge based on the knowledge differences put into explicit knowledge (see Combination in Figure 2.4).

The capability to recognize knowledge differences and create boundaries knowledge to accurately uncover new developmental elements in the Combination domain is related to the "common knowledge" of engineers (e.g., Star and Griesemer, 1989; Cramton, 2001; Carlile, 2002). Engineers require common knowledge to acquire the unique knowledge of each domain required for the target new product development. Common knowledge drives knowledge sharing and knowledge inspiration among engineers with differing specialties (Kodama, 2007), raises the ability to recognize knowledge differences among engineers, and is a factor that efficiently and effectively brings about boundaries knowledge.

Discovering and creating boundaries knowledge in this way enables the integration of diverse explicit knowledge. Combination happens when boundaries knowledge is incorporated into the integration process of diverse accumulated explicit knowledge. Integration of explicit knowledge does not only aggregate it into a generalized knowledge system, but also leads to the generation of new knowledge or new concepts through the combination of diverse explicit knowledge.

(d)   The internalization domain (explicit knowledge → tacit knowledge: the knowledge transformation process)

Internalization is the process of individuals acquiring new tacit knowledge from explicit knowledge. Specific behaviors are required for these processes. In other words, this is the process of consciously getting used to the theoretically understood explicit knowledge as tacit knowledge through actions. Internalization is not just simply practice, but is practice with awareness. This is an important perspective. The internalization phase is one in which practitioners turn explicit knowledge into skills and know-how as corporeal and experiential knowledge through conscious and introspective practice and behaviors. The thoughts and skills of individuals are crystallized as products, technologies and services, and when put onto the market trigger new interactions with customers, competitors, suppliers and localities etc., which further enriches the tacit knowledge of not only the individuals, but of organizations and corporations.

However, reflective practice through abduction processes is important for accumulating high-quality tacit knowledge in individuals and organizations. US Major League Baseball star Ichiro Suzuki says he has the sense that "another me is watching my hitting and the form of my bunt". This suggests he actually distinguishes his movements both theoretically and objectively while forming an image of his ideal form and body movement while constantly giving himself feedback on those differences (a knowledge difference) to continue to improve.

Behaviors that involve objectively looking at one's thinking and actions and correcting them have been described as "metacognitive ability" (e.g., Haynie et al., 2012), and are abilities that enable corporeal intake and embedding logically observed explicit knowledge as corporeal knowledge. This metacognitive ability prompts practitioners to become aware and discover, and at the same time forces them to recognize knowledge differences. Then, by generating new meaning from these knowledge differences, practitioners bring about boundaries knowledge through the abduction process of setting and verifying hypotheses through trial and error. Knowledge differences and boundaries knowledge born through the reflective practice in the Internalization phrase drive the knowledge transformation process, and enable practitioners to accumulate high-quality tacit knowledge as a source of differentiation (see Internalization in Figure 2.4).

Boundaries knowledge from new meaning generated from these knowledge differences is a factor that brings about high-quality tacit knowledge as a source of differentiation. Recent comments by athletes have led to a wealth of suggestions regarding these insights. In the July 2018 Wimbledon men's quarterfinals, Japan's Kei Nishikori lost to former world no. 1 Novak Djokovic (Serbia). In a press conference after the match, Nishikori said "Of course I wanted to attack, but it wasn't that simple. I expected the rallies to be long, but his defense was better than I expected, and he returned the deep balls. It was difficult." He continued, "The details of the play weren't bad, but something was missing, and because I couldn't knock him down all the way to the end, I'll have to find something in the future."

Also, having lost to a strong Belgium in the first round after advancing to the finals tournament for the first time in two tournaments at the Russian World Cup, Japanese national coach, Akira Nishino, said at a press conference after the game: "I was confident in my team's ability to get three points against Belgium. But the flow ended up changing on a very fine line. Just at 30 minutes. I questioned myself about what was missing – because the team wasn't unified in its direction."

The comments made by both Nishikori and Nishino about "something missing" suggests the necessity for discovery of knowledge differences and boundaries knowledge.

2.3.2   Forming strategic communities (SC) based on the creation of Ba

In each phase of the SECI process, it is possible to touch on another party's tacit knowledge, extract explicit knowledge from tacit knowledge, and create documentation for combination pivoting on the discovery and creation of boundaries knowledge through accumulated dialectical dialogue (or creative dialogue) with other parties. This knowledge can then be internalized by viewing the documented materials and information etc. Then, sharing and follow-up experiences with others and understanding things that have been put into explicit knowledge enables conversion to the tacit knowledge of the individual, which inspires the sharing of values and leads back to Socialization once again.

In particular, in each phase of the SECI process, the important thing is to expand the range of experience, and effectively acquire tacit and explicit knowledge by forming diverse strategic communities (SC) based on the creation of multilayered "Ba" in organizations (Kodama, 2001; Kodama and Shibata, 2016). The formation of SC prompts broad experiences that transcend specialist job functions, and leads to the generation of wide-ranging tacit and explicit knowledge in individuals. Broadening experiences is extremely effective in driving the SECI process efficiently.

As shown in Figure 2.3, SC based on the creation of Ba set the stage for creating new (tacit and explicit) knowledge through insights into latent market demands and synthesizing abstract spaces (life world domains – tacit knowing) and embodied spaces (formed world domains – explicit knowing). Ideas and concepts about new products and services do not suddenly appear out of the thinking of practitioners, rather, the key to success is whether the right tuning can be achieved for market demands through the discovery and creation of new boundaries knowledge by sharing experiential knowledge and customer tacit knowledge through practice, and the creation of tacit and explicit knowledge by repeated hypothesis setting, trialing and verification through abduction (see Figure 2.3).

Creating product plans and concepts is an act of bringing functional requirements and present conditions closer to the future (planning) through excellent hypothesis building capabilities, which entails multilayered, repeating interactions of synthesis and analysis of images and substance. Cognitive neuroscientist Professor Shinsuke Shimojo (California Institute of Technology) claims that "creative people grasp the overall situation and go back and forth between tacit knowledge and explicit knowledge" (Shimojo, 2008, p. 12). The overall situation is the "context" and can be said to be a global context from the social and technological viewpoints. The driving force of dynamic recursive movement between the tacit knowledge zone and the explicit knowledge zone centered on the discovery and creation of boundaries knowledge in global contexts can be said to be the boundaries vision and boundaries knowledge of practitioners (see Figure 2.3).

3.   IMPLICATIONS

This chapter has discussed and analyzed the framework for new "knowledge creation through boundaries knowledge" in the SECI model presented by Nonaka and Takeuchi (1995). Currently in the knowledge society, in addition to the necessity for individuals living in corporate society to create knowledge through the convergence of diverse knowledge across different values and in differing areas of specialization in organizations, it is most important to acquire creativity to form global networks of the best people and organizations around the world to converge the best knowledge with the knowledge of individuals and organizations.

The first aspect of this chapter's academic contribution is the new perspective on developing creativity. Centered on Amabile (e.g., 1988, 1995), there is an accumulation of academic research on creativity in the fields of psychology and business studies. However, much of this research presents only spot relationships regarding causes and effects and relationships between factors, and does not fully clarify why such outcomes occur, or the micro processes fundamental to the acquisition of creativity. These micro dynamic creativity development processes entail the generation of boundaries knowledge.

On the other hand, traditional organizational learning theory discusses the development of individual and organizational capabilities and the related processes of practice (e.g., Cyert and March, 1963). However, learning is not the same thing as creativity. Creativity entails producing something that has not existed in the past. However, this does not mean that something is created from nothing. Creativity is finding new combinations of existing knowledge and objects (which is equivalent to convergence) (e.g., Zhou and Shalley, 2007). Put in terms of cognitive science, as opposed to learning, which is the process of enriching networks by incorporating new information into existing knowledge networks, creativity is the process of bridging new links between existing and dissimilar networks (e.g., Fauconnier and Turner, 1998). The trigger that bridges these linkages for creativity is boundaries knowledge through boundaries vision.

Although both learning and creativity enrich knowledge networks, the processes to arrive at that state are not the same. In other words, learning involves information from outside forming linkages, while the spontaneous occurrence of information is creativity. Thus, learning comes from externalities such as teachers or teaching materials, while creativity requires spontaneously searching and new combinations of knowledge for self-realization from within. Opportunities come from the outside, but the discovery of solutions is a process that is spontaneous and generative. Here, boundaries vision is required on multiple boundaries to bring about new boundaries knowledge.

In the knowledge economy, to acquire creativity through the framework of knowledge creation through boundaries knowledge, diverse human knowledge (of which technology is one element) is a source of valuable products, services and business models that can give a company new competitiveness. By converging diverse technologies and different industries, new products, services and business models that transcend various boundaries are brought about, and new value chains are formed as new strategic models. Accordingly, companies must refresh their perspectives on management to span the boundaries between the knowledge of individuals, groups and organizations, bring about boundaries knowledge through boundaries vision, and achieve knowledge creation for new business.

The second aspect of this chapter's academic contribution is the new knowledge it provides to the knowledge management field. Polanyi's (1962) contribution clarified the dimension of tacit knowledge, but did not go as far as clarifying its interaction with explicit knowledge. Nonaka (2016) asserts that it is not possible to clarify the principle of knowledge creation only with Polanyi's (1962) knowledge theory. In contrast, Nonaka and Takeuchi (1995) clarify the knowledge creation process to bring about synergies through the interconversion (knowledge transformation) of the two types of knowledge – the tacit and explicit knowledge. Moreover, Nonaka et al. (2014) present practical knowledge (phronesis) as the third knowledge driving the spiral loop between tacit and explicit knowledge. With this existing research in mind, this chapter presents a new framework on the knowledge creation process that entails the inclusion of the concept of "boundaries knowledge (boundaries knowing)" in the processes of knowledge integration (tacit knowledge → tacit knowledge, explicit knowledge → explicit knowledge) and knowledge transformation (tacit knowledge → explicit knowledge, explicit knowledge → tacit knowledge) that occur on boundaries in the four phases of the SECI process (Nonaka and Takeuchi, 1995; Nonaka et al., 2014).

A future research perspective of this chapter would presumably be research on creativity development across a range of different research fields such as business studies, economics, psychology, the arts, sciences and engineering etc. In practice, while bearing in mind the importance of training creative people who can make large contributions to society (by innovating), there is promise for the interdisciplinary development across various dissimilar fields of research (business studies, economics, psychology, the arts, science and engineering etc.) to develop creativity to bring about knowledge convergence (knowledge creation).

4.   CONCLUSION

This chapter has focused on knowledge differences that occur between people and organizations, and between various "dissimilar things and events", and has presented the concept of "boundaries knowledge" or "boundaries knowing" that arises from the awareness, perception and discovery of such differences by people and organizations. The chapter has also described how the quality of boundaries knowledge and boundaries knowing influences the creativity of people and organizations, and hence influences innovation. Moreover, the chapter has presented that "boundaries knowledge (knowing) – "the fourth knowledge" following after tacit knowledge, explicit knowledge and phronesis – is strategic thinking and action for optimized creations, solutions and processes for new knowledge creation in the creation and execution of strategies by people, organizations and corporations, or as solutions to the problems and issues faced by people, organizations and corporations.

REFERENCES

Amabile, T. M. (1988). A model of creativity and innovation in organizations. *Research in Organizational Behavior*, *10*(1), 123–167.

Amabile, T. M. (1995). Attributions of creativity: What are the consequences? *Creativity Research Journal*, *8*(4), 423–426.

Anderson, D. R. (1986). The evolution of Peirce's concept of abduction. *Transactions of the Charles S. Peirce Society*, *22*(2), 145–164.

Baldwin, C. Y., & Clark, K. B. (2000). *Design Rules: The Power of Modularity* (Vol. 1). Cambridge, MA: MIT Press.

Brown, J. S., & Duguid, P. (2001). Knowledge and organization: A social-practice perspective. *Organization Science*, *12*(2), 198–213.

Carlile, P. (2002). A pragmatic view of knowledge and boundaries: Boundary objects in new product development. *Organization Science*, *13*(4), 442–455.

Carlile, P. (2004). Transferring, translating, and transforming: An integrative framework for managing knowledge across boundaries. *Organization Science*, *15*(5), 555–568.

Carlile, P. R., & Rebentisch, E. S. (2003). Into the black box: The knowledge transformation cycle. *Management Science*, *49*(9), 1180–1195.

Chesbrough, H. (2003). *Open Innovation*. Boston, MA: Harvard Business School Press.

Cramton, C. D. (2001). The mutual knowledge problem and its consequences for dispersed collaboration. *Organization Science*, *12*(3), 346–371.

Cyert, R. M., & March, J. G. (1963). *A Behavioral Theory of the Firm* (pp. 169–187). Englewood Cliffs, NJ: Prentice Hall.

Donnellon, A., Gray, B., & Bougon, M. G. (1986). Communication, meaning, and organized action. *Administrative Science Quarterly*, *31*(1), 43–55.

Fauconnier, G., & Turner, M. (1998). Conceptual integration networks. *Cognitive Science*, *22*(2), 133–187.

Giddens, A. (1984). *The Constitution of Society: Outline of the Theory of Structuration*. Cambridge: Polity Press.

Hacklin, F., Marxt, C., & Fahrni, F. (2009). Coevolutionary cycles of convergence: An extrapolation from the ICT industry. *Technological Forecasting and Social Change*, *76*(6), 723–736.

Haynie, J. M., Shepherd, D. A., & Patzelt, H. (2012). Cognitive adaptability and an entrepreneurial task: The role of metacognitive ability and feedback. *Entrepreneurship Theory and Practice*, *36*(2), 237–265.

Helfat, C. E., & Peteraf, M. A. (2015). Managerial cognitive capabilities and the microfoundations of dynamic capabilities. *Strategic Management Journal*, *36*(6), 831–850.

Jackson, M. C. (2003). *Systems Thinking: Creative Holism for Managers* (p. 378). Chichester: Wiley.

Johansson, F. (2004). *The Medici Effect*. Boston, MA: Harvard Business School Press.

Kodama, M. (2001). Strategic community management promoted by innovation communities. *Knowledge and Process Management*, *8*(4), 233–248.

Kodama, M. (2005). Knowledge creation through networked strategic communities: Case studies in new product development. *Long Range Planning*, *38*(1), 27–49.

Kodama, M. (2006). Innovation through boundary managing: Case of Matsushita Electric reforms. *Technovation*, *27*(1–2), 15–29.

Kodama, M. (2007). *The Strategic Community-Based Firm*. Basingstoke, UK: Palgrave Macmillan.

Kodama, M. (2009). Boundaries innovation and knowledge integration in the Japanese firm. *Long Range Planning*, *42*(4), 463–494.

Kodama, M. (2011). *Knowledge Integration Dynamics: Developing Strategic Innovation Capability*. Singapore: World Scientific Publishing.

Kodama, M. (Ed.) (2015). *Collaborative Innovation: Developing Health Support Ecosystems* (Vol. 39). Abingdon, UK: Routledge.

Kodama, M., & Shibata, T. (2014). Strategy transformation through strategic innovation capability: A case study of Fanuc. *R&D Management*, *44*(1), 75–103.

Kodama, M., & Shibata, T. (2016). Developing knowledge convergence through a boundaries vision: A case study of Fujifilm in Japan. *Knowledge and Process Management*, *23*(4), 274–292.

Kogut, B., & Zander, U. (1992). Knowledge of the firm, combinative capabilities, and the replication of technology. *Organization Science*, *3*(3), 383–397.

Lakoff, G., & Johnson, M. (1980). The metaphorical structure of the human conceptual system. *Cognitive Science*, *4*(2), 195–208.

Leonard-Barton, D. (1995). *Wellsprings of Knowledge: Building and Sustaining the Sources of Innovation*. Boston, MA: Harvard Business School Press.

March, J. (1972). Model bias in social action. *Review of Educational Research*, *42*(4), 413–429.

Nonaka, I. (2016). Cultivating organizational knowledge maneuverability: Tacit knowing, intersubjectivity, distributed leadership (in Japanese). *Hitotsubashi Business Review*, *64*(3), 68–85.

Nonaka, I., & Takeuchi, H. (1995). *The Knowledge-Creating Company*. New York, NY: Oxford University Press.

Nonaka, I., Kodama, M., Hirose, A., & Kohlbacher, F. (2014). Dynamic fractal organizations for promoting knowledge-based transformation: A new paradigm for organizational theory. *European Management Journal*, *32*(1), 137–146.

Nonaka, I., Toyama, R., & Hirata, T. (2008). *Managing Flow: A Process Theory of the Knowledge-Based Firm*. Basingstoke, UK: Palgrave Macmillan.

Polanyi, M. (1962). *Personal Knowledge: Towards a Post-critical Philosophy*. Chicago, IL: University of Chicago Press.

Rafols, I., & Meyer, M. (2010). Diversity and network coherence as indicators of interdisciplinarity: Case studies in bionanoscience. *Scientometrics*, *82*(2), 263–287.

Rosenkopf, L., & Nerkar, A. (2001). Beyond local search: Boundary-spanning, exploration, and impact in the optical disk industry. *Strategic Management Journal*, *22*(4), 287–306.

Shannon, C., & Weaver, W. (1949). *The Mathematical Theory of Communications*. Urbana, IL: University of Illinois Press.

Shimojo, S. (2008). *Subliminal Impact* (in Japanese). Tokyo: Chikuma Shobou.

Spender, J. C. (1996). Making knowledge the basis of a dynamic theory of the firm. *Strategic Management Journal*, *17*(S2), 45–62.

Star, S. L., & Griesemer, J. R. (1989). Institutional ecology, translations, and boundary objects: Amateurs and professionals in Berkeley's Museum of Vertebrate Zoology, 1907–39. *Social Studies of Science*, *19*(3), 387–420.

Teece, D. J. (2007). Explicating dynamic capabilities: The nature and microfoundations of (sustainable) enterprise performance. *Strategic Management Journal*, *28*(13), 1319–1350.

Teece, D. J. (2014). The foundations of enterprise performance: Dynamic and ordinary capabilities in an (economic) theory of firms. *The Academy of Management Perspectives*, *28*(4), 328–352.

van Rijnsoever, F. J., & Hessels, L. K. (2011). Factors associated with disciplinary and interdisciplinary research collaboration. *Research Policy*, *40*(3), 463–472.

Zhou, J., & Shalley, C. E. (2007). *Handbook of Organizational Creativity*. London: Psychology Press.

3. Knowledge convergence and design-driven innovation through boundaries knowledge: new knowledge from the knowledge convergence and design-driven innovation perspectives

Mitsuru Kodama and Masashi Kimura

1. THE IMPORTANCE OF COLLABORATING WITH CUSTOMERS

In increasingly dynamic business environments, companies are realizing the importance of collaboration for creating and sustaining competitive advantage. As the style of corporate strategy representative of the latter half of the 20th century, focus was placed on proactively incorporating knowledge and core competencies from outside the company through strategic partnering among corporations mainly involving business partners, suppliers and distributors, etc. For example, in the automotive industry, automotive manufacturers and parts suppliers have established long-term partnerships; while in the ICT field, notably with smartphones and tablets, business methods typically involve strategic alliances and M&A across various types of industries such as the appliance, communications, software and entertainment industries. Collaboration with partners and even competitors has become a strategic imperative for firms in the networked world of business (Brandenburger and Nalebuff, 1996; Gulati et al., 2000; Iansiti and Levien, 2004; Kodama, 2005).

These corporate strategies have been understood and accepted by many corporations as requirements to expand existing markets or pioneer new ones. In contrast, at the customer side, many customers have understood the acceptance of products and services to be a passive and natural flow, even though it is the customers who have the right to make decisions about purchasing the products and services offered by many companies.

However, with customers gathering high-level information and knowledge about products and services due to the rapid development of ICT in recent years and heightened customer interest in diverse applications, content and social networking services (SNS) using PCs and smartphones, customers themselves are now able to thoroughly learn about and become familiar with the products and services offered by companies and their associated business models. Accordingly, the assessment of products and services by customers with such high-level learning experience and the new value of their associated business models thus also have the potential to greatly influence the promotion of a company's products, services and business models.

Research on strategy and marketing in recent years has focused on collaboration with customers to co-create value (Thomke and Von Hippel, 2002; Prahalad and Ramaswamy, 2004). While collaboration with customers can span several business processes, one of the most important is collaborating to create value through product and service innovation. As identified by Prahalad and Ramaswamy (2000), and as a core element of corporate strategy, a pressing issue for corporate product and service developments and marketing with a 21st-century outlook is how to co-opt customer knowledge and competences. Rather than technological breakthroughs and user-oriented product development, the "design-driven innovation" of recent years (e.g., Verganti, 2003) differs greatly from conventional innovation in that it gives new meaning by providing people with never-before-seen customer experiences.

Therefore, due to external challenges necessitating high degrees of innovation, customers' needs, satisfaction levels and customer experiences with new meaning, many industrial firms need to transform their entire approach to product and service development through continuous innovation and learning process with customers (Kodama, 2007). The learning and knowledge creation process (Nonaka and Takeuchi, 1995; Kodama, 2007, Kodama, 2011b), can integrate the knowledge differences of companies and their customers to reduce the product and service development cycle time, and is inherent in collaborative innovation (Kodama, 2015) between companies and customers.

So, who are the main players in innovation (for new products, services or business models) at the heart of corporate strategy? Usually, the corporation developing products and services is considered to be the one doing the innovation. In contrast, "user innovation" is a phenomenon that means the user, as the traditional consumer of innovation, instead becomes the producer of it. In other words, users can also be innovators (Von Hippel, 1994).

Through user innovation, the roles of the user (the customer) and the vendor (the company) change as follows in the innovation process. In general, innovation is a chain of processes that follows a path beginning with the uncovering of user needs, product design to satisfy those needs, and then prototyping leading to mass production if all goes well. Conventionally, this was all done by the vendor company. However, with user innovation, the vendor is only involved in mass production – users are involved all the way through to the development of prototypes. Users do not just stop at conveying information about needs, they also contribute to the development itself. Why can users become innovators?

The first reason is due to the existence of a learning process called "learning by using". By actually using products or services, understanding of features or usage methods and forms can be deepened, and as a result knowledge or the existence of needs can be clarified (Rosenberg, 1982). This is equivalent to the "customer knowledge" discussed in this chapter. Rosenberg (1982) conceptualized the existence of this learning process as "learning by using". Learning by using entails the acquisition of knowledge that becomes clear for the first time in the actual experience of usage, and can be measured by an index called maintenance cost, and is observed as a reduction of maintenance costs. Users with rich usage experience do not only have valuable opinions about aspects of products that are deficient or that can be improved, but can also bring about new usage forms beyond the scope of the vendor's anticipation.

Accordingly, to provide customers with new products and services typical of ICT, vendors must both understand the importance of putting themselves in the customer position for marketing and product development for products, services and business models, and must absorb the opinions, hopes and criticism of customers who are familiar with the products and services as well as their comments through joint experimentation, etc. Also described as a case in this chapter, a particularly important perspective is the formation of strategic communities (SC) of innovative users (customers) and companies (manufacturers/vendors) to not only achieve new usage forms but also build new products and business models through "creative learning" (as discussed in Chapter 1) by proactive dialogue and collaboration within SC.

An important issue for vendors is promoting close dialogue and creative learning with customers. Corporations cannot establish one-sided product and business models to provide customers with products in the same way as the business models of the mass production and mass retail era, but instead must work to conceptualize new business models and product concepts at the same time as achieving new usage forms. This means nothing more than the customer is seen as a member of the vendor staff to jointly build business models and product concepts. It is important that customers and vendor project members resonate their values, visions, thoughts, etc. with each other as shared visions and thoughts to achieve new product concepts and new business models (including pioneering new product usage forms).

Thus, project members and customers must resonate values with each other through repeated dialogue to establish new concepts. Moreover, it is also important to build strategic communities (SC) between project teams and customers. Project members and customers must resonate values to drive the creative learning process in these SC.

Clarified through action research mainly conducted over the long term by the author's project team, this chapter describes the processes of bringing about boundaries vision and boundaries knowledge through the formation of SC between vendors and customers promoted by the significant differences that exist between the knowledge about product development of the project team at the vendor side (details of technical and market knowledge, herein called "vendor knowledge") and the knowledge possessed by various customers (knowledge linked to and embedded in knowledge and tasks through the customers' past market experience, herein called "customer knowledge").

2.   SUMMARY OF THE ACTION RESEARCH CASE[1]

The action research was conducted between 1994 and 1999 in the business processes from product planning and development to sales at the NTT Multimedia Business Development Department, where the author worked.

2.1   Commercialization of "Phoenix", the World's First Multimedia Conferencing System, Developed in Japan

The author's first encounter with a video conferencing system was at NTT (where the author worked) in February 1995. The author's team had a partnership with Picturetel, a US company with a proven track record in the field of video communications with multimedia, and embarked on joint development with Picturetel of the Phoenix next-generation desktop video conferencing system. The author's team worked hard in this partnership to complete negotiations ranging widely from details of the partnership through to technical specifications in just one month. During this time, the author also experienced contract negotiations in Boston USA, where Picturetel is headquartered, and 48-hour continuous contract negotiations with video conferencing between Japan and Boston.

At the time, many ISDN video conferencing systems were already available from a range of manufacturers both in and out of Japan, but these were expensive, costing around $10,000 for the desktop type, or several tens of thousands of dollars for the room type. Hence, the reason why video conferencing systems had not become common was not only because not very many people knew how to use them, but also because of their price. Taking advantage of the alliance with Picturetel, NTT aimed at releasing new video conferencing systems into society, as a driver of "multimedia available from today (Now-ISDN)" to heat up the video conferencing market at a burst.

Then, in March 1996, Phoenix went on sale as the world's first Windows 95 and PCI bus-compatible desktop multimedia conferencing system, as a killer application to achieve "multimedia available from today (Now-ISDN)".

2.2   Commercialization of "Phoenix Mini", the World's First Next-Generation TV Phone, Developed in Japan[2]

NTT then agreed on a wide-ranging alliance with Mitsubishi Electric Corporation covering everything from development through to sales in the field of video communications with multimedia to further popularize not only its Phoenix desktop multimedia conferencing system but also various applications using video conferencing systems. Both of these companies had already jointly developed video applications, etc. using ISDN, and in a first initiative, began selling the "Phoenix mini" ISDN videophone in 1998.

Phoenix mini was the world's first compact, lightweight, low-cost and high-quality ISDN videophone, and enabled easy-to-use video telephony with the same operations as a normal telephone, and was marketed with the catchphrase "anytime, anywhere, anyone" as a next-generation videophone shouldering a new culture of video communications. The unit had a 5.4-inch color LCD monitor with the handset all in one unit, and enabled video and voice communications with the feel of a normal telephone.

2.3   Establishment of NTT Phoenix Communications Network[3]

Video conferencing systems and videophones basically have a one-to-one communication function, so to communicate with large numbers of people, a very expensive server called a multipoint connection unit was required. This server had to be connected to multiple video conferencing terminals for nationwide corporate conferencing, remote learning or event broadcasts, etc.

There were cases of corporations purchasing this server to use the video conferencing regularly in multiple locations, although most companies only used these systems once or twice a week. However, as many corporate users wanted to use low-priced multipoint connection services, a business case could be made for multipoint connection units shared among many users.

Overseas, many type 1 and type 2 telecommunications carriers had already developed multipoint connection services for shared use, and some type 2 telecommunications carriers had already started up businesses on a small scale in Japan, but were not so popular due to their small scale and high usage fees.

NTT established its partnership with Picturetel so that many video conference users nation-wide could use a multipoint connection service at a low price, and hence established "NTT Phoenix Communication Network Inc.", a joint venture specializing in video conference multipoint connection services in 1998. It was a struggle to establish a company in a short time and get the business up and running. The multipoint connection video communication service was a service that required the use of H.320 international standard-compliant video conferencing systems simultaneously in multiple locations. NTT made this service available at national conferences and various seminars for its regional and branch offices, etc., to verify and confirm its functionality, operability and operation methods to study the business feasibility of the service. To commercialize the service, the author's team also asked various companies that had installed the Phoenix multimedia conference system terminal provided by NTT to try the service and give their opinions and hopes for it. As a result, the author's team came to believe the service could be used in wide-ranging fields such as business, education, welfare and entertainment, and decided to commercialize it.

Originally, the author's team established 30 access points across Japan making it possible to connect up to 1000 locations for video conferencing. The author's team also introduced an innovative nationwide fee structure of JPY 40 per three minutes per subscription. One year after commencing the service, approximately 500 companies had subscribed, and the service was used by approximately 40 company CEOs to give greetings at the beginning of the working year.

The mission for the author's project team was to expand the popularity of Phoenix, Phoenix mini and the multipoint connection service provided by the NTT Phoenix Communications Network. To fulfill this mission, the project team repeatedly learned through trial and error in its attempts to approach corporate customers in a range of businesses and industries. Some of these processes of learning through trials and errors are shown below, and are analyzed from the perspective of knowledge convergence of vendor and customer knowledge.

3.   ANALYSIS OF THE ACTION RESEARCH CASE: CUSTOMER USAGE SYSTEM DESIGN

3.1   Synergies of Vendor Knowledge and Customer Knowledge

3.1.1   Application from video communications to video IoT (Internet of things)

The strategy of the author's project team was to expand the popularity of video confer-encing systems to corporate customers and consumer users, based on the Phoenix series (Phoenix, Phoenix mini) and the multipoint connection service provided by the NTT Phoenix Communications Network. Through this action research undertaken by way of long-term sales activities, the author clarified that large differences exist between the knowledge that project team members at the vendor side have about product development (details of technical and market-learnt knowledge, herein called "vendor knowledge") and the diverse knowledge of customers (knowledge linked to and embedded in knowledge and tasks through the customer's past market experience, herein called "customer knowledge").

This perception of differences came about through dialogue with customers, and gave the vendor a new perspective of discovery and awareness at the same time. For example, the following episode occurred in daily sales activities.[4]

IBIZA Co., Ltd., headquartered in Saitama Prefecture, is a leading customer who quickly introduced and used the Phoenix multimedia conference system. The company is an industry-leading manufacturer of high-quality women's leather bags, and has established an integrated production system from careful selection of leather for bag materials through to manufacturing, wholesale, sales and aftercare, having approximately 800,000 customer members nationwide. In the business aspect, the company has also won several awards. With the company representing Saitama Prefecture, major examples of these awards include the 13th Excellent Management Award sponsored by the Nikkan Kogyo Shimbun, the SME Research Center Award – Kanto District Award, and the 1995 Saitama Prefecture Sainokuni Factory Designation.

At the time, company director Oguchi of IBIZA asked, "is it possible to convey color of a bag by videophone for repairs and maintenance?" As a result of various trial tests at the IBIZA headquarters, and through usage by IBIZA employees, the opinion was that although the network speed was narrowband, it seemed to be somehow usable. This is a usage form equivalent to modern-day video IoT. Our project team learned a new videophone usage form from the company. After that, the company deployed 52 Phoenix units, and promoted their usage for product information dissemination, taking orders and maintenance, etc. Specifically, this entailed the following:

(a)   Quickly getting product information to nationwide stores handling the products, and taking orders
At the time, the way of announcing products was limited to quarterly catalog issuances, previews and exhibits, etc. Introducing Phoenix to some dealers nationwide enabled easy setup of a place for product announcements to quickly and precisely provide information about new products and take orders on the spot using the system's bidirectional communications. Making product announcements via Phoenix also enabled the reduction of costs related to such things as modeling and business trips related to setting up presentation venues, as was necessary at the time.

(b)   Accurate response for customer's repairs and order-made goods
IBIZA-branded products have a lifetime warranty. For repairs also, Phoenix connected dealerships and factories so that repair staff could directly check items for repair at the repair facility, and respond accurately to nuanced customer orders without misunderstandings via video.

(c)   Quick and accurate ordering with stock confirmation
Phoenix demonstrates its power by confirming the products and the details of stock when receiving an order from a dealership, as leather, the material used for its bags, always has a different appearance (expression).

The IBIZA case is also an example where the project team (and customers) found differences on the boundaries between vendor knowledge and customer knowledge, and generated boundaries knowledge to design new customer usage forms. The creation of boundaries knowledge was enabled by the intersection (or sometimes collision) of the two opposites of how the project team can use its vendor knowledge for customer usage forms, and how customers can use vendor product technology in the customer knowledge (in other words in customer business processes).

In the vendor perspective, there was vendor knowledge rooted in the stereotype that video conferencing systems and videophones were mainly used for holding meetings and discussions, and at the time it was largely separate from customer knowledge that included ideas about using video conferencing systems and videophones for confirming products in real time in product maintenance processes. Generating boundaries knowledge for innovation to generate new customer usage forms in business processes of the customer from these separations (differences) enabled the knowledge convergence of vendor and customer knowledge, and brought about new usage forms as new convergence knowledge (see Figure 3.1).

Vendor knowledge and customer knowledge exist both as tacit and implicit knowledge, and converting these is the dynamic SECI process discussed in Chapter 2 (the interconversion of tacit and explicit knowledge). As discussed in Chapter 1, the vendor and the customer become aware of and recognize their knowledge differences through creative learning through prototype testing and opinion exchange, etc., and this creative learning promotes the acquisition of "boundaries vision" by the vendor and customer so that they can suitably respond to the context of these differences (see Figure 1.2 in Chapter 2) .

This process enables the emergence of the boundaries knowledge that exists between the vendor and customer knowledge, and such boundaries knowledge creation processes enable the dynamic convergence and integration of both the tacit and explicit knowledge in the vendor and customer knowledge. In other words, this is the achievement of dynamic tacit integration/tacit convergence, and explicit integration/explicit convergence between vendor and customer knowledge, as discussed in Chapter 2 (see Figure 3.1).

Boundaries vision is the insights and ideas practitioners have for recognizing differences on boundaries between vendor knowledge and customer knowledge, and the knowledge convergence and knowledge integration that bridge these boundaries leads to the design of new strategies. Boundaries vision is the ability to discover differences from the various discomforts and dissimilarities on boundaries, and is also the ability to seek out new knowledge such as new hints or ideas from those differences. Boundaries vision is also the ability to figure out what types of boundaries are discovered and how to link these together to trigger new knowledge for new ways of perceiving or discovery of things. Boundaries vision brings out the boundaries knowledge that exists between customer and vendor knowledge, and is an important factor in the convergence and integration of different knowledge. As shown in this case, the creation of new usage forms leads to design-driven innovation to bring about new meaning for customers and vendors.

Later, IBIZA introduced an optical fiber video information network system in 1998, which was the state-of-the-art at the time, to accumulate know-how about bag manufacturing with video. Company founder Shigeru Yoshida said this was "also an investment for our customers". At IBIZA, high-speed, high data capacity optical fiber networks and Phoenix systems that were compatible with the networks were used between the factory at HQ and its Annex (HQ building). This implementation enabled a video information distribution system that enabled discussions on design, etc. while viewing high-quality video to clearly confirm product materials (leather) as well as on-demand searching of video information about new products or outlets stored on a video server.

However, when the system was introduced, there was an issue related to faithful reproduction of the coloration of actual goods with the video system, due to the characteristics of handbags. This was solved by using the latest video compression technology, high-resolution video cameras and effective use of lighting. Also, because IBIZA sells high-end women's handbags, many of the managers in its dealerships are elderly and unable to use a computer. Hence, the use of Phoenix mini with its simple telephone-like feel that was easy for everybody to use solved this problem. After that, IBIZA began pouring efforts into direct marketing to customers using NTT DOCOMO's 3G mobile phone system (FOMA). IBIZA is an innovative company that is always practicing the business of creating customer value.

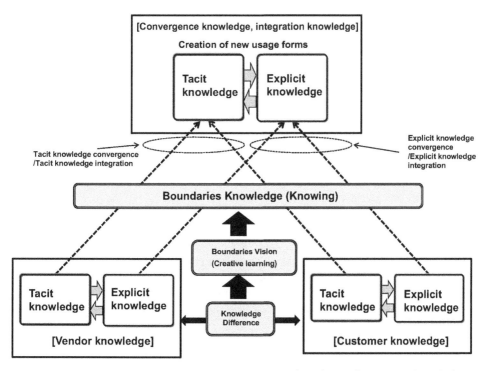

Figure 3.1   Dynamic integration and convergence of vendor and customer knowledge

3.1.2   Application of a remote healthcare system in veterinary medicine
(a)   Activating veterinary education and research, and local communities
In January 1996, the late Professor Emeritus Tsuneo Hirose[5] of Obihiro University of Agriculture and Veterinary Medicine, established the Research Institute of Information Science Development on Animal Medicine (in Obihiro City, Hokkaido, hereinafter referred to as "the laboratory"). Researchers at the laboratory consisted of people from different types of business such as university teachers, practicing veterinarians, group veterinarians, business owners, dairy farmers and the general public.

> To make veterinary medicine more meaningful in society, we have to not only gather veterinarians specializing in veterinary medicine, but also get participation from people in other fields (different

business types) to create opportunities to listen to peoples' experiences and ideas to avoid becoming fixated on narrow ideas. In particular, in preventing diseases to minimize economic losses with industrial animals, we can't ever expect to achieve useful outcomes without the producer (the farmer) participating in planning. In other words, knowledgeable veterinarians alone are not enough – we have to pay attention to the strong demands of farmers these days for veterinarians who are flexible in their thinking and can combine pieces of knowledge to uncover true value. Adopting free ideas is extremely important in order to break down veterinary medicine with strict rules – new ideas and human resources don't come about unless conventional frameworks are destroyed when required.

In the field of current clinical veterinary medicine, it's absolutely necessary to go beyond the framework of interdisciplinary research, and create interdisciplinary organizations of unprecedented collectives (collectives of dissimilar industries). In these collectives, original and ingenious ideas of individual veterinarians should be created through collaboration in groups. (Comment by the late Professor Emeritus Tsuneo Hirose)

Professor Emeritus Hirose also made the following comment.

In recent years, veterinary medicine has advanced with organ transplantation, prevention of various diseases at the genetic level, and greater elucidation of life phenomena. As bioethics-based veterinary medicine is currently being questioned, R&D fields with the distinctive veterinary medicine characteristics need to be established and human resources need to be developed with a scientific view of information about animal medicine, and veterinary medicine needs to be studied from a broad perspective that integrates medicine, engineering and science. The difference between veterinary medicine and other natural sciences is that it finds meaning and value in the existence of various animals and helps them to survive. Since social meaning and value systems exist about both industrial and companion animals, clinical veterinarians are working hard to fulfill their duties every day with a great sense of mission.

The goal of the laboratory was to build a virtual organization consisting of 54 researchers scattered throughout Japan, to create ideas that recognize local expectations and distinctive characteristics, and make use of the uniqueness of municipalities instead of centralized orientation towards Tokyo, the capital of Japan, and to create a base for information dissemination with an international perspective. Despite that, the development of new media environments in the clinical veterinary field had not progressed at the time. A key point was to use new media to invigorate veterinary education and research, and local communities.

Specifically, as explained in the following section, it became possible to expand video communications by broadening communications between veterinarians through information exchange and sharing using face-to-face videophone communications in the veterinary medicine setting.

(b)   Achieving design-driven innovation through convergence across dissimilar fields of business
For some time in veterinary medicine, large animals (cattle, horses, etc.) and small animals (dogs, cats, etc.) have been diagnosed with various pathologies using imaging technologies such as X-ray, CT and MR, etc., which have enabled significant achievements for early treatment and prevention, etc. In particular, with the trends in recent years, such as efforts to lower animal production costs due to intensifying international competition in agriculture and the elevated status of domestic companion animals due to the aging population and declining birthrates, there is an increasing weight on diagnostic imaging in veterinary medicine accompanying a major shift from treatment to prevention, similar to that in the human world.

In this shift, researchers led by the late Professor Emeritus Hirose made many pioneering efforts such as introducing Japan's first X-ray diagnostic car for large animals to universities all over Japan (Hirose, 1985). However, there was not much history of diagnosis with imaging in the veterinary medicine field at the time, and there were few specialists. Thus, joint business for education, diagnosis and treatment instructions between remotely located veterinarians became necessary in the process of developing and expanding diagnostic imaging.

On the other hand, recent years have seen the fences between the approaches to diseases of animals such as pets and those of humans become lower, which has resulted in demands on veterinarians to respond quickly with diagnostic imaging. This means there are strong demands for commercialization of bidirectional remote treatment in the field of clinical veterinary medicine using imaging, not just simply between veterinarians, but also between veterinarians and large animal producers, and veterinarians and small animal owners, etc. In light of this situation, the research group led by the late Professor Emeritus Hirose and the author's project group started research and development of remote diagnosis in veterinary medicine in early 1996.

The project team faced the challenge of popularizing the Phoenix desktop-type video conference system, which was launched in 1996. One target of the project was the development and use of applications using video conferencing systems in the medical field. The challenge for the project team was approaching customers with its newly developed system and getting them to understand the value of the product. In 1996 in Japan, customers had hardly any need to use PC-based video conferencing, nor was there much demand for video conference systems rooted in society as a whole. However, as part of its vision and ideas, the project team had a strong desire to realize the concept of creating a new video communication culture in Japan. Particularly, the challenge was to promote usage in education, welfare for the aged and general medical treatment including the veterinary field.

The project team thought hints could be uncovered by researching customer usage forms to popularize video conference systems – the tools of video communications. The team knew that video conferencing systems were generally used in business for meetings and discussions, but through analysis of the future market, estimated that demand for telemedicine would increase. However, as a telecommunications carrier, the vendor knowledge of the author's project team did not include accumulated knowledge and know-how regarding medicine or education, etc., and so the team had to learn a lot from doctors and teachers familiar with the field.

Nevertheless, the team believed there was plenty of latent potential to apply video conferencing systems in the medical field, from human treatment through to animal treatment, which meant that the partnership with the late Professor Emeritus Hirose, an authority on clinical veterinary medicine using radiology in Japan, was not only an important business chance, but also meant the project team's Phoenix development could contribute to the development of the clinical veterinary medicine field, which would be highly significant from the perspective of animal welfare.

Professor Emeritus Hirose's research group had also planned to build a unique information exchange system in the clinical veterinary field based on the customer knowledge accumulated to date. The system was built based on the opinions collected from the 54 researchers who had participated in planning, and focused on facilitating easy, two-way exchange of clinical images on the same level as other information. This specifically meant building a system in which all researchers had the same equipment to enable them to uniformly exchange information.

> Developing a remote diagnosis system for clinical veterinary medicine would not have been possible with only veterinarian knowledge. Our partnership with NTT, with its many years of knowledge and know-how in communications network and image communication technology was a great opportunity to create new innovations through collaboration that combined the intelligence of experts in industry and academia. (Comment by the late Professor Emeritus Hirose)

Thus, the project team and the late Professor Emeritus Hirose, the customer, matched their visions and values to establish a partnership to achieve a goal.

(c)   Customized product ideas through creative learning
New knowledge in terms of hardware and software was inspired and created as the remote diagnosis system concept and design, its construction and usage methods from the different perspectives of both vendor and customer knowledge while the team kept in mind what it was that they were providing – an application as a video communications usage method to create new value for many veterinarians.

However, in the initial startup stages, many problems arose. These were due to the differences that existed between vendor knowledge and customer knowledge. First, was the issue of usage via the veterinarians' PCs. At the time, there was no question that the PC was an incredibly convenient machine, but it was not always such an excellent information system. In other words, a device with advanced processing capabilities and a device that was easy for people to use were completely separate issues. The solution was in the boundaries vision that grew from these knowledge differences and led to the new idea of a system with information exchange functions that anybody could use (veterinarians of all ages), just like a household electrical appliance, instead of forcing people to get accustomed to utilizing PCs hence leaving out those not familiar with information technology.

The boundaries vision to discover new knowledge such as hints and ideas from various discomforts and the differences of dissimilarities on the boundaries between vendor and customer knowledge was shared among the project team and the veterinarians. One of the new types of knowledge brought about by boundaries vision was the decision to abandon application of the PC-based Phoenix video conferencing system to the remote diagnosis system.

In this way, the project team and veterinarians devised a method that allowed individual veterinarians to participate without feeling any discrepancies in their ability to operate the equipment. To overcome the problem of information literacy, and with the design concept of "easy operation for all veterinarians" in mind, a simple videophone (Phoenix mini) already developed for general use was adopted and customized to produce an optimal remote diagnosis system.

The system developed enabled discussion via face-to-face communications while also providing various types of images (x-ray, CT, MRI, pathology photographs) by sending and receiving voice and video through the communications network. All researchers had the same compatible model which enabled them to exchange information with each other easily. It was also possible to greatly expand the original functions of the videophone system by adding external cameras and monitors, etc. Also, in terms of cost, the system was achieved within a price range of about JPY400,000 per set. In addition, the author's team developed a system accessible to veterinarians all across Japan, in which various types of image information transmitted in real time such as case examples were successively stored as VOD (video on demand). Thus, the author's team established a relatively low-cost technology available to the veterinary field that was able to transmit various case images at a resolution enabling remote diagnosis (see Figure 3.2).

As described above, in the startup stage, the author's team achieved an optimal remote diagnosis system through a creative learning process which entailed trial and error processes, which took about a year and a half. This process enabled the emergence of the boundaries knowledge that exists between vendor knowledge and customer knowledge, and enabled the dynamic convergence and integration of both tacit and explicit knowledge in the vendor and customer knowledge (see Figure 3.1). In this remote diagnosis system case, differences on the boundaries between the vendor and customer knowledge were found, and, through boundaries vision, boundaries knowledge to design new customer (veterinarian) usage forms were found. Also, the creation of new usage forms and remote treatment system in the veterinary field is an example of design-driven innovation bringing about new meaning for customers and vendors.

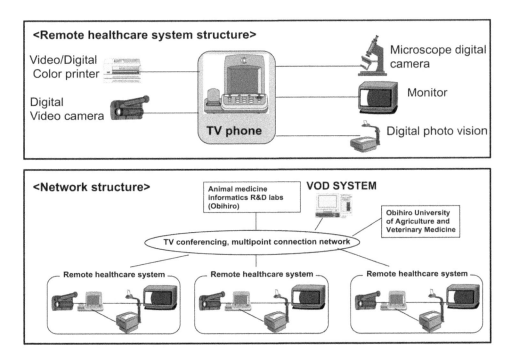

Figure 3.2   Remote healthcare system in the veterinary field

3.2   Further Exploration and Practice for Customer Usage Form Design

Other than the above two cases, the project team also engaged in sales activities at the same time, and drove initiatives to uncover various new usage forms. Beyond the idea of conference use, a customer-side usage form assumed from stereotypes rooted in existing vendor knowl-

[Vendor knowledge] (Assumed usage form at the customer side from a stereotype)

Industry / Usage form	Information communications	Manufacturing	Retail	Transportation/ passengers	Services	Broadcasting	Financial	Medical/welfare	Education	Security	Construction & real estate
Meetings											

- In-house meetings · Executive meetings · Management meetings
- Executive lectures · Meetings with trading partners, etc.

[Convergence knowledge] (New usage forms born from boundaries vision and boundaries knowledge)

Usage form	Information communications	Manufacturing	Retail	Transportation/ passengers	Services	Broadcasting	Financial	Medical/welfare	Education	Security	Construction & real estate
Education Training Guidance	- Technical guidance - Technicians support - Sales guidance	- Technical guidance - Technicians support	- Product description - Display (decorations) guidance - Sales supervisor guidance	- Check before starting/health check	- Guidance for sales methods/ customer interaction	- Staff training	- Guidance from HQ to branches, work support	- Medical training - Surgery guidance - Remote area guidance	- Interschool exchange - Remote lessons	- Security training	- Building site supervision work
Monitoring	- Systems operations monitoring	- Systems operations monitoring	- Store monitoring - Unmanned facilities (store) monitoring	- Garage, airport monitoring	- Store monitoring (Eateries such as pubs and conveyor-belt sushi bars)	- Broadcasting equipment (Unmanned) monitoring	- Monitoring of ATMs, etc.	- Patients through to hospitals, family homes	- Interlocked with crime prevention monitoring systems	- Interlocked with crime prevention monitoring systems	- Building site monitoring
Consultation	- Call center	- Call center	- Call center	- Call center	- Call center	- Call center	- Financial consulting (retail)	- At home medical treatment - Health consultations - interlocked with care support systems	- Call center	- Call center	- Model rooms remote sales
Broadcasting	- In-house broadcasting		- Fresh products auctions (flowers, foodstuffs, etc.) (Market to retailers) - Pet shops		- Wedding ceremonies broadcasting	- Broadcasting of TV programming/ program performers	- Real-time descriptions of financial information	- Conference broadcasting	- Remote lessons		
Others	- Confirmation of purchase (Manufacturing to distribution)	- Confirmation of purchase (Manufacturing to distribution)	- Online sales - Prototype publicity (In convenience stores, etc.)	- Employment interviews	- Worship (Religious organizations0	- Support of athletes by connection to video servers etc.	- Customer consulting	- Sign language support	- Remote lessons - Teacher interviews		- Installation in new homes and apartments

Figure 3.3   New usage forms from convergence of vendor and customer knowledge

edge, boundaries vision and boundaries knowledge arising from differences with customer knowledge gives rise to convergence knowledge for new usage forms (education, training, guidance, monitoring, consultation, broadcasting and maintenance, etc.) (see Figure 3.3).

Specific examples of convergence knowledge for new usage forms in the medical, welfare and healthcare field is introduced in Box 3.1, below. This example also has a common perspective on the process of achieving design-driven innovation as the creation of new usage forms by generating boundaries knowledge through the acquisition of boundaries vision through creative learning as experimenting to bridge the boundaries that arise from the differences in vendor and customer knowledge.

BOX 3.1   USE CASES IN THE MEDICAL, WELFARE AND HEALTHCARE FIELD

At Home Medical Treatment

Companies are making a wide range of service proposals to respond to the encroaching aging society and the advances in ICT of recent years. Against this backdrop, increasing numbers of elderly people are choosing at-home treatment instead of high-cost treatment at hospitals – healthcare service companies that specialize in home treatment have had their eye on the aging society and began home-visit medical care services at the beginning of the 1990s.

The important aspects of home treatment are regular confirmation of patient condition and having doctors respond quickly and appropriately if a patient's condition changes suddenly. The author's team believed that videophone systems would enable more fulfilling treatment by enabling regular "visits" and interviews in patient households, and if there was an emergency, they would demonstrate their power in providing a means to understand the patient's condition. Therefore, the project team and its customer, a home treatment company, devised a home-visit medical treatment support system using the videophone Phoenix mini, and began operations in 1998.

As well as enabling treatment visits via videophone, this system was linked to a patient database and could be used in cases of emergency to enable doctors to judge the patient's condition from their history and their appearance on the screen, and could be used for doctor dispatch and notification to supporting hospitals. In terms of medicine required for treatment also, pharmacists could make "video" visits to give instructions about dosage to patients who needed to know, and as well as providing regular pharmacist visits via videophone, the videophone system improved trust by increasing the opportunities for doctors and patients to talk through videophone interviews. Also, being able to grasp the patient's condition accurately at the time of an emergency call enabled efficient dispatch of doctors and reduced the number of emergency night visits, while videophone-based regular checkups reduced the amount of time staff spent traveling, which resulted in reduced labor costs. This new home-visit medical care support system as convergence knowledge was created in this way by combining vendor and customer knowledge.

Remote Area Treatment

As medical technological innovation progresses, regional disparities in healthcare are surfacing around the world. There are few large hospitals in depopulated areas, it is not possible to receive satisfactory treatment for diseases that must be handled by specialists, nor is it easy or even possible to travel to hospitals in urban areas to get treatment. As well as that, doctors at remote clinics have no other doctors in the vicinity with whom they can consult, and it is difficult for them to collect medical information because they cannot attend conferences and so forth due to the required travel time and geographical issues. Therefore, usage of video conferencing systems and videophones that enable image transmission could be applied to healthcare in remote areas.

The project team, its customer, a community medical department of a university, a medical center that conducts remote area healthcare, and multiple remote area medical offices were connected by video conferencing systems and videophones, and experiments were repeatedly conducted. This video transmission network was used to hold conferences on personal computer screens using data and simple images (such as X-ray photographs) and to attend university case studies remotely. As well as being able to collect the latest medical information, enhanced communications with doctors at other hospitals reduced the feeling of loneliness and anxiety when working in remote areas, and helped improve the quality of community healthcare. Thus, the convergence of vendor and customer knowledge enabled collection of cutting-edge medical information even in remote areas.

Emergency Medical Treatment

In the field of emergency medical care, there are cases where even the slightest delays in treatment can lead to significant differences in outcomes. Depending on patient symptoms, there are cases where supporting doctors are requested from other hospitals, or patients who require treatment by several doctors for visceral ruptures, etc. Thus, an information network for exchanging images of patient conditions in real time is an effective way to take the right measures. To achieve this, the project team and doctors devised a support system that entailed connecting the university emergency medical center with multiple hospitals across Japan to which doctors were dispatched from the center using a video conference system, so that the doctors at the center could see the condition of emergency patients brought to hospitals via video.

This video transmission enabled the center doctors to provide accurate judgments and instructions remotely, and enabled the center to dispatch support doctors as required. Even with emergency surgeries, a veteran doctor with a lot of experience can judge the execution of the surgery and provide support remotely while watching the video. The system was also used effectively to connect to related hospitals every morning to report on the progress of patients who had been brought in the night before. In addition, exchanging opinions in morning conferences on cases of illness contributed to the exchange of information between hospitals.

The biggest merit of the introduction of this system was the achievement of efficient treatment actions. Until then, when receiving a request for support from a related hospital, even if doctors could find out patient conditions over the phone, form teams, prepare for surgery, blood transfusions and intravenous drips, and rush to the hospital, often patients were still in a perilous state. This meant the costs of such preparations otherwise wasted could be saved if the patient's condition could be known in advance. A customer, a young doctor who had been dispatched, commented on the peace of mind that came with the support provided by the video conferencing system when it was not easy to make judgments alone. The convergence of vendor and customer knowledge in this way demonstrated significant effects in emergency treatments.

Health Consultation

In some cases it is difficult to properly conduct consultations or convey advice over the phone with the patient using only words like "I have scratches on my hands" or "I have an itchy back", and for the doctor to then make a judgment about whether it is okay to just apply medicine at home or whether the patient should quickly get to hospital, because it is not possible to make a proper judgment without seeing the actual symptoms. To address this issue, the project team and its customer, a health consultation provider, devised the use of easy-to-operate and low-cost videophones in the home.

With the help of dermatologists and ophthalmologists, and as a result of testing a range of items required for diagnosis such as the screen quality of the videophones, the health consultation provider concluded that standards were high enough for commercialization, and began providing the service in earnest in 1997. In actual fact, looking at data of past use of telephone consultation received by the health consultation provider, results showed that it was possible to get more accurate guidance in 70 to 80 percent of cases with the videophones.

As shown in Figure 3.3, consultation services including health using videophones are active in a number of fields. For example, in the real estate business, intense competition to sell has led to various options being added to apartments to give them distinct characteristics. The author's team proposed the option of videophone health and security services to the customer real estate company, which they adopted for apartments on sale.

A videophone was installed in the lobby at the back of the entrance hall of the apartment for residents to use freely. As well as apartments, this service can also be applied in aged care facilities in which residents' health is a constant concern. The system can also be used for remote and home care in combination with at-home care equipment. Health consultation services using videophones are services that respond to aging societies and the modern fitness and health boom. The convergence of vendor and customer knowledge in this way raised the level of added value of services in the healthcare field.

Sign Language Support Services

Sign language support services are services that provide sign language interpreting where it is required, such as businesses, local governments, hospitals or at department store counters by connecting to a sign language support center through an on-site videophone. The project team and its sign language support center customer deepened their common desire to advance initiatives to make services available nationwide to provide an easy way for the hearing-impaired to communicate.

To achieve a society in which all people can live more easily, barriers that prevent people with disabilities from self-reliance and participation in society must be removed. For example, the hearing-impaired mostly rely on writing to communicate with hearing people, but to communicate in more complicated conversations, they often have to go out accompanied by a sign language interpreter.

Thus, videophones, with which the hearing-impaired can hold a sign language conversation while facing a screen, and the hearing can understand the sign language interpreter's voice, are convenient for many people to use. In 1997, we trialed these devices in such locations as hotels, banks, department stores, hospitals, police stations and welfare center offices, and found that they were used up to 20 to 30 times per day, for such things as providing directions at urban police stations to the hearing-impaired, or for inquiries about the costs of giving birth at a hospital. The convergence of vendor and customer knowledge in this way brought about new value as a sign language support service.

3.3   Revitalizing Localities with Multimedia: New Lifestyle Design – the Multimedia Village Concept

Enhancement and expansion of local communities with ICT usage has become a major challenge in the 21st century. When the Internet was becoming popular around 1996, the project team had already partnered with the national and local governments to promote initiatives to form software and lifestyle-oriented communities using the state-of-the-art technology of the time. The examples of new forms of use shown in Box 3.1 and Figure 3.3 are cases of individual industries and corporations. On the other hand, the larger challenge of designing social systems is revitalization of localities through the use of multimedia such as videophones.

In April 1998, the project team began collaborating with Fukushima Prefecture and Katsurao Village in the prefecture on the world's first multimedia village using videophones. In this experiment, to revitalize this mountain village area and promote informatization, the author's team studied how anybody could inexpensively, easily and quickly use multimedia in a wide range of fields such as healthcare, welfare, education and government services.

Specifically, this entailed the use of easy-to-understand bidirectional communications with video information in remote areas and mountain villages, etc. to improve living environments and revitalize those areas. To achieve this, the author's team installed video transmission networks and videophones in all households as well as public facilities such as schools and government offices in Katsurao Village. In the village, information on administrative guidance, various services, shopping and entertainment, etc. was produced as video content and stored on a video-on-demand server.

This made it possible for users to search various video information on demand using a videophone, and easily obtain administrative information, go window shopping or enjoy karaoke, etc. A multipoint video connection service was also introduced to enable many people to interact in meetings and conferences, or participate in seminars at the same time. This enabled villagers to easily participate in video conferences around the country as well as in the village, from their homes.

The project team established the Katsurao Village Multimedia Village Promotion Council with Katsurao Village and Fukushima Prefecture to converge vendor knowledge and customer knowledge of local governments and local residents. The team then proactively engaged in experimentation and testing to verify the system, and began considering introduction of multimedia using videophones in villages nationwide. Health and welfare, and education subcommittees were set up in this council. The health and welfare subcommittee verified the possibility of future realization of telemedicine and various consultations using videophones in conjunction with aged care, and medical and health consultations. In addition, the education subcommittee provided various distance classes, seminars and inter-school exchanges using videophones to support lifelong learning in rural areas and achieve an educational environment free of regional differences.

In the Katsurao Village Multimedia Village Promotion Council, village representative members actively voiced their opinions and wishes such as their desire for lots of information on the video server focusing on lifestyle, questions about how children could enjoy the information while having fun, and their desires to communicate via videophone with family and friends outside the village. In the field of education, school-centered usage forms were established such as interactions with students in other schools involving research presentations and discussions with students in elementary and junior high schools outside the village, class visits via videophone with parents watching at their homes, and remote English conversation classes with foreign English language teachers.

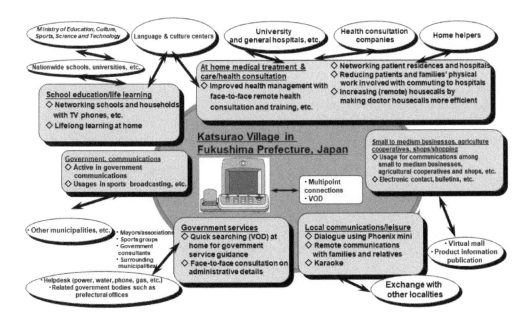

Figure 3.4   Lifestyle design with TV phone applications (in healthcare, education, governance and leisure, etc.)

In the field of health and welfare, the system clearly enabled the elderly people to feel at ease by enabling them to receive at home guidance on health exercises from a welfare center, and enabling them to consult clinics about health. Also, the system was highly praised for eliminating medication errors by enabling home helpers' guidance and individual consultations with health nurses through videophones. As well as that, various usages in a range of different fields such as life learning, and telemedicine using vital sign sensors contributed to local revitalization, and a new era of villager-centered multimedia dawned that began in Katsurao Village (see Figure 3.4).

This case also has a common aspect on the process of achieving new usage forms from the boundaries knowledge and boundaries vision acquired through the creative learning of the project team and stakeholders by establishing councils and subcommittees to bridge the boundaries that arise from the differences in vendor and customer knowledge.

4.   ACHIEVING DESIGN-DRIVEN INNOVATION THROUGH BOUNDARIES VISION

4.1   Forming Strategic Communities of Vendors and Customers to Accelerate the Creation of Convergence Knowledge

As discussed in Chapter 1, to create and execute concepts for excellent new products, services and business models, strategic communities (SC) and multilayered network SC formations are indispensable, and these SC must have mechanisms that enable practitioners in core departments in new product development such as marketing, R&D and production to create and share dynamic contexts across the boundaries of organizations. This enables practitioners to create and put into practice new knowledge (business concepts for new products and services, etc.). The necessity of forming these SC is the same in the cases of convergence of vendor and customer knowledge described in this chapter. The key is how densely these SC can be formed by the vendor project teams and their customers.

In these SC, it is crucial that project teams gain new recognition that they must plan products that will provide customers with new value, and find a way to grasp the latent needs of customers to plan products through "dialectical synthesis" (Kodama, 2007) through the synergy of their own subjective perceptions (a viewpoint to uncover latent demand by assimilating with customers), and objective perceptions (analysis of competing products and customer data).

Thus, vendors and customers must proactively form multilayered SC across organizations, collide their subjectivities together with market and technology contexts and perspectives, and bring about new energy and create contexts with a higher dimension through these paradigm collisions. Vendors and customers come to understand each other's diverse world views and values, and bring about mutual recognition and new rules in SC by acquiring boundaries vision through creative dialogue, dialectical dialogue and creative learning between different organizations. However, in SC, participants have to question how to create new knowledge by mutually understanding and sharing their thoughts and feelings, and combining both assertiveness and humility. This enables vendors and customers to develop in the dimension of higher thoughts and ideas. To bring about creativity, boundaries vision must be acquired through creative learning born from dialogue and practice in creative confrontations or conflicts between members.

These are "external knowledge convergence capabilities", which constitute the ability to generate and achieve new product concepts or the new usage forms discussed in this chapter through synthesis of dissimilar knowledge through "abduction" (Peirce, 1998). Practitioners' external knowledge convergence capabilities are the driving force behind the achievement of knowledge convergence.

4.2   Design-Driven Innovation through Co-Creation by Vendors and Customers

As discussed in Chapter 1, for companies (organizations) to demonstrate dynamic capabilities (DC) to create new markets or new value in dynamically changing markets, practitioners have to demonstrate (a) *context architect capabilities*, (b) *boundaries consolidation capabilities*, and (c) *strategy architect capabilities* (Kodama, 2011a, 2014, 2018). DC have to be demonstrated in the co-creation activities of vendors and customers (by both the vendors and the customers) at the same time as these three capabilities.

"Context architect capabilities" are also the practitioner capabilities of innovators (project members and their customers) who achieve design-driven innovation by generating new meaning between the dissimilar contexts of vendor knowledge and customer knowledge. Differences arise on the boundaries between the dissimilar contexts of vendor knowledge and customer knowledge (Carlile, 2002, 2004). These differences give rise to further diversity and contradictions of contexts, and are factors that drive boundaries vision for practitioners. Overcoming contradictions originating in contextual diversity dynamically gives rise to new contexts, which enables sharing of "specific contexts" (Kodama, 2006). In overcoming these contradictions, the execution of creative learning through dialectical and creative dialogue (Kodama, 2007), creative confrontations or abrasion (Leonard-Barton, 1995), productive friction (Hagel and Brown, 2005) and political negotiating practice (Brown and Duguid, 2001) and so forth among vendors and customers is an important factor. This process is similar to the "innovation process to generate meaning" to achieve design-driven innovation described by Verganti (2017).

To achieve their business visions or missions, the context architect capabilities of vendors and customers to bring about specific contexts enables the creation and practice of new concepts though constructive and creative dialogue and learning on questions asking why, how things should be, and how to achieve certain things. As a result, the quality of these specific contexts in turn determines the quality of the knowledge produced to achieve design-driven innovation.

Regarding boundaries consolidation capability, the building of strategic communities (Kodama, 2005) by practitioners both as vendors and customers is the basis of the aforementioned specific contexts. "Practitioners" does not mean simply anybody will do, but importantly means a number of "specific practitioners" (Kodama, 2006) who have the human capability of constantly pursuing self-improvement. Expressed in the contexts of technical experts, this also means specific practitioners who have common knowledge (shared language and knowledge) (e.g., Star, 1989). These people build strategic communities to proactively bring about specific contexts based on their beliefs and thoughts. In the cases in this chapter, "specific practitioners" means certain project team members or leading customers.

Strategic architect capabilities also mean practitioners' capabilities to formulate and implement strategy by dynamically forming strategic communities to bring about new business models (in the cases in this chapter, pioneering new usage forms or achieving customized product development, etc.) through context architect capabilities and boundaries consolidation capabilities.

5.   CONCLUSION

This chapter has provided new knowledge on the convergence of "vendor knowledge" and "customer knowledge" drawn from long-term action research in development and sales activities centered on a vendor project team. Significant differences emerge between the vendor knowledge of the project team about product development at the vendor side, and customer knowledge that diverse customers have about usage forms. However, as vendors and customers united to form strategic communities to bridge the boundaries that arise from the differences between vendor and customer knowledge, they acquired boundaries vision to bring about boundaries knowledge through creative learning involving experimentation, and achieved design-driven innovation as the creation of new usage forms by using boundaries knowledge.

NOTES

1. Please refer to the following website for an introduction to the practical experience of the author.
   https://www.vtv.co.jp/intro/taidan/02.html
2. Please refer to the following website for official news releases.
   https://www.ntt.co.jp/news/news97/970911b.html
3. Please refer to the following website for official news releases.
   https://www.ntt.co.jp/news/news97/970415b.html
4. In preparing this chapter, the author would like to express his deep gratitude to the founder, former chairman Yoshida and former director Oguchi. Its content reflects the various human and business philosophies that the author has learned from IBIZA in a long relationship over the past 15 years.
5. The late Tsuneo Hirose served as Director of the Research Institute of Information Science Development on Animal Medicine and Professor Emeritus at Obihiro University of Agriculture and Veterinary Medicine. Specializing in veterinary clinical radiology, using diagnostic imaging terminology for the first time in Japan, Professor Emeritus Hirose was a world leader in development and implementation of the large animal X-ray diagnostic cars and industrial animal diagnostic imaging vehicles, etc. still used on farms, and greatly contributed to the development of diagnostic imaging. In 1972, he received the Japan Veterinary Doctor's Award. Professor Emeritus Hirose served as Director of the International Veterinary Radiology Association and also served on the review Board of the Veterinary Radiology & Ultrasound Journal. He served as the chairman of the 12th International Veterinary Radiology Association (IVRA) held in Obihiro, Hokkaido in August 2000.

REFERENCES

Brandenburger, A. & Nalebuff, B. (1996), *Co-opetition: A Revolution Mindset That Combines Competition and Co-operation: The Game Theory Strategy That's Changing the Game of Business*, New York: Doubleday.

Brown, J.S. & Duguid, P. (2001), 'Knowledge and organization: A social-practice perspective', *Organization Science*, 12(6), 198–213.

Carlile, P. (2002), 'A pragmatic view of knowledge and boundaries: Boundary objects in new product development', *Organization Science*, 13(4), 442–455.

Carlile, P. (2004), 'Transferring, translating, and transforming: An integrative framework for managing knowledge across boundaries', *Organization Science*, 15(5), 555–568.

Gulati, R., Nohria, N. & Zaheer, A. (2000), 'Strategic networks', *Strategic Management Journal*, 21(3), 203–215.

Hagel III, J. & Brown, J.S. (2005), 'Productive friction', *Harvard Business Review*, 83(2), 139–145.

Hirose, T. (1985), 'Veterinary medicine: Results and research prospects', *Japan Veterinary Association*, 233–237.

Iansiti, M. & Levien, R. (2004), 'Keystones and dominators: Framing operating and technology strategy in a business ecosystem', *Harvard Business School, Boston*, 24–25.

Kodama, M. (2005), 'Knowledge creation through networked strategic communities: Case studies on new product development in Japanese companies', *Long Range Planning*, 38(1), 27–49.

Kodama, M. (2006), 'Knowledge-based view of corporate strategy', *Technovation*, 26(12), 1390–1406.

Kodama, M. (2007), *Knowledge Innovation: Strategic Management as Practice*, Cheltenham, UK and Northampton, MA, USA: Edward Elgar Publishing.

Kodama, M. (2011a), *Interactive Business Communities: Accelerating Corporate Innovation through Boundary Networks*, Aldershot, UK: Gower Publishing.

Kodama, M. (2011b), *Knowledge Integration Dynamics: Developing Strategic Innovation Capability*. Singapore: World Scientific Publishing.

Kodama, M. (2014), *Winning Through Boundaries Innovation: Communities of Boundaries Generate Convergence*, Oxford, UK: Peter Lang.

Kodama, M. (Ed.) (2015), *Collaborative Innovation: Developing Health Support Ecosystems* (Vol. 39), Abingdon, UK: Routledge.

Kodama, M. (2018), *Sustainable Growth Through Strategic Innovation: Driving Congruence In Capabilities*, Cheltenham, UK and Northampton, MA, USA: Edward Elgar Publishing.

Leonard-Barton, D. (1995), *Wellsprings of Knowledge: Building and Sustaining the Sources of Innovation*, Boston, MA: Harvard Business School Press.

Nonaka, I. & Takeuchi, H. (1995), *The Knowledge-Creating Company*, New York: Oxford University Press.

Peirce, C.S. (1998), *Chance, Love, and Logic: Philosophical Essays*, Lincoln, NE: University of Nebraska Press.

Prahalad, C.K. & Ramaswamy, V. (2000), 'Co-opting customer competence', *Harvard Business Review*, 78(1), 79–90.

Prahalad, C.K. & Ramaswamy, V. (2004), 'Co-creation experiences: The next practice in value creation', *Journal of Interactive Marketing*, 18(3), 5–14.

Rosenberg, N. (1982), *Inside the Black Box: Technology and Economics*, Cambridge, UK: Cambridge University Press.

Star, S.L. (1989), 'The structure of ill-structured solutions: Boundary objects and heterogeneous distributed problem solving', in Huhns, M. and Gasser, I.L. (eds), *Readings in Distributed Artificial Intelligence*, Menlo Park, CA: Morgan Kaufman, pp. 37–54.

Thomke, S. & Von Hippel, E. (2002), 'Customers as innovators', *Harvard Business Review*, 80(4), 74–81.

Verganti, R. (2003), 'Design as brokering of languages: The role of designers in the innovation strategy of Italian firms', *Design Management Journal*, 13(3), 34–42.

Verganti, R. (2017), *Overcrowded: Designing Meaningful Products in a World Awash with Ideas*, Cambridge, MA: MIT Press.

Von Hippel, E. (1994), '"Sticky information" and the locus of problem solving: Implications for innovation', *Management Science*, 40(4), 429–439.

4. Product and service innovation through boundaries vision and boundaries knowledge: new knowledge from the corporate strategy and innovation perspective

Mitsuru Kodama and Yoshiki Takano

1.   KNOWLEDGE CONVERGENCE AND TRANSFORMATION FOR NEW INNOVATION

The importance of raising the creativity of not only corporate organizations and wider social organizations, but also individual humans in all generations, to contribute to various social activities cannot be understated. In particular, in the business field in recent years, as an indicator of new product developments that differentiate from other companies and new business developments in dissimilar fields, there has been heightened interest in the development of new products and services through knowledge convergence (Kodama, 2014) and knowledge transformation (Nonaka et al., 2014) of dissimilar technologies and services. This is because there are many cases of never-before-seen creative new products and services achieved through the convergence of knowledge across dissimilar fields.

The necessity of business strategies for converging dissimilar technologies and services, developing products and services and building business models to create new markets is increasing. On the corporate side also, currently there is a strengthening of training and adoption of human resources with creative thinking. In light of this, this chapter focuses on the individual and organizational thinking and actions for creative thinking and innovation, and observes and analyzes two in-depth case studies involving the creativity development process for achieving knowledge creation.

This chapter focuses on knowledge differences that arise between people and organizations and between various different objects and actions, presents specific details of product development, in terms of the mechanisms of boundaries vision and boundaries knowledge (or boundaries knowing) that come about through the perception, awareness and discovery of such differences by people, and illustrates how boundaries vision and boundaries knowledge (knowing) impact the creativity and innovation of people and organizations to become capabilities that bring about innovation for the challenge of creating new knowledge by people and organizations.

2.   IN-DEPTH CASE STUDY ANALYSIS – THE DEVELOPMENT
      OF THE WORLD'S FIRST MOBILE TELEPHONE WITH
      BUILT-IN CAMERA AND THE COMMERCIALIZATION OF
      "SHA-MAIL"

In November 2000, J-Phone (later acquired by the UK's Vodafone, and in May 2006 acquired by Softbank – in October 2006 the company name changed to Softbank Mobile) launched a phone model with a built-in digital camera. The 74-gram device, the first cellular phone mounted with a camera, enabled users to transmit color photos to other mobile phones. Rollout started in Japan, the base of operations for J-Phone. In addition to the transmission of 256 color images, users could attach photos to email messages sent via the phone. Its screen also allowed users to display photos stored in memory, and caller photos could be set to appear when they dialed the device.

J-Phone was a leading mobile operator in Japan and a member of the Vodafone Group, the world's largest mobile community. J-Phone offered sophisticated mobile services including high-quality voice telephony, "Sha-mail" picture messaging, "Movie Sha-mail" video messaging, "J-SKY" mobile Internet and email access, and Java applications. Sha-mail was a service that allowed people to take pictures with a mobile phone with built-in camera and send them as email attachments. Encouraged by its ease of use, more and more customers recognized and adopted the Sha-mail brand, resulting in continued rapid expansion. After introducing its first mobile phone with a built-in camera in November 2000, J-Phone reached the milestone of 10 million Sha-mail users in approximately two years and seven months.

In December 2001, J-Phone adopted the J-Phone/Vodafone dual logo to visually promote its membership in the Vodafone Group, the world's leading mobile carrier. By adopting the Vodafone brand, J-Phone aimed to create an even stronger brand presence in the Japanese market by combining Vodafone's association with reliability and global services with the former J-Phone brand's reputation for innovation, as exemplified by the pioneering Sha-mail picture messaging service. As a member of the Vodafone Group, J-Phone strove to offer its customers even richer communications that were global in scope and advanced high-value-added products and service. Vodafone rolled out Sha-mail in Europe as Vodafone Live, capturing more than 380,000 users by December 2002.

By around 1999 to 2000, au, a competitor of J-Phone, was running a network with a higher speed (64 kbps) than J-Phone's (9.6 kbps), while both DoCoMo and au were planning the launch of a third-generation system. J-Phone was under a tremendous pressure to do something to offset their overwhelming disadvantage in data transmission speed. However, J-Phone knew that its strength lay in email and other communication aspects, as opposed to mobile Internet services like i-mode, and decided to build on that strength. Thus, J-Phone's basic policy for promoting the mobile market was to differentiate itself from DoCoMo and au by developing new mobile phones offering email-based mobile services. The development policy of the new mobile service was based on the concept of email, and offered customers various applications.

"Sha-mail – shoot, send, see-mail – begins here." At the end of June, 2001, J-Phone launched its new service campaign for mobile phones. By attaching digital data (images) to text and sending to the recipient as an attachment, Sha-mail "allows you to capture a face's expression or scenery at a particular time, something that a text mail alone couldn't express, by taking a photo and sending it to a partner" (Keiji Takao, J-Phone's mobile phone development project leader). The company set the goal of building a market for Sha-mail. Takao was trans-ferred to J-Phone from automaker Mazda in 1992 (he transferred again in 1996). At the time, Takao was inexperienced with mobile phones, but he and his colleagues undertook to develop the service progressively, and Sha-mail finally blossomed.

2.1   Socialization Phase – Generating Knowledge Differences and Boundaries Knowledge

The concept of the Sha-mail product started with the following episode. Takao's parents were visiting Tokyo from Kyushu. Wanting to relax and spend time with his parents, Takao went with them on a trip to nearby Hakone, a famous sight-seeing area. Together, the three of them rode on a cable car, and greatly enjoyed the fabulous views. But another sight also caught his eye: a woman talking into a mobile phone and saying "Hello? Hello? Oh, there's no connec-tion. Okay, now how do I send a message?" She was trying to communicate her feelings on seeing the beautiful view from the cable car through email, but the operation seemed to be very confusing. She did not seem to have a camera either, so she was unable to take a photograph.

The sight of the woman left a strong impression on Takao, who was left questioning how she had been trying so hard to send an email. At the time, Takao did not think so much about it, but days later he recalled the woman's valiant efforts to write email, and on thinking about it arrived at a hypothesis that she was making efforts to convey the beauty of the view in her email. Certainly, attempts to express such a wonderful view in writing would be quite difficult without carefully chosen wording. Although he thought taking a photograph would be okay, Takao felt that more than anything, she wanted her to share the feeling of the excitement of seeing the beautiful view in that moment, and with those feelings, was busy with the mail function working on the sentences. It certainly was possible to use a digital camera available on the market at the time to take a photograph of a view and save it for later, but to convey the feeling of excitement that arises in the moment is limited to the situation itself. Takao sensed that the woman certainly must have felt that she could convey her feelings as text with the mobile phone mail, albeit not very well. Thus, at the same time, Takao thought how great it would be to put a camera in a mobile phone, and had this revelation: "Of course! If mobile phones came with cameras, we could soon send our feelings to a recipient with a photograph!" This episode was the origin of the "Sha-mail" concept.

Takao reminisced that he wanted to realize such functions both as a developer and as a consumer for the Sha-mail development. This pinpointed direct experience also made Takao aware of valuable knowledge differences between the behavior of the woman that he saw at Hakone and the then-limited mobile telephone functionality for conveying feelings, and thus triggered boundaries knowledge as a need to implement the camera functions that were missing from the mobile telephones of the day.

2.2   Externalization Phase – Generating Knowledge Differences and Boundaries Knowledge through the J-Phone and Sharp Joint Development

At first three employees, including project leader Keiji Takao, set to work on drafting a devel-opment plan for establishing an email-based image communication market. Their vision was to create in Japan a new form of image communication out of conventional text-based email. They were presented with innumerable technical and business problems including the following:

- How to develop a low-cost, high-quality, digital mobile phone with built-in camera?
- How should J-Phone promote mobile phones with built-in cameras?
- How should J-Phone create and provide a service for customers?

Keiji Takao believed that collaboration with a mobile phone manufacturer would be important for developing the camera-mounted mobile handsets. In Japan's mobile phone industry, communications carriers do not just provide mobile phone services, but also supervise mobile handset marketing, product planning (they determine the handset's functions and usage – in other words, its specifications) and sales. Mobile phone manufacturers design their mobile phones based on the specifications determined by the communications carrier, and supervise the apportioning of parts development and manufacturing. Mobile phone brands are also sold with communications carrier brands (such as Vodafone, DoCoMo and au). The contract structure is for communications carriers to buy phones in bulk from manufacturers (the relationship between communications carriers and mobile phone manufacturers differs from that in the US and Europe, and is characteristic of relations among Japanese companies).

Japanese household appliance manufacturer Sharp (its large liquid-crystal Aquos TV is known throughout the world) came into mobile phone development and sales later than many other Japanese manufacturers (including NEC, Fujitsu, Matsushita, Mitsubishi and Toshiba), but jumped straight to number one in terms of market share (mobile phone shipping figures within Japan in fiscal 2005) with the development of the world's first mobile phone with built-in camera.

Before Sharp entered the mobile phone market, it focused its business resources on the PHS (Personal Handyphone System). The warning lights came on, however, when PHS users migrated to the mobile phone. In June 1998 Katsuhiko Machida, who had become CEO of Sharp, predicted the future profitability of the mobile phone business and concentrated business resources on the mobile phone. To begin with, he promoted collaboration with J-Phone centered on Sharp Communications Systems business headquarters in Hiroshima.

Taking the opportunity of the launch of J-Phone's SkyWeb content distribution service in December 1998, the first mobile phone incorporating Sharp's core liquid-crystal technology (SH-01) was launched. Sharp had exploited this unique technology through close collaboration with J-Phone. The phone, which incorporated a liquid-crystal panel (large for its time) became a great hit. In December 2000, J-Phone launched a mobile phone with built-in camera with a color liquid-crystal panel. By this time, however, NEC, Fujitsu and DoCoMo (for i-mode) had completed development of their color LCD-mounted mobile phones, and Sharp began to lose its competitive dominance. The leaders of the personal business division product and planning team and technology team at Sharp Communication Systems' business headquarters felt a sense of crisis and were impatient to act. They strongly felt the need to anticipate other companies' actions and to strike with a new development of their own.

What Sharp had in mind was to incorporate a camera module into a mobile phone and to create a mobile phone with a feeling of a "print club" (a photo booth found in malls and other places that creates photo stickers of the user with backgrounds of flowers or cartoon characters), which was then popular among Japan's junior high and high school girls. The new phone would be a "portable print club". There was logic to the reason why they resolved to use this idea. Looking back at the evolution of mobile phones to that point, a progression could be traced from voice communication to email and text, then to mobile Internet such as the i-mode service, then to ringtones and image download services. Considering the evolution of this kind of mobile phone technology and customer usage structures, the customer would naturally come to want a camera to take photographs. There was a down side to this reading of customer evolution, however, which was that the camera-mounted PHS, developed and sold by Kyocera, could be used as a TV phone, but was bulky and expensive, and was simply not selling.

Their interpretation of why the mobile phone with built-in camera would not sell was that it was a problem of lifestyle. The TV phone was ahead of its time, in that the culture of seeing someone's face while talking had not yet developed. However, the situation for still images rather than the moving images of the TV phone was different. The digital camera culture was spreading, and if pictures could easily be taken with a mobile camera, they could then be saved for later enjoyment or attached to an email and sent to a friend or family member. The leaders believed that such a phone was sure to sell. As mentioned above, J-Phone's Keiji Takao was thinking of exactly the same idea. J-Phone's and Sharp's expectations coincided exactly.

Around this time, Sharp approached DoCoMo with its idea for a mobile phone with built-in camera. DoCoMo, however, were at the peak of their success with the i-mode-loaded mobile phone, and sales were rising daily. DoCoMo's service strategy priority at that time was to maintain i-mode's distribution and expansion, and DoCoMo felt that adding a camera would raise the price of the handset. DoCoMo also predicted that even if users took photographs with the camera, they might save the pictures on the mobile phone, but few would use DoCoMo's communications networks to send photographic images. Since DoCoMo would be unable to charge a fee as a communications carrier unless the photographs were transmitted, the company saw no merit in the proposal, and responded negatively to Sharp's proposal. Sharp had seen this as an opportunity to land the coup of developing a mobile phone with a built-in camera while establishing a partnership with DoCoMo, but unfortunately, it was not to be. DoCoMo's logic had been impeccable.

To be sure, it became clear after the mobile phone with built-in camera became popular that users tended to save and enjoy the pictures, rather than sending them by email. Later, however, a mobile phone would not sell unless it was accessorized with a camera. Finding that it was falling behind J-Phone and au, in June 2002 DoCoMo decided to sell mobile phones with built-in cameras in collaboration with Sharp. Later DoCoMo exploited its brand strength to surpass J-Phone in mobile phone with built-in camera sales.

For Takao, who was project leader for initiating the joint development of mobile phones with built-in cameras with Sharp, it was important to cooperate with the in-house functional organizations of business planning, sales, equipment, maintenance and other divisions while at the same time strengthening collaboration with Sharp's development project. At this time, Kyocera's camera-fitted "Visualphone" was an influencing factor. Negative opinions about the development of the mobile phone with built-in camera were heard within J-Phone. Takao had the understanding and support of his immediate superior, however, but he also required strong commitment from the leaders and managers in related divisions, and he managed to gain their consent for the new development. At that time J-Phone was feeling the pressure from DoCoMo and au, and a sense of crisis pervaded the company. This crisis became the axis around which the entire company coalesced, and all the J-Phone employees became galvanized by the challenge of developing a mobile phone with a built-in camera. Leadership teams were formed within J-Phone as strategic communities (SC) between Takao's project teams and functional organizations.

Meanwhile Sharp, which J-Phone had contracted to develop the phone, was forming a development project involving various divisions within the company aimed at small-camera module development and camera mounting (see Figure 4.1). The frequent meetings with Takao's project in Tokyo were attended by the product planning team of Sharp's personal communications business division in Hiroshima, design and technology leaders, and Tokyo's sales team leaders. These groups engaged in discussions about the concept and idea of built-in camera mobile handsets (SC-0 in Figure 4.1: an SC for practicing abduction through the synergies of social contexts and technical contexts with the tacit knowledge and the explicit knowledge areas as user needs to properly absorb the needs and ideas of Sharp's customer J-Phone and to understand the specific functions and product specifications for the product).

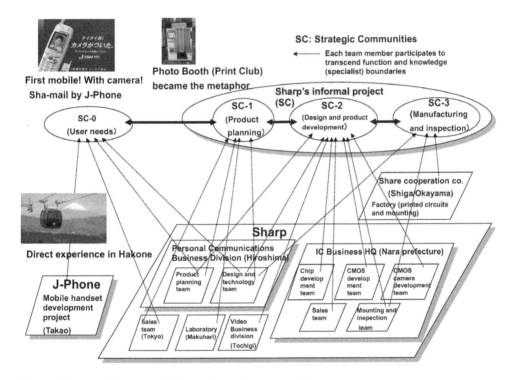

Figure 4.1   J-Phone and Sharp strategic communities

In the stages of this commercial planning process, Takao and Sharp's engineers became aware of valuable knowledge differences by thoroughly understanding the differences with "Visualphone", a past TV–telephone device of another company that failed, differences in strategy with competitive companies (NTT DOCOMO and au) and the reading of the changes (differences) in lifestyles using mobile telephones between the present and the future. As commercial planning concepts, this in turn triggered boundaries knowledge with a focus not only on the installation of a compact camera module, a function that had not been included in mobile phones of the time, but also on three developmental functions: not destroying the design of the mobile phone itself, preventing spy photos by forcefully generating shutter noise in silent mode and the ability to take pictures of oneself. These were different from the products that had failed in the past.

Also, regarding commercial planning documentation, materials on the judgments of decision-making at the start of the new product development, Sharp's engineering team had to "read" the technical potentials (differences in product development processes to date: grasping the knowledge differences) to get approval from top management of both companies (J-Phone and Sharp). This "reading" (grasping the knowledge differences) entailed the acquisition of boundaries knowledge to enable knowledge transformation (tacit knowledge → explicit knowledge) to achieve Combination and Integration (the closed innovation process shown by Pattern A in Figure 4.1) of the mobile phone, camera module, image-processing and miniaturization (mounting) technologies, etc. that Sharp had fostered. Also, the metaphor of "a portable photo booth" prompted knowledge transformation, which gave the product development team the high-quality explicit knowledge required for the design of the mobile phone with a built-in camera and its functional specifications.

2.3   The Combination Phase – Creating Elements of a New Development with Knowledge Differences and Boundaries Knowledge

At Sharp's personal communications business division, the ideas and specifications discussed with J-Phone were consolidated as specific design data (overall system architecture, hardware and software, and individual module level elements). Then designers and staff members (where necessary) became involved and exchanged their views (SC-1 in Figure 4.1: an SC for practicing abduction through the synergies of social and technical contexts for product planning in the manufacturer). The focus of the new development elements was the small camera module. The engineers in the personal communications business division were an expert group regarding mobile phone communications technology, but they had no specialist knowledge of lenses or image-processing. Realizing a mobile phone with built-in camera, however, required the fusion of heterogeneous technologies including communications, lenses and image-processing ICs. Fortunately, Sharp had accumulated image and camera technology from the Zaurus PDA hit product and the liquid crystal Viewcam video camera. Without delay, the Hiroshima engineers accessed the CCD division of the IC business division in Tenri, Nara Prefecture.

In Tenri, technology staff from the personal communications division and the CCD division held numerous meetings to discuss how to develop a small camera module (unifying image elements, lenses and image-processing ICs) and include it in a small mobile phone while maintaining the phone's size. The investigation progressed energetically through discussions that included the new development of low-energy IC chips dedicated to image-processing, development of small CMOS camera modules and methods for loading the new components (SC-2 in Figure 4.1: an SC for practicing abduction through the synergies of micro-social and technical contexts for design and component development). Regarding the development period required by the J-Phone customer, Sharp's engineers directly faced development process issues, such as CMOS sensor noise correction and miniaturization of the lens-integrated CMOS sensor.

Many of the issues were solved, however, by transcending organizational barriers and sharing individual specialist skills. In this way, they succeeded in reducing the thickness of the camera module used in the Zaurus PDA (a hit product for Sharp) by about half.

Next came the need for technology to mount more than 50 new components, including a miniature camera module and dedicated IC chip, onto a compact circuit board. The IC business headquarters' mounting and inspection team outsourced volume manufacture of the circuit on which the components would be loaded to a Sharp collaborative company named Sumitomo Electric Printed Circuits in Shiga prefecture.

A flexible circuit board for loading components was adopted as an industry first. But the problem occurred that the circuit pattern, or electronic wiring, could not be seen clearly after surface processing, and the percentage of good-quality boards was an atrocious 20 percent. With a predicted sales figure of 10,000 units a day, this kind of situation was unacceptable. To address this issue, the IC business head office's mounting and inspection team and Hiroshima's Production Control supervisor gathered at the cooperative company in Shiga prefecture, reconsidered product standards and reviewed circuit patterns and surface processing while implementing a trial and error approach. The quality ratio rose steadily.

New problems arose, however. After manufacturing the printed boards, loading a large number of components onto the boards' small surface area disrupted the circuit pattern during the mounting process. The heat of the soldering also caused the circuit board to distort. These major problems were solved through cross-divisional cooperation (in this case with support from a mounting technology specialist in Hiroshima) within Sharp. This was the first time that this level of high-precision mounting had become possible in the mobile phone industry (SC-3 in Figure 4.1: an SC for practicing abduction through the synergies of micro-social and technical contexts for manufacture and inspection).

In this way, it became possible to surmount obstacles and develop a mobile phone with built-in camera. A key point for the formation of cross-organizational project teams is that teams sharing various contexts to solve problems should be formed informally on the boundaries between generally different organizations and among individuals with different specializations (knowledge). Then, context and knowledge can be inspired and shared among the informal teams (SC). In Sharp's case, the project networks mediated by the SC (SC-0) created with the customer, J-Phone, were formed between different companies (see Figure 4.1).

After surmounting the problems, Sharp, in a joint development project with J-Phone, launched the Japanese-developed, world- and industry-first, mobile phone with a built-in camera (J-SH04) in November 2000. J-Phone gave the name "Sha-mail" to the service that enabled a picture taken with the built-in camera to be sent out as an email attachment.

In the micro-technical contexts for developing a new IC chip specialized for image-processing to lower power consumption, a new compact CMOS camera module, and new part mounting, the engineers became aware of knowledge differences as the elements of the new development were different from the conventional mobile telephone functions. This awareness triggered boundaries knowledge for new core technology developments. Then finally, top-quality explicit knowledge was completed as the commercialization of the world's first mobile phone with built-in camera and Sha-mail.

**2.4   The Internalization Phase – Accumulating New Developmental Capabilities
with Knowledge Differences and Boundaries Knowledge**

The mobile phones with built-in cameras flew off the shelves. The J-Phone marketing and sales teams did not just focus on consumers, but carried out numerous application development tests exploiting Sha-mail for practical use targeting corporate clients from different industries, then quickly and widely publicized the product and acquired good sales figures (see Box 4.1).

In strategies to expand the sales of mobile phones, normally, consumers are targeted, but the J-Phone marketing and sales team noticed the existence of particular usage methods by particular corporate customers. These knowledge differences noticed through the reflective practice of executing special sales strategies different from the norm entailed the generation of boundaries knowledge to develop new solutions for corporate customers.

The marketing and sales divisions, functional organizations at J-Phone, formed corporate networks with specific corporate customers to strengthen and drive the advertising of Sha-mail in society as a sales strategy. As well as that, with various opinions and technical support for the functionality of the mobile phone with a built-in camera, the company configured full technical and after service systems centered on its functional organizations. Thus, centering on the marketing and sales activities of Sha-mail, the chain of know-how and skills in the business activities from product development, sales, after sales services and promotional activities were accumulated in both staff members and organizations.

Close collaboration through the formation of an SC with Takao's product development project and functional organization such as marketing and sales departments drove the Sha-mail development. In-house at J-Phone, leadership teams (Kodama, 2005) were formed as SC between leaders and managements in all departments, including top management. Thus, the leadership teams established robust linkages in the business processes of mobile phone with built-in camera development, marketing, sales, advertising and PR, facilities and after sales services to optimize the entire business.

BOX 4.1   J-PHONE'S INCUBATION WITH SPECIFIC CORPORATE
CLIENTS: COLLABORATION BETWEEN BUSINESSES
IN DIFFERENT INDUSTRIES

**(1)   Accelerating The Popularization of "Sha-mail" Applications in the
Medical Field**

Collaboration is based on interactive relationships between businesses and customers in other industries, with the goal of finding new markets and expanding existing markets for products and services generated in the strategic creation of new businesses. Leaders and managers must discover and search out key people in businesses in other industries, and then work with them to cultivate and expand new markets. These elements are also essential for raising the quality of the products and services generated in the process of strategic business creation to create new value for customers (Kodama, 2002). Taking customers as important strategic partners and working with them to improve the quality of products and services makes it possible to create new businesses and expand markets. J-PHONE, in the course of increasing the diffusion of the "Sha-mail" into various medical institutions (such as medical universities) or companies, has moved forward with a business strategy of successively winning over medical institutions throughout Japan.

J-Phone's task was to exploit Sha-mail and mobile networks to realize an environment in Japan that would allow large numbers of patients to overcome the limitations of space and time, and apply to the emergency medical field, anywhere, any time, and without inconvenience. The key to achieving this goal lay in popularizing Sha-mail among medical institution customers. To this end, it was important to first create strategic partnership-based business teams with medical institutions and companies, and to succeed with a Sha-mail-based medical information network as part of a one-point penetration strategy.

It was also important for J-Phone to take the knowledge, expertise and new ideas gained in creating its first team and put them to work in the business with its second strategic partner. This, along with innovative leadership on the part of leaders and managers to further popularize Sha-mail, provided important knowledge for the company.

The strategic collaboration that J-Phone promoted in the field of medicine could be seen in the business expansion the company achieved through a series of consecutive strategic partnerships with universities, large medical institutions and technical companies, including the following:

- May 2001: Partnership in the joint development of mobile medical systems with Philips Medical Corp. and Infocom Corp.
- October 2001: Launched CT and MRI Sha-mail image transmission experiments with several medical institutes and companies.
- January 2002: Partnership in the emergency medical field with Kyourin Medical University using Sha-mail.

In this manner, J-PHONE created and succeeded with Sha-mail applications in the medical fields. Such new virtual medical services combining these types of multimedia technologies and services in the medical fields can be viewed as a new form of knowledge-based service (Kodama, 1999).

(2)   New Business Model Combining Communication and Broadcasting Services

Other J-Phone challenges were to collaborate with TV broadcasting companies, and to create a strategic partnership with TV-Aichi Corp. to trial a service combining Sha-mail and TV programs. This trial service enabled Sha-mail users to interactively participate in live TV by sending an image, pictures or text information through Sha-mail in advance. While enjoying a program on television, for example, a user would be able to participate interactively by using a Sha-mail mobile phone after going to J-Phone's web site (J-SKY) and sending image, pictures, or text. In addition to the strong entertainment value of the trial service, broadcasters would be able to obtain basic demographic information about their interactive viewers, such as age, gender and general location, for marketing purposes.

3. CONCLUSION

This chapter has observed and analyzed a new concept and framework of knowledge creation through boundaries vision and boundaries knowledge from an in-depth case study. Currently in the knowledge society, for individuals living in corporate society, in addition to the necessity to create knowledge through the convergence and transformation of diverse knowledge across differing values and areas of specialization in organizations, it is most important to acquire creativity to converge (or transform) the best knowledge distributed across the globe with the knowledge of individuals and organizations by forming global networks of the best people and organizations around the world.

In the acquisition of creativity through the framework of knowledge creation through boundaries vision and boundaries knowledge, in the knowledge economy, diverse human knowledge (of which technology is one element) is the source of valuable products, services and business models that can give a company new competitiveness. New value chains are formed as new strategic models by merging diverse technologies and different industries to bring about new products, services and business models that transcend various boundaries. Accordingly, a company must refresh its perspectives on management spanning the boundaries between the knowledge of individuals, groups and organizations, bringing about boundaries knowledge through boundaries vision to create knowledge as new business.

REFERENCES

Kodama, M. (1999), 'Customer value creation through community-based information networks', *International Journal of Information Management*, 19(6), 495–508.
Kodama, M. (2002), 'Transforming an old economy company through strategic communities', *Long Range Planning*, 35(4), 349–365.
Kodama, M. (2005), 'Knowledge creation through networked strategic communities: Case studies on new product development in Japanese companies', *Long Range Planning*, 38(1), 27–49.
Kodama, M. (2014), *Winning Through Boundaries Innovation: Communities of Boundaries Generate Convergence*, Oxford, UK: Peter Lang.
Nonaka, I., Kodama, M., Hirose, A., & Kohlbacher, F. (2014), 'Dynamic fractal organizations for promoting knowledge-based transformation: A new paradigm for organizational theory', *European Management Journal*, 32(1), 137–146.

5. Interpersonal cognitive traits and interactional traits that support boundaries vision: the basis of group creativity

Takashi Oka and Mana Yamamoto

1. INTERPERSONAL COGNITIVE AND INTERACTIONAL TRAITS SUPPORTING BOUNDARIES VISION

Psychological research on creativity has focused on clarifying personality traits that define an individual's creativity. However, studies on the personal traits that define the creativity of groups involving multiple individuals have so far been limited. Just like the Gestalt principle that the whole is more than just the sum of its parts, the creativity of a whole group is more than just the sum of the creativity of its individual members. This research aims to explore the traits of individual members that bring about group creativity, which cannot be reduced to the creativity of individual members. Several studies have examined personality factors as individual traits of members that influence the creativity of a group. For example, the "big five" traits are attracting attention due to their stability. The big five traits are: openness to experience, conscientiousness, extraversion, neuroticism and agreeableness. These personality traits directly affect teamwork self-efficacy and motivation at the individual level, although it is possible that they affect the overall creativity of groups due to their connection with group efficacy and motivation at the group level (e.g., Tagger, 2019). Put differently, these personality traits are not thought to directly define group creativity as proximal antecedents, but are thought to define group creativity as distal antecedents via various processes.

This research focuses on the interactional relationships among members within a group, assuming that the dynamism of these interactions makes the creativity of the group more than the simple sum of the creativity of its members, and considers the proximal individual traits that directly define the dynamism of these interactions. In Chapter 1 of this book, Kodama focuses on the knowledge differences between group members and names new knowledge born through the perception of such differences as "boundaries knowledge" and believes that this boundaries knowledge is the mother of group creativity and innovation. Perceiving boundaries between oneself and others, and boundaries between others in a group, and accurately assessing the knowledge and traits of members within the group including oneself and bridging the boundaries between members who mutually control themselves, brings about new knowledge and traits within the group. Kodama (2019) calls the characteristic that agents should possess to enable such creation "boundaries vision".

Rethinking the function of boundaries vision in terms of the relationships among members of the group from a psychological perspective reveals that boundaries vision can be divided into two functions – interpersonal cognition and interpersonal interaction. Interpersonal interaction, whether within a group or not, begins with discerning and recognizing others who are different from oneself. Whether this interpersonal cognition is performed correctly and properly is key to the success or failure of subsequent interpersonal interactions. Reasonable interpersonal cognition does not guarantee that subsequent interpersonal interactions will be efficient and effective. For successful interpersonal interaction, it is important that the parties involved interact appropriately. When these people interact and expose their fixed unaltered selves, they may by chance be able to harmonize with each other, although there is often a tendency for collisions which end in unproductive interaction. On the other hand, if one or more of the parties in the interaction has a variable self, and can accurately recognize the other person's self and interact while controlling their own self, the interaction will be suitable. In interpersonal interactions involving many selves, the nature of interaction in which many selves are included is the key to the success or failure of such interpersonal interactions.

2.   COGNITIVE COMPLEXITY

In this research, we focus on cognitive complexity as tendencies in personality that allow a person to accurately and in detail recognize others as individuals. Cognitive complexity is a cognitive trait that defines interpersonal cognition, and is the degree of differentiation of constructs in recognizing others in social environments (Bieri, 1955). Individuals with low cognitive complexity engage in interpersonal cognition on an intensive and single dimension, whereas individuals with high cognitive complexity engage in interpersonal cognition on differentiated and multiple dimensions. More than individuals with high cognitive complexity, individuals with low cognitive complexity have been shown to be more likely to make decisions using stereotypes for the groups to which others belong rather than with information about individuals that distinguishes others from others (Ben-Ari, Kedem, and Levy-Weiner, 1992). In other words, individuals with high cognitive complexity do not judge others by applying their own prejudices, but by obtaining detailed information about others through observation from various viewpoints. This can be stored as knowledge of others and used in various places of interpersonal interaction by searching out required information from the abundant stored information.

3.   PERMEABILITY CONTROL POWER

Transactional analysis is a system of psychotherapy and personality theory with a focus on interpersonal interaction, and was founded by Eric Berne (1964). This theory aims to understand interpersonal interactions by measuring the structure of the ego and how it works in relation to others, and attempts to intervene as a psychotherapy for treating hindrances to interpersonal interaction. In the analysis of the interactions of the people involved, it is assumed that there are three "I's" in the minds of people, i.e., three ego states, that perform the following five functions. These functions are assumed to have certain amounts of respective energy and become dominant or inferior in certain interpersonal interactions.

1. Parent: "I" as a parent. An ego state adopted from a parent or caregiver, and which appears when persuading someone or doing something for a person. This ego state has the following two functions:
   (1) Critical Parent: "I" that is strict towards others. This entails bossing people about, dominating them or criticizing them.
   (2) Nurturing Parent: "I" that is gentle towards others. This entails helping people out, looking after them or protecting them.
2. Adult: "I" as an adult. The "I" that appears when handling situations in reality. This entails judging things objectively and logically based on facts and tries to act rationally.
3. Child: "I" as a child. An ego state adopted from experiences as a child, and which appears when doing something for oneself. This ego state has the following two functions:
   (1) Free Child: The "I" that is free from people. Behaving freely according to one's feelings and desires.
   (2) Adapted Child: The "I" adapt to people. Trying to live up to the expectations and demands of surrounding people.

Katsura et al. (1997) measured the ability of an individual to freely switch between the above five ego state functions according to the situation and other parties, by introducing the concept of permeability control power. If this ability is low, only certain ego states will appear, regardless of the situation or other person, maybe leading to maladaptation. Conversely, if this ability is high, the display of the optimal ego state to suit the situation or other party is possible so that effective interpersonal interaction can be facilitated. Katsura, Sinzato, and Mizuno (1997) assert that people who have this ability highly have the psychological characteristics of a positive perception of themselves, strong self-control, proper understanding and awareness of themselves, are future-oriented, and have a strong commitment to their work, etc.

4. SOCIAL SKILLS AND EMPATHY

Cognitive complexity and permeability control power that support boundaries vision are latent psychological traits, and are ineffective unless manifested as specific interpersonal behaviors in actual interpersonal interactions. These traits can be realized as various interpersonal behaviors, but will be manifested as behaviors accompanied by empathy and social skills if they are to affect the success or failure of interpersonal interaction.

Rather than using oneself as the frame of reference in order to understand others, empathy entails using other people as frames of reference so that one can experience the perceptions, thoughts and feelings of others. Empathy is thought to be composed of cognitive elements such as acquiring the viewpoint of others, and emotional elements such as importing the feelings of others. In contrast to people with lower empathy, individuals with higher empathy do not understand and act in a way that assimilates others with themselves without recognizing the boundaries between themselves and others – they instead recognize the boundaries between themselves and others and differences between themselves and others, and they place themselves in the positions and roles of others to understand and act in ways to assimilate themselves with others. It could be that such understanding and behaviors do not converge the knowledge of others with themselves, but create new knowledge by combining one's own knowledge with the knowledge of others, i.e., boundaries knowledge that will become the mother of group creativity.

In the narrow sense, social skills are the abilities and behaviors required to respond appropriately in interpersonal situations. Typically, these skills include assertiveness, communication, relationship building and maintenance, and coping, but more broadly include problem-solving, decision-making and self-control skills in both interpersonal and personal situations. It is conceivable that behaviors involving these social skills can create new knowledge, i.e., boundaries knowledge, the mother of group creativity, by expanding and sharing one's own knowledge and the knowledge of others in interpersonal interactions within a group.

5.   THE OBJECTIVES OF THIS RESEARCH

This research explores whether interpersonal cognitive traits and interactional traits supporting boundaries vision define group creativity through behaviors accompanied by empathy and interpersonal skills. Specifically, as shown in the conceptual model in Figure 5.1, this research studies (1) the way interpersonal cognitive traits and interactional traits are related to empathy and social skills, and (2) how empathy and social skills are related to group creativity. According to the above discussion, the following predictions should hold: the higher the cognitive complexity in interpersonal cognition and the higher the permeability control power in interpersonal interactions, the more the empathic and socially skillful interpersonal behaviors in interpersonal interactions within a group, which should lead to greater group creativity.

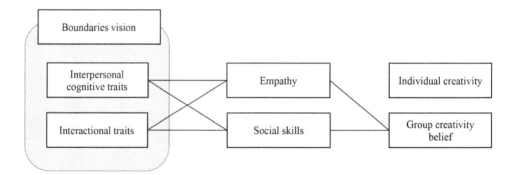

Figure 5.1   Conceptual model of this research

6.   METHODOLOGY

Survey Participants

One hundred and fifty-five university students (75 males, 79 females, 1 unknown, average age 19.45 years old, $SD = 1.29$) participated in the survey.

Procedure

The survey was conducted in two separate sessions after university classes finished in November 2018. As well as providing verbal explanations, the researchers distributed questionnaires to participants, which explained on the cover the voluntary nature of cooperating with the research and the fact that personal information will be protected. Next, participants were asked to enter their student ID numbers so that the first questionnaires could be matched with the second questionnaires. At that time, it was explained that the questionnaires would not be used for any purpose other than research and no individual would be identified. This study underwent an ethical review by the Research Ethics Review Committee of the College of Humanities and Sciences, Nihon University, and was approved (approval number 30-43).

Questionnaire Structure

The first questionnaire was titled (in Japanese) "A Survey on Social Psychological Research on University Students (1)", and consisted of the following contents.

Measuring individual creativity
To measure individual creativity, we asked participants to answer the Unusual Use Test (UUT; Guilford, 1967). The questionnaire was created based on Yamaoka and Yukawa (2017). First, to explain the implementation method printed on the questionnaire was

> You will be asked to list as many unusual uses of some ordinary things used in daily life. You will be asked to answer about two things. Please spend two minutes answering about each thing. First, as an example exercise, please spend 30 seconds answering about a brick. Please answer in accordance with the researchers' signals to start and finish answering.

This was also instructed verbally. Next, the participants did the example exercise for 30 seconds, and after confirming that everybody understood everything, the main exercises were performed. As the main exercises, we asked for two-minute answers each for "socks" and "canned food cans". Participants were given one page for each exercise. At the top of each page was printed the instruction "Please list as many ways of using the following item that are different from normal". Participants were asked to answer freely in a given frame.

Measuring group creativity
There are no established methods of measuring group creativity. In this research, we created a group creativity belief scale, and compared individual creativity with group creativity to measure the belief that group creativity is superior to individual creativity. Beliefs do not always manifest in behavior and therefore outcomes based on beliefs are not always produced. However, social psychology research on the relationship between beliefs and behavioral outcomes shows that beliefs sufficiently predict behavioral outcomes through behavioral intentions. In this research, first, two researchers created the 12 items shown in Table 5.1 to measure the belief in group creativity. In the questionnaire, the 12 items were placed at random, and participants were asked to answer about each item on a scale of 1 to 7 (1: Not applicable to 7: Very applicable).

Table 5.1   Group creativity belief scale items and principal component analysis results

Number	Item	1st		2nd
		I	II	II
2	New ideas are born more easily by thinking together rather than alone	.827	.081	.824
7	Working in a team produces many ideas easily	.807	.167	.826
4	A team approach makes thinking from various perspectives easy	.797	.196	.823
6	Overall team creativity rises easily when members stimulate each other	.741	.256	.780
8	Creative jobs are easier to do in groups rather than alone	.724	-.102	.702
12	Diverse concepts come about more easily by thinking together with other people rather than alone	.702	.110	.716
1	Discussions with everybody more easily produce ideas that an individual might not think of alone	.669	.229	.697
3	Creative ideas emerge easily by brainstorming with everybody	.566	.364	.611
10	The creativity of individuals is easily sacrificed when working in teams (R)	-.347	.648	Excluded
11	Many ideas emerge easily when thinking alone rather than in groups (R)	-.571	.575	Excluded
5	Ideas never before conceived emerge easily when thinking alone rather than in groups (R)	-.477	.558	Excluded
9	Unique feats can be easily achieved by a lonely genius (R)	-.262	.352	Excluded
	Eigenvalue	5.046	1.532	4.513
	Cumulative contribution (%)	42.052	54.820	56.411

Note: (R) Indicates a reversal item.

Measuring cognitive complexity

To measure cognitive complexity, we employed a Japanese version of the Role Construct Repertory Test (Kelly, 1955) created by Hayashi (1976). In this test, participants were asked to identify five character roles (liked men, disliked men, liked women, disliked women, and themselves) from their surroundings, and rate 20 adjectives about their impressions of those characters on a scale of 1 to 7 (1: Not applicable to 7: Very applicable). There were 20 positive and negative adjectives used that Ohashi, Miwa, Hirabayashi, and Nagato (1973) judged to be suitable for evaluating such impressions.

Finally, we asked about gender and age.

The second questionnaire was titled (in Japanese) "A Survey on Social Psychological Research on University Students (2)", and consisted of the following contents.

Measuring interactional traits

We used a PC egogram survey form developed by Katsura et al. (1997). The questionnaire consisted of a 70-item self-rating psychological test with statements such as "I often criticize people", "I often take care of people", "I respond to things calmly", "I often decide things with intuition", "I often match with what people say". There were three possible responses: "yes", "?" and "no". In addition to the five ego states of critical parent, nurturing parent, adult, free child and adapted child, the questionnaire also enabled measurement of the permeability control power that adjusts these ego states. Permeability control power was measured with items such as "I have good self-control" and "I'm good at switching feelings". The questionnaire also included items for checking the reliability of responses.

Measuring empathy

To measure empathy, the multidimensional empathy measurement scale (Sakurai, 1988) was used. This scale is based on the multidimensional empathy model of Davis (1983) and measures four dimensions of empathy, i.e.: perspective-taking, fantasy, empathetic consideration and personal distress. In the questionnaire, the survey participants were asked to respond to 28 statements such as "Before criticizing a person, I try to think about what I would think if I were that person", and reversal items such as "even if someone is upset, I don't feel particularly sorry for them", using a scale of 1 to 4 (1: Not applicable to 4: Very applicable).

Measuring social skills

To measure social skills, the daily life skills scale (Shimamoto and Ishii, 2006) was used. This scale measures not only social skills in a narrow sense but also life skills in general. Specifically, this scale measures affinity, leadership, sensitivity and interpersonal manners as interpersonal skills, and planning, information summarization, self-esteem and positive thinking as personal skills. The questionnaire asked participants to respond to 42 statements such as "When I'm in trouble I can easily consult my friends", "I can summarize everyone's opinion in a discussion", "I can plan for what's ahead", and "I am satisfied with my life so far" on a scale of 1 to 4 (1: Not applicable to 4: Very applicable).

Finally, we asked about gender and age.

7.   RESULTS

Subjects of Analysis

Of the 155 survey participants, 16 who did not respond at all to one or more of the scales were excluded from the analysis. This left 139 participants (70 men, 69 women, average age 19.45 years, $SD = 1.24$) whose data was used for analysis. Of the 139 participants, 36 had some missing values, but these missing values on one scale were less than or equal to two items, so the average of the remaining items was calculated and substituted for those items.

Individual Creativity Score Calculation

To calculate the individual creativity score, scores for answers to the Unusual Use Test (UUT) were obtained as follows.

Fluency
Fluency scores were obtained by calculating the average value calculated for the two stimuli (the two things, specifically "socks" and "canned food cans") to obtain the frequency of answers (Guilford, 1967) according to Yamaoka and Yukawa (2017) (Table 5.2). The intra-participant correlation between the two stimuli was $r = .733$ ($p < .01$).

Flexibility
Each of two evaluators assessed how many categories could be applied to responses to each stimulus (Guilford, 1967). For example, for ways of using canned food cans, the responses "use to hold garbage" and "used to hold water" both entail using the canned food can as a container, and so were classified as one category and given 1 point, whereas the responses "use to hold garbage" and "melt and recycle the metal" were classified as two different categories and given 2 points (Yamaoka and Yukawa, 2017). To study the match ratio of the number of categories between evaluators, correlation coefficients were calculated, which were $r = .922$ ($p < .001$) for "socks", and $r = .921$ ($p < .001$) for "canned food cans". The average number of categories between evaluators was calculated for each stimulus, and the average calculated using the two stimuli was used as the flexibility score (Table 5.2). The intra-participant correlation between the two stimuli was $r = .752$ ($p < .001$).

Uniqueness
(1)   Non-redundant uniqueness
To score non-redundant uniqueness using the average of the two stimuli, 1 point was awarded to answers that did not overlap with the answers of other participants, 0 points were awarded to answers that overlapped (Table 5.2; Wallach and Kogan, 1965; Yamaoka and Yukawa, 2017). The intra-participant correlation between the two stimuli was $r = .700$ ($p < .001$).

(2)   Rare uniqueness
Of all the answers of all participants in the experiment, 1 point was awarded to answers that held a 5 percent share or less and 2 points were awarded to answers that held a 1 percent share or less. The average value calculated for the two stimuli was used as the score of the rare

Table 5.2   *The mean, standard deviation and coefficient of correlation for individual creativity and group creativity beliefs*

	M	SD	Fluency	Flexibility	Non-redundant uniqueness	Rare uniqueness	Evaluative uniqueness
Individual creativity							
Fluency	4.09	2.35					
Flexibility	3.47	2.03	.957**				
Non-redundant uniqueness	1.77	1.85	.849**	.855**			
Rare uniqueness	6.26	4.36	.962**	.931**	.921**		
Evaluative uniqueness	2.71	1.02	.741**	.774**	.569**	.692**	
Group creativity belief	4.89	1.06	−.057	−.101	−.132	−.058	−.007

Note: **$p < .01$.

uniqueness (Guilford, 1967; Yamaoka and Yukawa, 2017). The intra-participant correlation between the two stimuli was $r = .702$ ($p < .001$).

(3)   Evaluative uniqueness
Two evaluators were asked to rate the creativity of each answer on a scale of 1 to 5, from "1: Not creative at all" to "5: Very creative". The average value calculated for the two stimuli was used as the score of the evaluative uniqueness (Table 5.2; Silvia, Winterstein, Willse, Barona, Cram, Hess, Martinez, and Richard, 2008; Yamaoka and Yukawa, 2017). Evaluators were asked to base their assessments on whether answers were intelligent in that they entailed usage of the stimulus unimaginable from the usual use of the stimulus, and that was unlikely to be thought of by another person. Evaluators were also asked to award 0 points to unanswered items. To study the match ratio of the number of categories between evaluators, correlation coefficients were calculated, which were $r = .666$ ($p < .001$) for "socks", and $r = .814$ ($p < .001$) for "canned food cans". The intra-participant correlation between the two stimuli was $r = .528$ ($p < .001$).

Group Creativity Belief Scale Creation and Score Calculation

Principal component analysis was performed to confirm the one-factor structure of the group creativity belief scale (Table 5.1). As a result, there were two items in which the load of the first principal component was low, and two items in which the load was high over both the first and second principal components. As a result of deleting these four items and performing reanalysis, all items showed a high load of the first principal component ($\alpha = .885$). Note that the reliability coefficient of the 12 items before item deletion was $\alpha = .858$, and was higher after the deletion of four items. From these results, eight items were selected for the group creativity belief scale. The average of these eight items was used as the group creativity belief score (Table 5.2).

Calculating Scores for Cognitive Complexity

Total cognitive complexity (TCC; Hayashi, 1976) was used as the index for cognitive complexity. TCC looks at how each adjective differentiates from the evaluation dimension. In other words, with TCC, the more positive or negative the match of the adjective rating, the lower the cognitive complexity. TCC for each role person is the total value obtained by calculating the total number of matches for the median score of positive and negative ratings respectively. The procedure for calculating TCC is as follows. First, the results of the seven-step ratings were coded with 0 as the median score, "+" for positive ratings, and "–" for negative ratings. Next, for each role person, the total number of matches of the codes given to each of the 20 adjectives was calculated. The formula used was $kC_2 + lC_2 + mC_2/2$, where k is the positive rating constant, l is the negative rating constant, and m is the median rating. The sum of the TCCs of all role persons is the TCC score of the participant. In the method by Sakamoto (1991), the calculation cannot be performed if even one value is missing among the 20 rating values for one role person. Thus, if these were two or fewer missing values for a role person, those values were replaced with the average ratings for that role person. Higher TCC scores indicate lower cognitive complexity. Therefore, in this research, we subtracted the raw score from the highest possible TCC score of 190, to give the cognitive complexity score (Table 5.3). Thus, with the scores shown below, higher scores indicate higher cognitive complexity. The alpha coefficients for the scores of the five role persons (liked men, disliked men, liked women, disliked women, themselves) were .567.

Interactional Traits Score Calculation

According to Katsura et al. (1997), to calculate the score of interactional traits from the answers in PC egogram survey form, 2 points are given for "Yes", 1 point for "?", and 0 points for "No" and the total value of ten items for measuring permeability control power is obtained for each participant (Table 5.3).

In addition, in this research, we created an index of permeability control power potential independently. Ego states must have a potential so that their respective energies can be increased to freely switch and adjust ego states. In this research, according to Katsura et al. (1997), the total value of ten items for measuring factors were calculated, and the scores of the factors were calculated for five factors of critical parent, nurturing parent, adult, free child and adapted child. A high score for a particular ego state means that energy can be allocated to that ego state up to the level of its score. Accordingly, being able to freely switch across ego states means that the scores must be high for any of those ego states. In this way, potential can be indexed as the height of the total score of the multiple ego states. Therefore, in this study, the total score of the five ego states was calculated and used as the score for permeability control power potential (Table 5.3).

Empathy Score Calculation

To confirm the reproducibility of the scale configuration (four-factor structure) of the multidimensional empathy measurement scale, factor analysis (principal factor method and promax rotation) was performed on 28 items. This analysis was done with the factor loading standard set to $|.400|$. As a result, seven items that did not meet the standard values for any of the factors were found and deleted, and the analysis was performed again. Then, two items that showed a load higher than the standard value were found in factors different from Sakurai (1988) and were deleted, and analysis was performed for the third time, to confirm a similar four-factor structure to Sakurai (1988).

The first factor was "fantasy", and was $\alpha = .821$ (6 items). The second factor was "perspective-taking", and was $\alpha = .779$ (5 items). The third factor was "empathetic consideration", and was $\alpha = .724$ (4 items). The fourth factor was "personal distress", and was $\alpha = .715$ (4 items). The item averages were calculated for these factors to score the factors.

In this research, we examined the content validity of these four factors, and found that "fantasy" and "personal distress" have a focus on the thinking and emotions that occur in people who empathize, while "perspective-taking" and "empathetic consideration" have a focus on the thinking, emotions and behaviors directed at the object of the empathy. Therefore, in this research, we independently calculated the former total score as the score for "intra-personal empathy" and calculated the latter total score as the score for "interpersonal empathy" (Table 5.3).

Table 5.3   *The mean, standard deviation and coefficient of correlation for each scale score*

	M	SD	Interactional traits		Empathy		Social skills		Fluency	Flexibility	Individual creativity			Group creativity
			Permeability control power	Permeability control power potential	Intra-personal empathy	Interpersonal empathy	Personal skill	Interpersonal skill			Non-redundant uniqueness	Rare uniqueness	Evaluative uniqueness	Group creativity belief
Interpersonal cognitive traits														
Cognitive complexity	98.76	17.07	−.230**	−.158†	.131	−.213*	−.159†	−.308**	.086	.117	.048	.054	.080	−.108
Interactional traits														
Permeability control power	10.56	4.43		.485**	−.288**	.269**	.752**	.580**	−.017	−.044	−.037	−.018	.028	.148†
Permeability control power potential	12.43	2.18			.108	.451**	.455**	.540**	.004	−.027	−.040	.001	.017	.198*
Empathy														
Intra-personal empathy	2.76	.42				.267**	−.156†	−.039	.136	.139	.078	.133	.162†	−.039
Interpersonal empathy	2.73	.44					.334**	.455**	.037	.043	−.011	.018	.023	.232**
Social skills														
Personal skills	2.38	.52						.607**	−.021	−.015	−.013	−.011	.033	.106
Interpersonal skills	2.73	.48							.011	−.023	−.027	.001	.011	.224**

Note: †*p* < .10, *p < .05, **p < .01.

Social Skills Score Calculation

To confirm the reproducibility of the scale configuration (eight-factor configuration) of the daily life skills scale, factor analysis (principal factor method and promax rotation) was performed on 24 items. When the analysis was performed with the factor loading standard set to |.400|, one item was found that showed a load higher than the standard value for factors different from Shimamoto and Ishii (2006), which was deleted, and analysis was re-done. As a result, an eight-factor structure similar to Shimamoto and Ishii (2006) was confirmed.

The first factor was "affinity" and was α = .849 (3 items). The second factor was "interpersonal manners" and was α = .799 (3 items). The third factor was "planning" and was α = .786 (3 items). The fourth factor was "information summarization" and was α = .788 (3 items). The fifth factor was "leadership" and was α = .858 (2 items). The sixth factor was "sensitivity" and was α = .717 (3 items). The seventh factor was "self-esteem" and was α = .736 (3 items). The eighth factor was "positive thinking" and was α = .596 (3 items). The item averages were calculated for these factors to score the factors.

Since this daily life skill scale can be divided into personal skills and interpersonal skills as higher factors, these scores were also calculated and used for analysis. Specifically, the average of the scores of planning, information summarization, self-esteem and positive thinking included in personal skills was used as the score for "personal skills", while the scores for affinity, interpersonal manners, leadership and sensitivity included in interpersonal skills were averaged and used for the score for "interpersonal skills" (Table 5.3).

Relationship between Individual Creativity and Group Creativity Belief

To examine the relationship between individual creativity and group creativity belief, the coefficient of correlation between each index was calculated (Table 5.2). Although the five indicators of individual creativity showed a significant positive correlation with each other (r = .569 to .962, ps < .01), they showed almost no correlation with group creativity belief (r = −.132 to −.007).

Relationships between Interpersonal Cognitive Traits, Interactional Traits, Empathy, Social Skills and Creativity

Table 5.3 and Figure 5.2 were obtained when the correlation analysis progressed according to the conceptual model shown in Figure 5.1 discussed above. As predicted by the conceptual model, no significant path from interpersonal cognitive traits, interactional traits, empathy or social skills to individual creativity was obtained. The following focuses on the path to group creativity.

Path from interpersonal cognitive traits to group creativity
Cognitive complexity shows a significant negative correlation with interpersonal empathy (r = −.213, p < .05) and interpersonal skills (r = −.308, p < .01); moreover, interpersonal empathy and interpersonal skills had a significant positive correlation with group creativity belief (r = .232, r = .224, ps < .01, respectively). Thus, contrary to our predictions, the result showed that

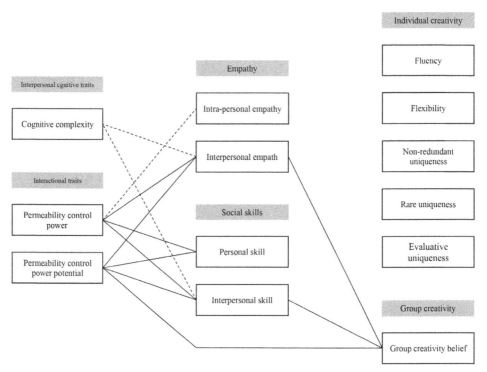

Note: The solid line indicates a positive correlation, and the dotted line indicates a negative correlation.

Figure 5.2   Relationship between creativity and interpersonal cognitive traits, interactional traits, empathy, and social skills

the lower the cognitive complexity, the higher the interpersonal empathy and interpersonal skills, resulting in higher group creativity belief.

Path from interactional traits to group creativity

Permeability control power and permeability control power potential showed a significant positive correlation ($r = .485$, $p < .01$). With these also, there was significant positive correlation between interpersonal empathy (respectively, $r = .269$, $r = .451$, $ps < .01$) and interpersonal skills (respectively, $r = .580$, $p = .540$, $ps < .01$). Moreover, interpersonal empathy and interpersonal skills were significantly positively correlated with group creativity belief, as discussed above. The permeability control power potential also showed a significant positive direct correlation with group creativity belief ($r = .198$, $p < .05$). Although it did not reach a significant level, permeability control power also showed a significant direct positive correlation with group creativity belief ($r = .148$, $p < .10$). As described above, the higher the permeability control power and permeability control power potential, the higher group creativity belief, although results showed that parts of those relationships are mediated by interpersonal empathy and interpersonal skills.

Note that permeability control power and permeability control power potential showed a significant positive correlation with personal skills ($r = .752, r = .455, p$s $< .01$). Permeability control power also showed a significant negative correlation with intra-personal empathy ($r = -.288, p < .01$).

8. DISCUSSION

Group Creativity Belief Scale

Although various methods for measuring individual creativity have been developed, no method for measuring group creativity has been established. Therefore, in this research, we independently developed a group creativity belief scale. This research measured the belief that group creativity is superior to individual creativity, assuming that belief can be sufficiently fulfilled as actual behavioral results through behavioral intentions. This scale has sufficient internal consistency. Also, group creativity belief has a distinctive validity among criteria-related validities, in that it measures psychological traits that differ from individual creativity. Furthermore, this group creativity belief has a significant positive correlation with interpersonal empathy and interpersonal skills. Therefore, this can be considered to have convergent validity among criteria-related validities, in that orientation towards others and groups match. Note that in general, belief scales should also have predictive validity among criteria-related validities. In this investigation, predictive validity was not studied, and is therefore an issue for the future.

Interactional Traits, Empathy, Social Skills and Creativity

By psychologically reinterpreting boundaries vision that should be facilitated in agents that drive the formation of boundaries knowledge, the mother of creativity, as advocated by Kodama (2019) and in Chapter 1 of this book in the relationships between members of groups, this research has attempted to study how group creativity is brought about by dividing the function of boundaries vision into interpersonal cognition and interpersonal interaction functions. Specifically, we focused on cognitive complexity as the interpersonal cognition function and permeability control power as the interpersonal interaction function, and attempted to clarify the path that leads to group creativity through the interpersonal behaviors of empathy and social skills.

As this research suggests, if the permeability control power of interactional traits is high, and the more freely egos can be switched to appropriately suit the situation or other party to demonstrate interpersonal empathy and social skills in interpersonal interactions in groups, this could result in raising the level of group creativity. Group members with high permeability control power determine the boundaries between group members and between themselves and others, while switching their ego state to suit others in interpersonal interactions within the group, and recognizing the knowledge differences between those boundaries. Thus they can expand boundaries knowledge by efficiently and effectively managing interpersonal interactions through viewpoint acquisition and empathetic consideration towards others, and leadership behaviors through interpersonal manners, affinity and sensitivity towards others. In this way, irreducible to individual creativity, boundaries knowledge enriched in a group can be considered to be the mother of new creation and innovation.

Interpersonal Cognitive Traits, Empathy, Social Skills and Creativity

This investigation produced a result that was the opposite of our prediction regarding the cognitive complexity of interpersonal cognitive traits. In other words, the results obtained showed that when cognitive complexity is high and there are many constructs for perceiving and judging others in interpersonal interactions, the more differentiated the constructs, the less interpersonal empathy and interpersonal skills are demonstrated. In contrast, when cognitive complexity is low, i.e., cognitively simple, and interpersonal interactions are perceived and judged with fewer specific constructs, the less differentiated the constructs, the more interpersonal empathy and interpersonal skills are demonstrated.

Why the opposite result was obtained, i.e., low rather than high cognitive complexity being more likely to bring about interpersonal behavior with interpersonal empathy and interpersonal skills in interpersonal interactions within a group, could be for the following two reasons. First, in dynamically changing human interactions, the higher the cognitive complexity of interpersonal cognition, the more difficult it is to engage in efficient and effective interpersonal behavior. The higher the cognitive complexity, the more time is spent gathering information about individual members in a group and using that information for multidimensional analyses using various constructs to make holistic and multifaceted judgments about group members. In dynamic interactions, such complex perceptions, analyses and judgments are inefficient. Furthermore, it may be difficult to determine effective interpersonal behaviors towards others seen as having such diverse and complex characteristics. Complicated cognitive customs aiming for thoroughness can lead to indecisiveness (Yates, Ji, Oka, Lee, Shinotsuka, and Sieck, 2010), which makes it difficult for efficient and effective interpersonal interactions to occur. In contrast, the simpler the cognition, interpersonal behaviors based on judgments using specific constructs for specific points in time and specific people occur more easily. Based on the observed results of those behaviors, subsequent interpersonal behaviors occur more easily based on judgments of others made by appropriately switching to different specific constructs at subsequent points in time. While involving some trial and error, this could make management of efficient and effective dynamic interpersonal interactions easier.

The second reason for being the opposite of our prediction is that the scale for cognitive complexity measures the availability of constructs for interpersonal cognition without depending on specific contexts, despite the fact that interpersonal behaviors take place within a particular group in the context of particular interpersonal interactions. Interpersonal interactions that take place within a particular group are goal-oriented, with individual members playing roles towards achieving that goal. In such contexts, making complex and multidimensional judgments using constructs that are not related to the goals or roles is not only inefficient but also ineffective – from the viewpoint of the goals and roles, judgments using specific but relatively simple constructs in interpersonal cognition could lead to more effective interpersonal actions. Again, in these contexts, in the course of time, efficient, effective and dynamic interpersonal interactions might conversely be more efficiently managed through repeated trial and error.

Thus, the lower the cognitive complexity in interpersonal cognition, i.e., the cognitively simpler, the easier it is for interpersonal judgments using tentative constructs considered appropriate in the context of the interpersonal interaction to occur, and thus easier interpersonal behaviors based on those judgments. The results of this interpersonal behavior with interpersonal empathy such as perspective-taking, and social skills such as sensitivity, show appropriate switching between constructs for interpersonal judgment and the addition of modifications for efficient and effective interpersonal behaviors. Repeating such trial and error could lead to boundaries between self and others and group members being appropriately defined in the group, and the expansion of the boundaries knowledge based on recognition of knowledge differences between those boundaries, and thus could bring about group creativity and innovation as a result.

9.   PROVISIONAL CONCLUSION OF THIS RESEARCH

This research suggested that interpersonal cognitive traits and interactional traits supporting boundaries vision may contribute to group creativity through specific interpersonal behaviors. Specifically, this research showed that the lower the cognitive complexity in interpersonal cognition and the higher the permeability control power in interpersonal interactions, the higher the group creativity belief through interpersonal behaviors based on interpersonal empathy and interpersonal skills.

REFERENCES

Ben-Ari, R., Kedem, P., and Levy-Weiner, N. (1992). Cognitive complexity and intergroup perception and evaluation. *Personality and Individual Differences, 13*, 1291–1298.

Berne, E. (1964). *Games People Play*. New York: Grove Press.

Bieri, J. (1955). Cognitive complexity–simplicity and predictive behavior. *Journal of Abnormal and Social Psychology, 51*, 263–268.

Davis, M.H. (1983). Measuring individual differences in empathy: Evidence for a multidimensional approach. *Journal of Personality and Social Psychology, 44*, 113–126.

Guilford, J.P. (1967). *The Nature of Human Intelligence*. New York, NY: McGraw-Hill.

Hayashi, F. (1976). Measurement of individual differences in interpersonal cognitive structures (1): Preliminary study on measurement of cognitive complexity. *Bulletin of the Faculty of Education*, Nagoya University (Department of Educational Psychology), *23*, 27–38 (in Japanese).

Katsura, T., Shinzato, R., and Mizuno, M. (1997). *PC egogram*. Aptitude Science Research Center (in Japanese).

Kelly, G.A. (1955). *The Psychology of Personal Constructs*. New York: W.W. Norton.

Kodama, M. (2019). Boundaries knowledge (knowing): A source of business innovation. *Knowledge and Process Management, 26*(3), 210–228.

Ohashi, M., Miwa, H., Hirabayashi, S., and Nagato, K. (1973). Research on impression formation by photography (2): Selection of scale items for impression rating. *Bulletin of the Faculty of Education*, Nagoya University, *20*, 93–102 (in Japanese).

Sakamoto, A. (1991). Familiarity, favorability, cognitive complexity: Integration of interaction and alert hypotheses. *Japanese Journal of Psychology, 61*, 392–399 (in Japanese).

Sakurai, S. (1988). The relationship between empathy and helping behaviors in college students: Using a multidimensional empathy measurement scale. *Bulletin of Nara University of Education, 37*, 149–154 (in Japanese).

Shimamoto, K., and Ishii, M. (2006). Development of a daily life skill scale for university students. *Japanese Journal of Educational Psychology, 54*, 211–221 (in Japanese).

Silvia, P.J., Winterstein, B.P., Willse, J.T., Barona, C.M., Cram, J.T., Hess, K.I., Martinez, J.L., and Richard, C.A. (2008). Assessing creativity with divergent thinking tasks: Exploring the reliability and validity of new subjective scoring methods. *Psychology of Aesthetics, Creativity, and the Arts*, *2*, 68–85.

Tagger, S. (2019). The cognitive underpinnings of creativity in teams. In Paulus, P.B., and Nijstad, B.A. (Eds.), *The Oxford Handbook of Group Creativity and Innovation*. Oxford, UK: Oxford University Press, pp. 11–32.

Wallach, M.A. and Kogan, N. (1965). *Modes of Thinking in Young Children: A Study of the Creativity–Intelligence Distinction*. New York, NY: Holt, Rinehart, and Winston.

Yamaoka, A., and Yukawa, S. (2017). The relationship between creativity and mind wandering and awareness. *Japanese Journal of Social Psychology*, *32*, 151–162 (in Japanese).

Yates, J.F., Ji, L.-J., Oka, T., Lee, J.-W., Shinotsuka, H., and Sieck, W.R. (2010). Indecisiveness and culture: Incidence, values, and thoroughness. *Journal of Cross-cultural Psychology*, *41*(3), 428–444.

6. The process of creating knowledge between different actors in co-creation ba: a case study of the Panasonic smart city project

Nobuyuki Tokoro

1. INTRODUCTION

There is increasingly high interest in creating new value through co-creation among different actors. Since it is well known that innovative concepts and ideas are more likely to come about through the interactions of various actors, the formation of organizational communities that ensure diversity is considered key to bringing about innovation. However, even though the knowledge exchange and fusion that occurs in the interactions of diverse actors is a template for the creation of new value, it is not easy to say that these specific processes and their details are well understood. In other words, so far, no theoretical framework on the series of processes that lead to value creation from the exchange and fusion of knowledge has been established.

This chapter aims to theorize and build a framework for this series of processes that leads to value creation from the exchange and fusion of the knowledge of diverse actors. Firstly, the chapter reviews research to date on knowledge creation, co-creation, open innovation, and "knowledge differences", "boundaries vision" and "boundaries knowledge" presented in Chapters 1 and 2 to extract essences for forming a theory. Next, the chapter builds a hypothesis to build a theory based on the existing research and the knowledge accumulated to date by the author. Then, the chapter verifies the hypothesis through a case analysis. The case study presented is a smart city construction project by Panasonic – a major Japanese electronics manufacturer that the author has studied over many years. Finally, the chapter presents the implications and issues obtained through verification of the hypothesis.

2. REVIEW OF EXISTING RESEARCH

The proposition of creating new value through co-creation between diverse actors has been a major focus of innovation research, and many studies have been conducted so far. For example, the knowledge creation theory advocated by Nonaka and Takeuchi (1995) conceptualizes the process of creating new knowledge through the exchange and fusion of knowledge between individuals as the SECI model. In short, in this model, the tacit knowledge of individuals is shared and converted into organizational tacit knowledge through shared or direct experiences of things and events (Socialization). Then, tacit knowledge is converted to explicit knowledge by expressing it as language or charts using metaphors, analogies and so forth (Externalization). Next, explicit knowledge is combined with other explicit knowledge to create a system of explicit knowledge (Combination). This systemized explicit knowledge is then internalized by individuals through their actions and practices to become new tacit knowledge (Internalization). In other words, the SECI model asserts that the conversion of tacit knowledge and explicit knowledge circulates knowledge between individuals and organizations, amplifies it, and creates new knowledge.

Moreover, knowledge creation theory focuses on the role played by "ba" in the creation and transformation of knowledge (Nonaka and Konno, 1998). The concept of ba does not only refer to a physical location such as a conference room, but also includes such things as mental connections like the sharing of thoughts and values. In other words, a ba is a conceptualization of the relationships built between people under a specific context. In knowledge creation theory, it is assumed that the conversion and creation of knowledge takes place with ba as the stage, and as such, building and properly managing ba is essential for knowledge transformation and creation to take place. Knowledge creation theory conceptualizes the processes of knowledge creation between diverse actors, and presents a theoretical model, although it does not provide details about the tacit knowledge ↔ explicit knowledge transformation process. In other words, there are not any clear explanations about the steps where the tacit knowledge of individuals is shared and converted into organizational tacit knowledge, or what processes are followed to convert tacit knowledge into explicit knowledge. Nevertheless, Chapter 2 discussed the importance of the creation of boundaries knowledge (knowing) in each step of the knowledge transformation processes of [tacit knowledge → tacit knowledge], [tacit knowledge → explicit knowledge], [explicit knowledge → explicit knowledge], [explicit knowledge → tacit knowledge].

Research into co-creation has become more prevalent in the service marketing field in recent years. In service-dominant logic (S-D logic) advocated by Vargo and Lusch (2004), it was perceived that companies do not provide services to customers one-way, but rather services become built-in as customers and companies co-create. S-D logic emphasizes that corporate value creation is not a model standardized for pricing of products, but instead is changing to a model that focuses on the systems and logic of services. Others who have researched from the S-D logic perspective include Payne et al. (2008), Vargo et al. (2008), Mele et al. (2010), Echeverri and Skälen (2011), Saarijärvi (2012), Grönroos and Voima (2013), Gummerus (2013) and Karababa and Kjeldgaard (2014). All of this research has a focus on analysis of the processes of value creation that take place between companies and customers, although they do not necessarily present clear knowledge about the processes or mechanisms of co-creation.

Meanwhile, research by Prahalad and Ramaswamy (2003, 2004) analyzed the relationship between a company's competitiveness and co-creation between the company and its customers. They argue that in the 21st-century marketplace, value is created through co-creation between companies and their customers, and that markets do not only function as places where products and services are traded, but also function as places where customers and companies co-create. They go on to state that an accumulation of a variety of experiences is required to enable co-creation, and that "dialogue" plays a key role in those experiences because corporate logic and customer logic are not the same. Nonaka above also emphasized the same thing regarding the creation of value through dialogue, so it seems dialogue among many actors holds great significance for value creation.

The assertions of "open innovation" advocated by Chesbrough (2003, 2006) also offer important suggestions in considering co-creation among diverse actors. In the past, many companies maintained full independence and secrecy when creating innovative technologies and services – the idea of opening up their own technologies and know-how to create new products, technologies and services by co-creating with other companies did not exist. This was because companies thought that such actions would lead to loss of competitive edge because important technology and know-how would be stolen and imitated by other companies. Open innovation is the idea of breaking down such conventional ways of thinking to enable a company to open up its technologies and know-how to co-create with other companies and bring about value that would otherwise be impossible to produce independently. However, practicing this concept entails two prerequisites. First is fostering relationships of trust between companies – as argued by Vangen and Huxham (2003), it is not possible to succeed with collaboration if there are no relationships of trust between organizations. Secondly, opening technology and know-how does not mean opening all of it – it is important to select what should be opened and what should remain closed. If such selections are not done well, the value lost will be greater than the value gained. Thus, strictly speaking, open innovation is actually open and closed innovation.

The latest research findings on knowledge creation through co-creation among different actors include the concepts of "knowledge differences", "boundaries vision" and "boundaries knowledge" presented in Chapters 1 and 2 (Kodama, 2018, 2019). Chapter 2 focuses on "knowledge differences" that arise between people, organizations and various different objects and events, describes how these differences are sensed with "boundaries vision", and names the new knowledge of people recognizing objects and events that comes about through their awareness, perception and discovery as "boundaries knowledge (knowing)". Although similar concepts have been advocated such as Sensing (Teece, 2007, 2014), or Wide lens (Adner, 2012), the concepts of boundaries vision and boundaries knowledge are theoretically important, because it is necessary to know differences from the outset when embarking on co-creation with different actors.

3.   THEORETICAL FRAMEWORK BUILDING: HYPOTHESIS SETTING

Regarding the creation of knowledge through co-creation with different actors, the author has reviewed existing research, but found that this research does not lead to a clear theory on the processes of creating value through co-creation. Existing research proposes new thinking on the overall picture of co-creation systems by presenting novel concepts such as tacit knowledge, explicit knowledge and boundaries knowledge in individual domains, and perceiving open innovation and markets as places for co-creation between companies and customers, but has not actually established any theoretical frameworks for specific processes and mechanisms for creating value through co-creation.

Thus, this chapter attempts to construct a theoretical framework for the processes and mechanisms of knowledge creation through co-creation between different actors. Firstly, as a prerequisite, the different actors have to meet and build a ba as the stage for their co-creation. A ba has been discussed as a critical concept to create knowledge in the above knowledge creation theory, and is a concept that has been developed mostly in the fields of physics and psychology. Notably, famous research on ba was done in the field of psychology by Lewin (1951). Lewin defined "ba" as all coexisting facts generally considered to be interdependent, and argued that living spaces that encompass people and their reality have to be seen as one kind of ba in psychology. In Lewin's way of thinking, ba are formed spontaneously in society. However, this chapter does not take that view, and perceives ba as something that should be formed intentionally. In other words, the author would like to define the relationship between people in physical, virtual and mental spaces that are formed intentionally in specific contexts as "ba". In this chapter, if co-creation between different actors is equivalent to such a specific context, and the ba formed in such specific contexts, the author calls such ba "co-creation ba".

Presuming that the co-creation ba is built, this chapter freshly presents the knowledge creation process between different actors on the co-creation ba (exploration → resonance → fluctuation → synchronization → concentration and distribution → fusion → trajectory → convergence) and also presents the relationships between the co-creation ba and the three core elements (knowledge difference sensing, sensing through boundaries vision and boundaries knowledge creation) that enable the spiral conversion of the SECI model presented in Chapters 1 and 2 (see Figure 6.1).

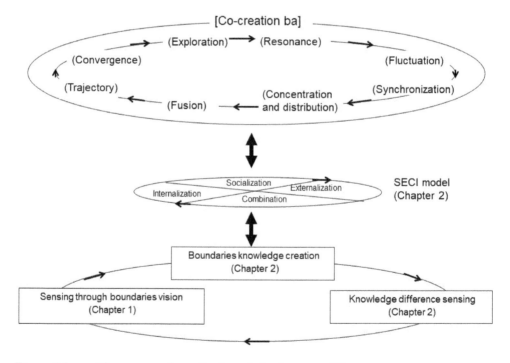

Figure 6.1   The process of creating knowledge between different actors

3.1   Exploration

Exploration is the first step in co-creation between different actors. In other words, this means trying to find out who other people are when actors with various backgrounds meet. For example, in relationships between individuals, when meeting for the first time, it is possible to find out the social position of another person through the exchange of business cards, etc., and to find out various aspects of the other person's background (age, educational background, career, etc.) through conversation. It is also possible to guess the other person's abilities and propensities from the content of their speech, their use of words and their behavior, etc. The first step in co-creation is to recognize what type of people other people are through a series of such "exploration" actions.

The concepts of knowledge difference sensing and sensing through boundaries vision presented in Chapters 1 and 2 are similar to these exploration actions. Actors with excellent exploration capabilities are able to grasp the state of other actors with greater accuracy. Teece (2007, 2014) and Helfat and Peteraf (2015) call this ability a cognitive capability.

3.2   Resonance

Following from exploration, the second step is "Resonance". The phenomenon of resonance between one's inherent resources and those of another person occurs at the stage in which people have come to understand each other's existence. A range of cases could be assumed – for example, finding that you have had similar experiences and feel mutually sympathetic, or conversely, finding that clearly you and the other party have followed completely different paths and feel that the other party has an ability that you do not have. It is important to note that resonance does not simply mean that people with similar thoughts and behaviors will have a sense of friendship and solidarize. Resonance is also finding abilities that you do not have in the other person and showing respect for such abilities. This means that resonance is the act of making certain evaluations and judgments about the other person that you have come to know through exploration. In the stage of resonance, knowledge differences between different actors are sensed, and this sensing triggers the induction of sensing through boundaries vision between different actors.

3.3   Fluctuation

Following from exploration and resonance, the third step is "fluctuation". Fluctuation refers to ripples that form in relationships that have been maintained between different actors, and that lead to imbalances and instability. Mutual recognition of abilities and propensities through exploration and resonance leads to subtle changes in the sense of distance between each other, and specifically triggers the encouragement of the thinking and actions of knowledge difference sensing and sensing through boundaries vision presented in Chapter 2. This could mean similar positions, circumstances or ways of thinking leading to a sense of familiarity and close relationships forming as the sense of distance quickly and mutually shortens, or it could mean changes appearing in a relationship that has been maintained by actions such as finding that the other person has completely different qualities to you, and hence attempting to get closer to that person to know them more deeply, or conversely, keeping a certain distance due to a sense of caution. Organizational theory identifies a necessity for managers to bring about imbalance and instability by occasionally and intentionally causing fluctuation in organizations to break through the status quo and give rise to innovative ideas. Such fluctuation also leads to encouraging different actors to create new boundaries and knowledge. Nevertheless, fluctuation should occur spontaneously if the exploration and resonance steps have been properly taken.

3.4   Synchronization

Fluctuation occurs between different actors, and new movements occur when the balance of relationships that have been maintained is destroyed. This phenomenon is called "synchronization". From the outset, the purpose of various actors' participation in a ba is to create new value through co-creation with other actors, and synchronization is the act of grasping those seeds. In other words, synchronization is a phenomenon in which things that have complementary relationships, or things that have the potential to bring about new value by their multiplication and so forth in mutually held resources, become attracted like magnets and resonate. Synchronization of resources enables the specific shape and direction of co-creation between different actors to be seen for the first time. In this stage, the outline of new boundaries knowledge begins to appear between the different actors from their thinking and behaviors of knowledge difference sensing and sensing through boundaries vision.

3.5   Concentration and Distribution

The concentration and distribution of resources is triggered through the occurrence of synchronization of resources. Resources are attracted like magnets and synchronized for co-creation among actors, and the various actors engage in selection work regarding their resources. Here, the actors make judgments about what will be advantageous for themselves to achieve the open and closed strategy of "hybrid innovation" (Kodama, 2011). In other words, actors have to weigh the size of the value that will be born through opening their resources to other actors and then combining them with other actors' resources, with the size of the value that will be gained by keeping resources secret, and make judgements about which will be advantageous for themselves. Provisionally, if actors judge the latter to be advantageous, they will not open their resources to other actors even if resource synchronization occurs. Conversely, if actors judge the advantage to be gained by opening their resources to be large, those resources will be opened and separated from other resources, and clearly and precisely managed. This is concentration and distribution. On considering hybrid innovation, it is necessary to identify boundaries knowledge among resources (knowledge) owned by individual actors, and to clearly evaluate and analyze its quality and quantity.

3.6   Fusion

Resource concentration and distribution clarifies the resources to mobilize for co-creation between actors so that a kind of chemical reaction occurs when those resources are mixed together. This is fusion. This is like the color change that occurs when different liquids are mixed and a change occurs. However, at this stage it is still not possible to clearly predict what kind of change will occur – it is the stage of repeated trial and error, similar to increasing or decreasing the amount of liquids to mix. Actors have to search for the most optimal fusion pattern between different resources (tacit and explicit knowledge) by uncovering boundaries knowledge between different actors through trial and error to figure out what form the fusion of their resources, in other words their knowledge, should take to bring about substantial value.

3.7   Trajectory

If it is possible to discover an optimal fusion pattern by the process of repeatedly fusing resources through the creation of boundaries knowledge, a pathway to creating value will appear. This is the trajectory stage. In the trajectory stage, resource fusion accelerates, and an overall image of the value to be created becomes clear. Each actor operates their resources at full speed to create value while verifying the resource fusion process.

3.8   Convergence

Convergence is the final step in co-creation between different actors. When new value is created through the previous seven steps, the series of actions leads to convergence. In this way, through the series of processes of "exploration → resonance → fluctuation → synchronization → concentration and distribution → fusion → trajectory → convergence" in the co-creation ba, the knowledge transformation process is executed as the three core elements (knowledge difference sensing, sensing through boundaries vision and boundaries knowledge creation) that enable the SECI model for spiral transformation (Socialization → Externalization → Combination → Internalization) interlock (see Figure 6.1).

   Also in this convergence stage, it is conceivable that new value creation stimulates actors to continually develop further actions by the sensing through boundaries vision that arises from the perception of new knowledge differences, but these should strictly be regarded as new movements for different value creation – this value creation process finishes with this convergence.

4.   CASE ANALYSIS

This section verifies the hypothesis set in the previous section through a case analysis. The case study presented is the smart city project by major Japanese electronics manufacturer Panasonic (Fujisawa Sustainable Smart Town). This project involves participation from companies in various different industries, and aims to create value through co-creation between companies in different industries. The author held three interviews (February 2014, September 2016, March 2019) with directors at Panasonic, the company leading the project, and accepted the related materials that were offered. The author has also published other research findings analyzing this project (Tokoro, 2015, 2016, 2017). This section verifies the hypothesis based on these materials and knowledge.

4.1   The Fujisawa Sustainable Smart Town Project (Fujisawa SST)

Fujisawa SST is an urban development project with construction ongoing in Fujisawa City in Kanagawa Prefecture by major electronics manufacturer Panasonic, on the former site of one of the company's factories. Fujisawa City is a seaside town about 50km from Tokyo and rich in nature. Begun in 2011 with the aim of completion by 2022, the overall cost of the project will be around JPY 60 billion. Including Panasonic, the leader corporation, the project involves participation from companies in various different industries, governing bodies, universities and autonomous citizen organizations, and aims to create new value through co-creation between these various actors (Figure 6.2).

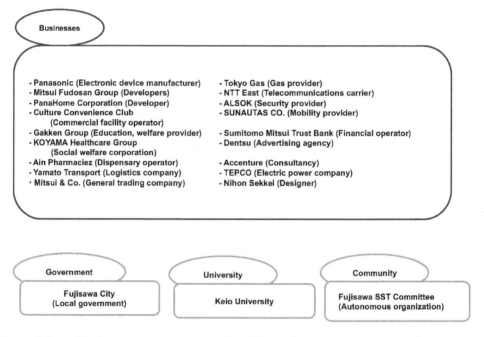

Figure 6.2   Businesses, governments, universities and autonomous organizations participating in Fujisawa SST

Under the concept of "bringing energy to life", the project aims to create new value in the five areas of energy, security, mobility, healthcare and community.

4.1.1   General overview of the town

Fujisawa SST covers a site about 19 ha (600m east–west × 300m north–south), and contains detached houses (600 households), collective residences (400 households), health, welfare and education facilities, commercial facilities, a meeting place, a next-generation distribution center and an urban development base, etc.

(1)   Smart houses

All detached houses are equipped with solar power generation systems and batteries as standard. Connecting the solar power generation system, storage batteries and the "ENEFARM" household fuel cells with the latest linked system enables households to cleverly use electricity made at home and sell the surplus. In an emergency, power can be allocated to a preset minimum number of necessary devices such as household lights, refrigerator or TV to secure a lifeline for three days. The objective of this is local energy production for local consumption and self-sufficiency.

(2)   Smart infrastructure
A community solar installation on public land in one corner of the city contributes to lowering the local carbon footprint by supplying power to the power grid during normal times. In an emergency, this power can be opened to provide emergency power to Fujisawa SST as well as the residents in the surrounding area. The town also features about 50 security cameras mainly installed at the entrances to the town, public buildings, in park shadows and at main street intersections in an effort to strengthen crime prevention by linking them with lighting.

(3)   Wellness SQUARE
Wellness SQUARE is a facility for healthcare, welfare and education. A special nursing home for the elderly, serviced housing for the elderly, various clinics, nursery and cram schools, etc. are built on a block called "Well SITE". These facilities are seamlessly connected to provide optimal services to residents. This is called a "comprehensive community care system", and ICT is used to centrally manage the health-related information of residents on a common server, which enables hospitals, pharmacies and nursing homes, etc. to connect to the server and provide services appropriately.

(4)   SHONAN T-SITE
There is a block called "SHONAN T-SITE" with about 30 bookshop and theme-based shops. In this area, companies running shops are able to discuss spatial design, shop design, and the lineup of products to try to bring about their own unique cultures. This not only entails simply selling products, but also entails proposing new lifestyles to residents. For this, all shops have books, so that this unique mall seamlessly links bookstores with specialist shops.

(5)   Community center
The central park in the town features a community center where residents can meet. The purpose of the community center is to provide a place for residents to interact, and a place where parties or cooking classes, etc. can be held. Not limited to those, the center also functions as a base for disaster prevention. The center is designed as an evacuation point for about 100 people in the event of a tsunami, and is ready for emergencies with disaster prevention supplies (food, beverages, toilets, fuel, etc.) on hand.

(6)   Next-generation distribution center
Fujisawa SST also has an ecologically friendly and smart distribution system that makes use of ICT. Yamato Transport collects packages addressed to Fujisawa SST from couriers and delivers them in batches to residents. In addition to increased logistic efficiency, the company also collects and distributes packages with trolleys and provides electrically assisted bicycles to reduce environmental impacts. Yamato Transport also runs an "on demand delivery" service which notifies recipients on residential smart TVs of the date and time of package arrival and contact details if the resident was not home at the delivery time, to reduce secondary deliveries.

(7)   Fujisawa SST SQUARE

Fujisawa SST SQUARE has been created as a base for promoting urban development. In this facility, Fujisawa SST Management Co., Ltd. is responsible for, and in charge of the town management.

4.1.2   Verification: co-creation between different actors to create value

Although Fujisawa SST is oriented towards value creation through co-creation between various companies in dissimilar industries, here, the author verifies the co-creation case involving three companies – Mitsui Fudosan Residential, Tokyo Gas and Panasonic. The descriptions here are based on interviews conducted by the author with Panasonic supervisors in March 2019, and materials provided on that occasion.

While smart houses with solar power generation systems, storage batteries and household fuel cells as standard equipment in detached houses are the main selling point at Fujisawa SST, the above three companies engaged in co-creation to create living spaces with even higher added value. Of these three companies, Tokyo Gas and Panasonic are responsible for some of the housing hardware such as gas and home appliances, but do not have knowledge of housing in its entirety. In contrast, Mitsui Fudosan Residential is a housing specialist that buys and sells houses and has a wealth of knowledge about housing in general. Thus, the co-creation between these three companies started with Mitsui Fudosan Residential taking the initiative. However, in discussions between the three companies to create new living spaces, it was found that Tokyo Gas had important knowledge – according to the Tokyo Gas Urban Life Research Institute, hard-working 30–50-year-olds get tired, and when questioned what they would like to do in their free time at home, it became clear that they had high demands to use their free time to rest and relax so they could revitalize themselves.

Instead of the original assumption that ideas would be drawn from the rich knowledge accumulated by Mitsui Fudosan Residential, a specialist in housing, and that the three companies would co-create with Tokyo Gas and Panasonic providing various hardware in line with those ideas, Tokyo Gas proactively took the initiative to contribute to proposals for ideas and concepts, leading to the idea that many hard-working 30–50-year-olds did not have an acceptable body–mind balance; a problem that could be rectified by aiming for a beautiful lifestyle in which the body and mind were more naturally aligned in daily life. Thus, as a concept proposing new living spaces, the "house that will keep you beautiful if you live in it" was born.

When the new living space was conceptualized, the co-creation between the three companies proceeded to the next step. Based on this concept, the companies cooperated to figure out how to specifically design the new housing. In their cooperation, the opinions of the three companies were aligned about building houses that would provide rest for the body and rest for the mind. Therefore, the concept of a house that will keep you beautiful if you live in it was further divided into two elements – health and beauty – from which seven items were derived: stress care, beauty care, sleep, bathing, community, exercise and meals.

When these seven index items for the residential design were clarified, the three companies' resources were mobilized to bring the design to reality. Mitsui Fudosan Residential used its knowledge to design spaces and position greenery in living rooms to reduce stress, and design interiors with relaxing effects matched with audiovisual devices and so forth, while Tokyo Gas supervised facilities such as ENEFARM to generate electricity and provide hot water by using city gas as well as gas hot water floor heating to warm the feet. Panasonic also provided appliances for health and beauty, and sleep environment support systems, etc. Hence, the three companies used their own resources to co-create new value as a house that will keep you beautiful if you live in it. The three companies' co-creation did not stop there – they also engaged in a different concept. This other co-creation was done under the concept of "a house where time is born if you live in it". Double-income households raising children have high demands to shorten housework. To respond to such needs, the three companies derived the concept of "a house where time is born if you live in it", which meant the companies co-created to shorten housework time by designing the layout and storage in consideration of the flow of housework, by designing spaces so that robotic cleaners can be used easily, and by providing remote housing equipment controllers that can be used from anywhere in the house to look after visitors.

What can we say about how this case study fits with the theoretical framework (see Figure 6.1) discussed in the last section? In other words, to what degree is the knowledge creation process of exploration → resonance → fluctuation → synchronization → concentration and distribution fusion → trajectory → convergence between different actors justified, and how are the processes of knowledge difference sensing, sensing through boundaries vision, and boundaries knowledge creation related to these knowledge creation processes?

The first thing that can be identified in this case study is that processes from the third step of fluctuation and beyond can be confirmed to some degree. Regarding fluctuation, it can be seen that Tokyo Gas, the company that was initially expected to handle the provision of gas-related equipment and devices, also had important knowledge about housing that affected the relationship between the three companies in their co-creation. In other words, at the outset, Mitsui Fudosan Residential took the initiative to derive ideas and concepts using its rich knowledge about housing, and it was assumed that Tokyo Gas and Panasonic would provide equipment and devices based on those ideas and concepts. Instead, it was Tokyo Gas that took the initiative to derive ideas and concepts. At this point, Tokyo Gas engaged in knowledge difference sensing between the three companies, and engaged in sensing through boundaries vision to inspire boundaries knowledge between the different knowledge of the companies.

Moreover, it can be confirmed that concepts were clarified through the creation of boundaries knowledge, objective directions for value creation were determined, and the three companies created value by mobilizing their resources through the stages of synchronization, fusion, trajectory and convergence. Notably with fusion, the author was told in detail in interviews about how the house was built to embody the concept while fusing the three companies' resources by the creation of boundaries knowledge through trial and error to figure out which equipment and facilities should be placed in which rooms of a two-story detached house, how the equipment should be connected and how the spaces should be designed, etc.

However, it is not possible to clearly confirm concentration and distribution in this case. In the process of clarifying what value should be created and what resources should be mobilized to that end, the three companies should have been engaging in a hybrid innovation strategy to select resources to open and resources to close, although this was not clarified in interviews. However, the director interviewed responded that there was an implicit understanding that inviolable areas existed in each others' companies.

It was neither possible to sufficiently verify the first and second steps of exploration and resonance in the knowledge creation process. In other words, it is possible that in this case the three companies may have already taken the first and second steps when they came together to create new living space value. Although in different industries, the three companies may have chosen each other as co-creation partners because they were aware of who each other was and what resources they had, and because they understood each others' competencies. If that were the case, it would be difficult to verify the exploration and resonance processes in a normal interview survey with the companies. This is because if questions about the processes of exploration and resonance were asked in interviews, a clear answer could be unobtainable because the companies might not have any awareness of those processes. The following perspective is important in this regard: co-creation between companies in dissimilar industries ultimately entails relationships between humans. For some purpose, strangers come together, exchange greetings, and "explore" each other through dialogue to determine each other's capabilities, which results in these actors sensing knowledge differences between their companies. Also, the act of "resonance" between actors is based on human psychology, which basically does not change even in the act of supporting an organization such as a company. Therefore, an approach not only from the business administration perspective but also from that of psychology is required to understand the actions of exploration and resonance.

5.   IMPLICATIONS AND ISSUES

This chapter established a theoretical framework based on hypotheses about the process of creating knowledge through co-creation between different actors, which has not necessarily been clarified in previous research, and verified it through a case study. As mentioned above, among the eight steps that make up the process of creating knowledge, fluctuation, synchronization and fusion, etc., could be clarified by case analysis. Moreover, the chapter was able to confirm some of the dynamic processes of the three elements of knowledge difference sensing, sensing through boundaries vision, and boundaries knowledge creation between the different knowledge of different companies.

In particular, the author would like to identify the processes from fluctuation through to synchronization. Depending on how you look at it, it is possible to arrive at synchronization even if fluctuation does not occur. With prior planning, it should be possible to create new value by bringing together the technologies and know-how possessed by companies and combining them. However, if fluctuation occurs, there is a possibility that changes will occur in subsequent developments. In other words, situations that might not have been anticipated in planning could come about, and the processes of sensing through boundaries vision and boundaries knowledge creation that lie behind the processes of synchronization and fusion occur in forms different to those that had been initially predicted. Even in the case study in this chapter, if fluctuation had not occurred, the development may have followed some completely different path. Viewed from the perspective of creating innovation, there is a tendency to give importance to the creation of "unintentional value" that is different from planned "intentional value". In this sense, fluctuation is an important step in the knowledge creation process.

Several issues were clarified in this chapter. Firstly, exploration and resonance, parts of the theoretical framework on the knowledge creation process set out in this chapter could not be sufficiently verified. In this regard, an approach from psychology is required, as described above. For example, enacting measures such as having a psychology specialist cooperate when conducting fact-finding surveys can be cited as an issue. Collaboration between management and psychology is required to build a more sophisticated theoretical framework.

Another thing is to examine the validity of the theoretical framework established in this chapter by looking at cases of co-creation under different circumstances to this case. The case example discussed in this chapter is a case of co-creation under the leadership of Panasonic, and the relationships between the companies participating in this co-creation are not necessarily equal. The impact of this on the co-creation process will not be clarified without analyzing cases of co-creation in different environments from this case. Focusing on, and analyzing examples of co-creation under a wide variety of environments will raise the universality and validity of this theoretical framework.

REFERENCES

Adner, R. (2012), *The Wide Lens: A New Strategy for Innovation*, London: Penguin UK.

Chesbrough, H. (2003), The Era of Open Innovation. *Sloan Management Review*, Vol.44, No.3, pp.35–41.

Chesbrough, H. (2006), *Open Business Models: How to Thrive in the New Innovation Landscape*, Boston, MA: Harvard Business School Press.

Echeverri, P., Skälen, P. (2011), Co-creation and Co-destruction: A Practice-theory Based Study of Interactive Value Formation. *Marketing Theory*, Vol.11, No.3, pp.351–373.

Grönroos, C., Voima, P. (2013), Critical Service Logic: Marketing Sense of Value Creation and Co-creation. *Journal of the Academy of Marketing Science*, Vol.41, No.2, pp.133–150.

Gummerus, J. (2013), Value Creation Process and Value Outcomes in Marketing Theory: Strangers and Siblings? *Marketing Theory*, Vol.13, No.1, pp.19–46.

Helfat, C.E., Peteraf, M.A. (2015), Managerial Cognitive Capabilities and the Microfoundations of Dynamic Capabilities. *Strategic Management Journal*, Vol.36, No.6, pp.831–850.

Karababa, E., Kjeldgaard, D. (2014), Value in Marketing: Toward Sociocultural Perspectives. *Marketing Theory*, Vol.14, No.1, pp.119–121.

Kodama, M. (2011), *Interactive Business Communities: Accelerating Corporate Innovation through Boundary Networks*, Aldershot, UK: Gower Publishing, Ltd.

Kodama, M. (2018), Boundaries Innovation through Knowledge Convergence: Developing Triad Strategic Communities. *Technology Analysis & Strategic Management*, Vol.30, No.5, pp.609–624.

Kodama, M. (2019), Boundaries Knowledge (Knowing)–A Source of Business Innovation. *Knowledge and Process Management*, Vol. 26, No.3, pp.210–228.

Lewin, K. (1951), *Field Theory in Social Science: Selected Theoretical Papers*, Edited by Dorwin Cartwright. New York: Harper.

Mele, C., Spena, T.R., Culurcio, M. (2010), Co-creating Value Innovation through Resource Integration. *International Journal of Quality and Service Science*, Vol.2, No.1, pp.68–78.

Nonaka, I., Konno, N. (1998), The Concept of Ba: Building a Foundation for Knowledge Creation. *California Management Review*, Vol.40, pp.40–54.

Nonaka, I., Takeuchi, H. (1995), *The Knowledge Creating Company*, New York: Oxford University Press.

Payne, A.F., Storbacka, K., Frow, P. (2008), Managing the Co-creation of Value. *Journal of the Academy of Marketing Science*, Vol.36, No.1, pp.83–96.

Prahalad, C.K., Ramaswamy, V. (2003), The New Frontier of Experience Innovation. *Sloan Management Review*, Vol.44, No.4, pp.12–18.

Prahalad, C.K., Ramaswamy, V. (2004), Co-creation Experience: The Next Practice in Value Creation. *Journal of Interactive Marketing*, Vol.18, No.3, pp.5–14.

Saarijärvi, H. (2012), The Mechanisms of Value Co-creation. *Journal of Strategic Marketing*, Vol.20, No.5, pp.381–391.

Teece, D.J. (2007), Explicating Dynamic Capabilities: The Nature and Microfoundations of (Sustainable) Enterprise Performance. *Strategic Management Journal*, Vol.28, No.13, pp.1319–1350.

Teece, D.J. (2014), The Foundations of Enterprise Performance: Dynamic and Ordinary Capabilities in an (Economic) Theory of Firms. *The Academy of Management Perspectives*, Vol.28, No.4, pp.328–352.

Tokoro, N. (2015), Achieving Health Support Innovation in a Smart City Concept. In Kodama, M. (ed.), *Collaborative Innovation: Developing Health Support Ecosystem*, London: Routledge, pp. 135–158.

Tokoro, N. (2016), *The Smart City and the Co-creation of Value: A Source of New Competitiveness in a Low-carbon Society*, Tokyo: Springer.

Tokoro, N. (2017), Green Innovation Based on Ma Thinking: The Lessons of the Japanese Smart City Vision. In Kodama, M. (ed.), *Ma Theory and the Creative Management of Innovation*, London: Palgrave Macmillan, pp. 147–177.

Vangen, S., Huxham, C. (2003), Nurturing Collaborative Relations: Building Trust in International Collaboration. *The Journal of Applied Behavioral Science*, Vol.39, No.1, pp.5–31.

Vargo, S.L., Lusch, R.F. (2004), Evolving to a New Dominant Logic for Marketing. *Journal of Marketing*, Vol.68, pp.1–17.

Vargo, S.L., Maglio, P.P., Akaka, M.A. (2008), On Value and Value Co-creation: A Service System and Service Logic Performance. *European Management Journal*, Vol.26, No.3, pp.145–152.

7. Regional revitalization through cultural innovation and creativity development

Takehiko Yasuda

1. ISSUE AWARENESS AND OBJECTIVES

Currently, Japanese society is facing the problem of a shrinking population. As birthrates fall and people get older, aging and depopulation are becoming especially serious problems in regional areas. How can rusting rural and fishing villages be revived? Creative regional revitalization through contemporary art projects have been gaining attention in this regard. Previously, regional revitalization measures mainly focused on attracting industries to regions to create employment and prevent the flow of young people into large cities. However, there are already few young people left in many aging and depopulated rural and fishing villages, and it is not easy to attract young people to such villages from large cities.

Additionally, in cities, there has been serious hollowing out of industries and decline in central urban areas due to factories relocating overseas, etc. In some cities, local revitalization through cultural industries has been attempted and has been successful. Developing cultural industries in cities has required the building of cultural clusters. This entails a focus on how to form creative "Ba" to accumulate cultural capital and transmit new culture in regions. It is a fact that cultural capital will not develop unless it is linked not only to economic capital but also to social capital (Yasuda, 2017).

In this chapter, we look at the Setouchi Triennale as an example art project, and a framework that leads to value creation as social capital through the exchange and fusion of knowledge between various actors, from the perspective of the "knowledge differences", "boundaries vision" and "boundaries knowledge" discussed in Chapters 1 and 2.

2. URBAN REVITALIZATION IN CULTURAL ECONOMICS

The influence of arts and culture on urban development has been studied in cultural economics as a creative cities theory (Goto, 2003). From the policy perspective, Charles Landry (2000) looked at how to create, operate and maintain "Creative Ba (Milieu)" to enable creative solutions to urban problems such as urban regeneration. This concept is similar to the "Innovation Milieux" concept raised in Europe. An "Innovation Milieu" is a complex that has regional characteristics but is also open to the outside of the region, and is defined as the inclusion of know-how, rules and related management resources, etc. Within a Milieu, social networks are formed within enterprises, or between individuals across enterprises, so that active exchange of information and knowledge and collaborative learning take place. The concept is similar to the definition of the regional cluster.

Landry looks at the issues of creative "Ba", mainly in European cities. As added value in cities is generated by intellectual capital applied to products, processes and services rather than by manufacturing industries, Landry analyzes cities as creative "Ba" for generating such intellectual capital. A creative "Ba" is a material condition setting, with a necessity for "hard" and "soft" aspects of urban infrastructure to generate related ideas and inventions, especially for the soft aspect. This is a system that consists of structures that connect objects and events, social networks, and connections and interactions between people. The system includes regular meetings of clubs and informal organizations, networks of common interests like business clubs, and public and private partnerships. Demonstrating the power of such networks in creative "Ba" requires high levels of trust, self-responsibility and flexible organizational management, with strong yet undocumented principles. Trust is central to the success of creative "Ba", and brings about related creative ideas and innovations.

In cultural economics, areas where cultural industries are concentrated and where cultural innovation is actively occurring have been analyzed as a "cultural clusters". Much of the research on cultural clusters has been done using a cluster approach based on urban theory by Jane Jacobs (1985). Cultural clusters form in cities due to their diverse labor markets, generosity and word of mouth that leads to efficient operations, etc. This is because they are connected with the rarefied, valuable and diverse knowledge that exists in cities, and ensuring access to such knowledge is a source of an enterprise's competitive advantage. Another reason is that rapid recombination of diverse knowledge becomes possible within cultural clusters. This need for rapid recombination of knowledge is exactly where traditional and cultural industries differ. An important feature of the cultural industry is that it is project-based. Most projects are distinctly different from previous ones, and thus require new project teams with different competencies to be brought together for short periods of time to gain a competitive advantage. Therefore, according to Jacobs' approach, cultural clusters need diverse local human capital – a feature mainly of large cities. This means cultural clusters form in cities with high levels of tolerance and openness.

3. ACCUMULATING CULTURAL CAPITAL AND FORMING CREATIVE PLACES BA

According to David Throsby (2001), who presented the concept of cultural capital in cultural economics, economic capital and cultural capital are distinguishable. Economic capital only brings about economic value, while cultural capital creates both cultural and economic value. Cultural capital takes two forms.

According to Throsby, tangible and intangible cultural capital differs greatly in the process of deriving economic value. With tangible cultural assets such as historic buildings, the economic value of the asset is greatly enhanced thanks to its cultural value. Works of art such as paintings also derive much economic value from their cultural content. Intangible cultural capital, on the other hand, has a different relationship between cultural and economic value. Existing stocks of music and literature, cultural customs and beliefs and languages, etc. have strong cultural value but no economic value. This is because they cannot be traded as assets, except where they can be bought and sold if they have rights to income such as royalties.

Instead, it is the service flows brought about by these stocks that create the cultural and economic value of the assets. In most cases of usage, the economic value of the service flows generated by these cultural assets tends to be highly valued as a result of their cultural value. In other words, with intangible culture, cultural value as stock creates economic value only when intangible culture flows. Therefore, intangible cultural capital becomes depleted unless investments into cultural capital are constantly made. However, continuous investments into cultural capital can benefit consumers as flows. Put differently, public support for culture can be thought of as investment in cultural capital.

Also, if relations between individuals and groups in society are a problem, cultural capital must be considered in combination with social capital. Robert Putnam (1993) showed circumstances in which social capital as a social infrastructure contributed to the economic development of a region in Italy. Essentially, the concept of social capital relies on relationships of trust and social networks among citizens. An important difference between social capital and physical capital is that social capital loses its value not by being used, but by not being used. Social capital is positioned as a complement to economic and cultural capital.

The value of arts and culture needs to be considered from three aspects – economic capital that generates income and grows economies; social capital that promotes communication and formation and maintenance of communities; and cultural capital that inspires people mentally and spiritually. Culture relates to urban and industrial development, and even corporate management, because it has not only the cultural capital aspect but also the social and economic capital aspects. In many regions, efforts are being made to re-evaluate resources unique to regions from the three aspects of cultural, social and economic capital, and position them in town development.

4.   BOUNDARIES VISION AND BOUNDARIES KNOWLEDGE TO BRING ABOUT CREATIVE PLACES BA AND INNOVATION

4.1   Design Discourse

In Milan in Italy, a global center for design, Roberto Verganti (2009) of the Polytechnic University of Milan, who studies the process of creating innovative new products, is critical of user-centered innovation, and advocates design-driven innovation. As empirical management research progresses, pioneers of radical innovation achieve meaning innovation in innovation processes that consist of undocumented networks of synergies.

In design-driven innovation, external capital has to be used to give meaning to things. Corporations use external research processes to put the focus on meaning. Thus, design discourse is research that is done on spreading informal networks, which are networks of interpreters of meaning as creative "Ba". This design discourse consists of interpreters in the two areas of cultural production and technology. Interpreters that belong to cultural production are directly involved with investigating and producing social meaning. Artists such as painters, writers, film directors, and musicians in the upstream in cultural production engage in cultural production as the most powerful and iconic creators in society. Next, cultural associations, such as associations, foundations and museums in which artists are involved, contribute to the interpretation and production of social meaning. Not only do they act as representatives of existing culture, but also present new meanings and visions in special exhibitions, etc., and promote research and experiments in culture. There are specialists who interpret these activities and the social effects of cultural phenomena from studies of meaning and language. These are researchers in psychology, consumer sociology, cultural anthropology, marketing and communications. Finally, there is also the media that observes cultural phenomena and influences the processes by which people internalize cultural phenomena. In the technology area, research and educational institutions that research and investigate not only technology itself but also the evolution and impacts of technology on culture and society are at the center. Technical suppliers also play a major role. Designers and design firms, corporations in other industries, retail and distribution companies, and users, also form parts of design discourse.

4.2 Meaning Innovation and New Cultural Social Paradigms from the Perspective of Boundaries Vision and Boundaries Knowledge

In contrast to novel, user-centered innovation, Verganti advocates radical innovation of meaning. Meaning reflects the psychological and cultural dimensions of humankind. Because it is strongly dependent on values, beliefs, norms and traditions, meaning represents a model of culture. Therefore, radical innovation of meaning represents a fundamental change in the socio-cultural model. Socio-cultural models periodically undergo significant changes. These are caused by rapid changes in the economy, major changes in public policy, arts, demographics, lifestyles, and science and technology. Innovations that occur within a currently dominant socio-cultural model are gradual, but radical when a completely new socio-cultural paradigm is created.

What is the source of new meaning? According to Verganti (2016), to cause meaning innovation, four points that should be reviewed are: (1) "market gaps", (2) "commoditization", (3) "new technology opportunities" and (4) "lack of analysis of one's own company". In terms of innovation of meaning from the socio-cultural paradigm, (1) gaps in awareness among people are important. In the ongoing fourth industrial revolution, people's lives are changing, and latent desires must be identified to lead to new awareness. Also, with rapidly developing technological innovation, (3) the unknown potential of new technologies must be derived without replacing technology.

Such gaps in recognition cause a sense of wrongness. "Knowledge" that seeks to find something in that wrongness is "boundaries knowledge" – the "knowledge" found on boundaries. From asking the question why to uncover the truth about such wrongness brings about innovation of meaning as new "knowledge". This finding new meaning from the inside to the outside in intrinsic processes is not the same as the current mainstream creative problem-solving approach that goes from the outside to the inside.

In design discourse, new discoveries arise in perspectives on objects and events from differences in the varied knowledge of their interpreters. Interpreters perceive the knowledge differences between dissimilar actors. This perception is a trigger that inspires sensing through boundaries vision between dissimilar actors. In other words, this specifically prompts interpreters to the thinking and actions of knowledge difference sensing and sensing through boundaries vision presented in Chapters 1 and 2. Thus, an outline of new boundaries knowledge begins to appear between the dissimilar actors from the thinking and actions of knowledge difference sensing and sensing through boundaries vision. This new knowledge is also boundaries knowledge (Kodama, 2018, 2019). Interpreters discover or create boundaries knowledge, and boundaries vision is used to bridge these boundaries. Boundaries vision and boundaries knowledge are the source of the knowledge creation process in the SECI model presented in Chapter 2.

5. ART PROJECTS WITH MODERN ART AND CREATIVE DEVELOPMENT: THE PERSPECTIVE FROM BOUNDARIES KNOWLEDGE

5.1   Art Projects up to the 1980s

While exhibitions in facilities other than art galleries, or outdoors, began to increase in the 1970s, it was "Sculpture Projects Münster", which began in Münster, Germany, which had a major impact on Japanese art projects. This project was held once every ten years, with works installed in urban areas and parks, some of which remain in the town. This is a project that includes not only the exhibition that takes place in the year it is held, but also the subsequent processes. Sculpture Projects Münster is characterized by the adoption of the "work-in-progress" method, in which artists stay on site and create their works while engaging in discussions with the citizens, and install the works outdoors. This method of producing works is recognized for its relationship with creative regional regeneration and development, and has spread worldwide.

Unlike art works displayed in architectural spaces such as museums, art works installed in public spaces such as towns and parks are called public art. Often contemporary art is intentionally installed in public spaces through urban planning. These are objects in parks, media art using water and light, and installations that strongly reflect the meaning of the location. Installations of public art in public spaces aim to bring art closer to citizens. Because it creates attractive spaces and raises the cultural value of cities in conjunction with town development, public art has become mainstream in urban redevelopment.

There are several streams of public art. First is the creation of new spaces by positioning abstract forms such as stone and metal in town squares and parks, like those typical of Isamu Noguchi's modeling. Second, like the modeling of Dani Karavan, who developed this trend, the strong monumental form is incorporated into the context of wider urban and natural environments. Third, there is "land art" which makes the environment itself the art. This has two directions. One is "earthwork", entailing artworks created in the natural environments like those in the western United States in which the art is carved into the earth as if the earth were an infinite canvas. Another one is land art which is eco-friendly and creatively questions the meaning of climate. The art projects currently booming in Japan are the latter.

5.2   Art Projects from the 1990s Onward

The 1980s and the 1990s in Japan was the period in which Japan faced the bubble economy. In the aftermath of the bubble economy, corporate involvement in cultural activities increased, and the Association for Corporate Support of the Arts (Kigyo Mecenat Kyogikai) was established in 1990. That same year, the Japan Arts Council was established with government and private funding, expanding the scope of grant allocations. Local governments also became more interested in culture, and art galleries and museums were constructed one after the other as the so-called "hakomono" administrations (a word used to ridicule governments that overly prioritize facilities construction) reached their peak. This was not only due to increased tax revenues from the bubble economy, but also due to the tailwind of support from government-run hometown revitalization projects aimed at promoting local culture.

After that, in the 1990s, the concept extended from "space" to "Ba". As the cultural environments in societies have changed, movements towards new artistic environments have emerged. Creative and collaborative artistic activity entered the social context in the same period to develop in connection with individual social events.

An important example of how art began to engage with social systems was the "Museum City Tenjin", centered on the Tenjin district in Fukuoka City, Fukuoka Prefecture, which was an urban art exhibition held every other year since 1990. At that time, the concept of public art was beginning to become popular, and many works, mostly sculptures, were installed in cities. This project was groundbreaking because it was operated by various volunteers – not only those involved in art, but also people from corporations and governments. At the outset, in the bubble economy, there was a new tendency for funding to be covered by the finances of private companies. This project ran until 2004, but towards its end many projects had come to more intensely influence social systems. Since this time, the number of works belonging to "places" and works that make use of the characteristics of places have increased. In this way, the concept of "site-specific" became widespread (Kumakura, 2014).

5.3   Art Projects from the Beginning of the 21st Century

The bubble economy collapsed in the early 1990s, heralding the end of the real estate development boom. Criticism of the hakomono administrations increased, and people began to turn their attention to soft culture rather than the hard culture of museums and theaters. The Great Hanshin-Awaji Earthquake of 1995 made people question how art could help rebuild society, and was marked by the appearance of a movement to create connections between art and society. The collapse of the bubble economy changed values that had been dominated by economic efficiency, and a direction to seek connections with society was born. Instead of staying within the framework of art, creative art projects began to appear that connect to other areas such as urban development and hence influence social mechanisms.

One of these established directions is the "Echigo-Tsumari Art Triennial" which is a large-scale international art exhibition that has been held once every three years since 2000 in the Echigo-Tsumari area in the high-snowfall region of Niigata Prefecture. The works are scattered in regional settlements to enhance the accessibility to typical Japanese farm villages so that people can rediscover original Japanese scenery through these "Ba". The art project is sponsored by a local government and characteristically involves young people and local citizens who work as volunteers called "Kohebitai" to assist in production and operations. Local women refurbished an old house in a depopulated village and launched a community business called a "farmer restaurant", which has become a hot topic and has earned recognition as a way to create new and creative communities. With the Echigo-Tsumari Art Triennale as a trigger, local community-linked art projects have been highly praised not only for their economic ripple effects but also for their revitalization of local communities.

In 2010, the urban art project "Aichi Triennale" and the large-scale international art exhibition "Setouchi Triennale" held on depopulated islands began. From the era of rising interest in the relationship between space and creations, the nature of interest shifted to concepts of "Ba" that include the historical and contemporary nature of a location and its social context, etc., and concepts of "base" that act as hubs for new communities and networks where friends and acquaintances can gather. This has resulted in an increase in activities that can be perceived as art projects.

This connecting of art projects with local communities entails sensing of knowledge differences between dissimilar actors. This perception is a trigger that inspires sensing through boundaries vision between dissimilar actors. The outline of new boundaries knowledge begins to appear between the dissimilar actors from the thinking and actions of knowledge difference sensing and sensing through boundaries vision. The dynamic processes of the three elements of knowledge difference sensing, sensing through boundaries vision and boundaries knowledge creation between the different knowledge of actors creatively achieves connections between art projects and local communities, and are factors that grow new "community networks" (Kodama, 2011, 2014).

6.   CASE STUDY: THE DEPOPULATED ISLANDS OF THE SETO INLAND SEA AND THEIR DEVELOPMENT INTO A CONTEMPORARY ART FESTIVAL

6.1   From the Naoshima Project to the Setouchi Triennale

In decline due to depopulation and aging, the islands of the Seto Inland Sea are being revitalized through modern art. This endeavor, which began on Naoshima island in Kagawa Prefecture, was originally started by Fukutake Shoten (now Benesse Holdings) with its Naoshima Cultural Initiative, and entailed the acquisition of sites where tourism development had been abandoned due to the bursting of the bubble economy in the 1980s. In 1989, the company opened an international campsite, and three years later in 1992, opened the Benesse House Museum that combines an art museum with a hotel. With its rooms having no televisions, the hotel is a luxury resort designed for the enjoyment of art and landscape. In 1998, in the Naoshima Honmura district, a "house project" was started in which an old vacant house was assigned for exhibiting branded works of modern artists. While staying on Naoshima, artists listen to the history of the area and the stories of the original residents of the unoccupied house to envision their artworks. A feature of Sculpture Projects Münster, the house project adopts the so-called "work-in-progress" method in which artists stay on site and create and install their works while engaging in discussions with the local citizens. This has resulted in the spreading of the "site-specific" production philosophy.

In 2004, the Tadao Ando-designed Chichu Art Museum opened. With coverage in overseas travel magazines and so forth, the number of visitors to the island rose dramatically. In 2008, the Inujima Smelter Museum opened, using the remains of the nearby Inujima Smelter. In 2010, the Lee Ufan Art Museum designed by Tadao Ando opened on Naoshima and the Teshima Art Museum designed by Ryue Nishizawa opened on Teshima island. Based on the success of Naoshima, the Naoshima Fukutake Art Museum Foundation announced the

"Setouchi Art Network" initiative to connect the islands of the Seto Inland Sea with art, and art infrastructure in the Seto Inland Sea was steadily built.

Benesse held a "Standard Exhibition" in 2001 using the entire island of Naoshima as a venue for contemporary art, and successfully encouraged the volunteer activities of residents as well as the economic effect of dispersing tourists throughout the island. This led to the 2006 "NAOSHIMA STANDARD2". Using contemporary art successfully boosted island tourism, with 10,000 tourists in 1990 increasing to 40,000 in 2000 and 340,000 in 2008. This developed into the "Setouchi Triennale" first held in 2010 (see Box 7.1).

6.2   Boundaries Knowledge Creation: Soichiro Fukutake and the Setouchi Triennale

The most important role in the island revitalization using contemporary art that began in Naoshima was played by Benesse Holdings CEO and Chairman of the Fukutake Foundation, Soichiro Fukutake. Hailing from Okayama Prefecture, Soichiro Fukutake is the son of the founder of Fukutake Shoten. Initially, Benesse led the project, but due to restrictions on corporate involvement, the Fukutake Foundation began to take center stage. Soichiro Fukutake argues that "economy is the servant of culture". His basic thinking on the influence of culture and his strong commitment to Naoshima and its residents have led to the success of these art projects. The Fukutake Foundation was established around the Fukutake Family essentially as its philanthropy organization. It could be said that Fukutake had boundaries vision to fill the gaps between economy, arts and culture.

The Fukutake Foundation and Kagawa Prefecture played the central roles in envisioning the Setouchi Triennale. In 2003, Kagawa Prefecture had been promoting "art tourism". Thus, the Kagawa government, led by its young staff, made a proposal to the governor to hold an international art exhibition on the islands. During the same period, the Naoshima Fukutake Art Museum Foundation announced the Setouchi Art Network to connect islands in the Seto Inland Sea with art, based on the success of Naoshima. However, the most influence in all this came from Soichiro Fukutake. Fukutake visited the Echigo-Tsumari Art Triennale, which had already achieved success, to participate in the event. He spoke with its director general, Fram Kitagawa, about the concept of the Setouchi Triennale, which resulted in these two unique leaders running the Setouchi Triennale.

Soichiro Fukutake's beliefs are reflected in the revitalization of Naoshima, Inujima and Teshima through art. The islands of the Seto Inland Sea were one of the first national parks to be designated in 1934, and they also supported Japan's modernization and post-war high growth. However, they are also saddled with a dark legacy. Smelters that emitted acidic sulfurous gases were built on Naoshima and Inujima, and the natural environment on Teshima was damaged by massive illegal dumping of industrial waste. Thus, it can be said that strong resentment against such distortions of modern society and rebelliousness against Tokyo are the source of these activities (Fukutake, 2013). The questioning and resentment of modern society, lingering thoughts about depopulated hometown islands, and the sense of mission to change society have all lent support to these endeavors over the long term.

Fukutake felt greatly uncomfortable that the islands of the Seto Inland Sea had been left behind after Japan's rapid growth and subsequent period of post-industrialization. Boundaries vision is the ability to recognize such wrongness, identify its true character, and inspire "knowledge" to try to find something therein. The knowledge to drive boundaries vision to bring about creative regional generation is boundaries knowledge (Kodama, 2014, 2019). Overcoming such wrongness can be achieved by relativizing the situation or object on which you feel the wrongness subjectively, and taking a bird's-eye view of the discomfort to objectify it and transform it into an incongruity (gap) to overcome it. In the SECI model discussed in Chapter 2, boundaries knowledge drives the process of formalizing tacit knowledge. Put differently, boundaries knowledge is itself just the ability to transform uncomfortable situations themselves, and such self-transformation directly leads to human creativity. Good, positive examples of this are works of art. Although Fukutake himself is not an artist, through publishing and educational businesses, he had the idea of overcoming modernization through art, and so took up the challenge of transforming localities suffering from depopulation into creative places.

BOX 7.1   THE OVERVIEW OF THE SETOUCHI TRIENNALE

1.   Holding the Setouchi Triennale

With the main theme of the Setouchi Triennale as "reinstatement of the sea" the event is held with the aim of reviving the islands of the Seto Inland Sea where beautiful nature and humans mix and are in residence with each other so that the Seto Inland Sea becomes a "sea of hope" for all the regions of Earth. The first Setouchi Triennale was held from July to October 2010 on seven islands in the Seto Inland Sea and around Takamatsu Port. Seventy-five groups of artists and projects from 18 countries participated. The festival was held under the sub-theme of "A 100-day adventure of art and sea", and attracted a total of 940,000 visitors, nearly three times that expected. The event was presented by the Setouchi Triennale Executive Committee chaired by the Governor of Kagawa Prefecture. The Executive Committee Secretariat was located in the Kagawa Prefectural Office. The producer general was Soichiro Fukutake, and the director general was Fram Kitagawa. After the great success of this first event, it was decided to hold the event again three years later. From the initial event to the fourth held in 2019, the event has been steered by the strong leadership of the two.

   The second Setouchi Triennale was held from March to November 2013, and was divided into three spring, summer and autumn sessions for a total of 108 days. The event was held on 12 islands and at Takamatsu and Uno Ports. With 200 participants from 26 countries, the sub-theme was "around the arts and islands of the Seto Inland Sea in four seasons". The number of visitors rose to 1.07 million.

   The third Setouchi Triennale was held from March to November 2016, and again was divided into three sessions over a total of 108 days. The sub-theme was the same as that of the second event. Similarly, the venues were also 12 islands and around Takamatsu and Uno Ports. Increasing to 230 groups, participating artists came from 33 countries with approximately 150 new exhibitor groups. Organized by the Setouchi Triennale Executive Committee, the producer general again was Soichiro Fukutake, the director general again was Fram Kitagawa. The communication director was designer Kenya Hara. The number of visitors was 1.4 million, about the same as the second time.

   The fourth Setouchi Triennale was held from March to November 2019, and again was divided into three sessions spanning a total of 107 days. The event was also held on 12 islands and around Takamatsu and Uno Ports. This fourth time, local culture and food was pushed to the forefront and links with Asia were strengthened. The event attracted a lot of attention from overseas, and in 2019, the UK edition of *National Geographic Traveler*, a leading and internationally known U.S. travel magazine that offers new travel ideas to travelers seeking alternatives, selected The Seto Inland Sea for first place in "The Cool List 2019", and introduced the Setouchi Triennale. In addition, the event was featured in *The New York Times* and *The Guardian*.

2.   Interaction between Local Residents and Artists and Koebi-Tai: Volunteer Organization

Koebi-Tai was established in October 2009 as a volunteer organization for the Setouchi Triennale. At the first Setouchi Triennale, this group included up to 8,500 people with 800 people actually active, and in the second event it included up to 7,000 people with 1,300 people actually active in Koebi-Tai, also with participation from overseas. Koebi-Tai's main activity is to help artists create works. Then, after the festival opens, Koebi-Tai provides reception, guidance and descriptions in the various venues. Koebi-Tai is a separate organization from the executive committee and was incorporated as an NPO in 2012. In addition to coordinating volunteers, Koebi-Tai also manages restaurants and sells related products.

Koebi-Tai has been highly praised as a factor of success of the Setouchi Triennale. This is because the interaction between local residents, the young Koebi-Tai volunteers and artists from other places has stimulated local creative activities. In the process of creating art projects, the cooperation of volunteers and local residents with artists to create works has been highly praised for the energy for creativity it has brought to the region. In addition, through the festival, many tourists visited the depopulated islands from both Japan and abroad, attracting attention and giving the islanders pride. Works that were left after the festival have become cultural capital, and have become objects of affection. In these depopulated and aging island communities, it can also be said that interaction with the young volunteers has led to improvements in the quality of life for the elderly residents.

7.   DISCUSSION: ART PROJECTS AND SOCIAL CAPITAL FORMATION THROUGH THE CREATION OF BOUNDARIES KNOWLEDGE

Currently in the islands of the Seto Inland Sea, depopulation is progressing rapidly. Youth are being swept away to the cities, and those left on the islands are aging, making it difficult to maintain their local communities. Interactions and communications within communities have declined significantly, leading to their decay. In addition, clinging to relations specific to the community and the will of conservative residents who hate change are rigidifying these local communities. In contrast, artists usually aim to create their own original works in their studios, which will then be valued in the modern art scene. Thus, these depopulated localities and the modern art of artists inherently do not mix.[1]

However, as seen in the success of the Echigo-Tsumari Art Triennale, attention has come to be focused on the role of art in creative regional regeneration. Rather than have a traditional festival with a strong orientation towards art, many works are created with the work-in-progress method through dialogue with local residents. Thus, the local culture, social climate and history are important factors in the production of these works, which are site-specific. In the process of producing, publicly opening and exhibiting these works, these regions have been creatively activated and regenerated.

How can one evaluate the relationship between local residents and artists and volunteers from other places? In the diversity of forms of social capital, Putnam (2000) identifies inward-looking "bonding" and outward-looking "bridging" as being the most important elements. "Bonding" social capital is good for stabilizing specific reciprocity, and enacting solidarity. In contrast, "bridging" social capital is good for collaboration with external resources and information propagation. Playing the major role of creating "bridging" social capital, artists from other places and representative activists in regions demonstrate boundaries vision to create works that will belong to local places and that make use of the characteristics of such places. Thus, they perceive knowledge differences between different actors (for example, the difference between desirable local creation through regional revitalization and the current situation). Such sensing is a trigger that inspires sensing through boundaries vision between dissimilar actors.

The thinking and behavior of those involved by their sensing through boundaries vision can create a wider identity and reciprocity as bridging social capital. Artists who come from other places play a bridging role with the local citizenry and volunteers through their work-in-progress approach, and create new site-specific value. Through these processes, local citizens can reassess the cultural capital of their region from a new and external perspective. Furthermore, as installed artworks are sometimes left in the locality after the art festival, they continue to maintain the pride of the region. It is necessary to consider art as cultural capital and social capital in combination. As cultural capital that inspires the human spirit, the art, the artist as its creator, volunteers and local citizens are brought together through trust. This promotes communication within local communities, and revitalizes local communities that were headed for decline.

The dynamic processes of the three elements of knowledge difference sensing, sensing through boundaries vision and boundaries knowledge creation between the different knowledge of actors creatively achieves connections between art projects and local communities, and make the connections grow to become new "community networks" to bring about social capital through the knowledge creation process (Kodama, 2011, 2014). These approaches and processes have generated economic ripple effects in cultural tourism (e.g., the opening of island kitchens during the event, the creation of employment in the region, and an increase in population due to the influx of young people).

8.   CONCLUSION

This chapter has discussed creative regional regeneration through contemporary art based on existing research on cultural economics, from the boundaries vision and boundaries knowledge perspectives. The chapter has clarified why art projects have been accepted in Japan and their historical background in terms of the expansion of the concept of "space" to "Ba". As a case study art project, this chapter has looked at Japan's "Setouchi Triennale", and discussed its success factors and the process of creating boundaries knowledge from the viewpoint of cultural economics. The chapter has discussed a framework that leads to value creation as social capital through the exchange and fusion of knowledge between various actors, from the perspective of "knowledge differences", "boundaries vision" and "boundaries knowledge". In this regard, this chapter has confirmed some of the dynamic processes of the three elements of knowledge difference sensing, sensing through boundaries vision and boundaries knowledge creation between the different knowledge of various actors.

NOTE

1.   Also, many people and local governments have opposed the holding of art festivals, stating that contemporary art is something that only a few people can understand or grasp.

REFERENCES

Fukutake, Soichiro (2013). A management perspective is essential for town revitalization, *Nikkei Architecture*, vol. 998, pp. 22–25 (in Japanese).

Goto, K. (2003). Theoretical approach to creative city, with special reference to the concept of creative milieu and social interaction in cultural policy, cultural economics and economic geography, *Cultural Economics* (Japan Association for Cultural Economics), vol. 3, No. 4, pp. 1–17.

Jacobs, J. (1985). *Cities and the Wealth of Nations*. New York: Vintage.

Kodama, M. (2011). *Interactive Business Communities: Accelerating Corporate Innovation through Boundary Networks*. Aldershot, UK: Gower Publishing, Ltd.

Kodama, M. (2014). *Winning Through Boundaries Innovation: Communities of Boundaries Generate Convergence*. Frankfurt: Peter Lang.

Kodama, M. (2018). Boundaries innovation through knowledge convergence: Developing triad strategic communities, *Technology Analysis & Strategic Management*, Vol. 30, No. 5, pp. 609–624.

Kodama, M. (2019). Boundaries knowledge (knowing)–A source of business innovation, *Knowledge and Process Management*, Vol. 26, No. 3, pp. 210–228.

Kumakura, Junko (supervisor) (2014). *Art Projects: Art and Co-creating Societies*. Suiyosha, pp. 19–20 (in Japanese).

Landry, C. (2000). *The Creative City*. Chapter 6. Earthscan Publications.

Putnam, R.D. (1993). *Making Democracy Work*. Princeton, NJ: Princeton University Press.

Putnam, R.D. (2000). *Bowling Alone: The Collapse and Revival of American Community*. New York: Simon & Schuster.

Throsby, D. (2001). *Economics and Culture*. Cambridge: Cambridge University Press.

Verganti, R. (2009). *Design-Driven Innovation*. Boston, MA: Harvard Business Press.

Verganti, R. (2016). *Overcrowded*. Cambridge, MA: The MIT Press.

Yasuda, T. (2017). Industrial innovation with ma thinking: Lessons from Singapore's economic development, in Kodama, M. (ed.), *Ma Theory and the Creative Management of Innovation*. Basingstoke, UK: Palgrave Macmillan, pp. 103–124.

8. Product innovation through boundaries vision and boundaries knowledge: new knowledge from the corporate transformation and innovation perspective

Mitsuru Kodama and Yuji Mizukami

1. NINTENDO'S TRANSFORMATION OF THE GAME INDUSTRY: A SENSE OF CRISIS IN THE GAME INDUSTRY AND NINTENDO'S INNOVATIONS

Nintendo is a company that has gained global attention in the game device field for its "Pokémon go" and "Nintendo Switch" devices. Although Nintendo had maintained a high competitive advantage in terms of its share of stationary game consoles, many of its markets were taken away by Sony Computer Entertainment's (SCE, currently Sony Interactive Entertainment Inc.) PlayStation (Kodama, 2007: Chapter 5). Also, software shipments trended downward in the Japanese game market between 1997 and 2004, not only because the secondhand game market became flooded, the birthrate was declining and mobile phones became popular, etc., but also because of the shift away from games due to their increasing complexity and more sophisticated operations, even among the so-called "gamers". Game consoles had undergone technological innovation since the Famicon ("family computer", Nintendo Entertainment System) era, their performance had improved and many game users had been satisfied. However, signs began to appear that these technology-oriented business models were gradually changing.

Nintendo's ex-President and CEO, the late Satoshi Iwata (died 2015, aged 55) asked himself, "What is needed in the game industry now to expand the gaming population?" "Is the game market able to grow in the future with technology-oriented business models?" and "What is needed to expand the game market?"

> I became president of Nintendo in 2002, the year after the GameCube was released. I thought I had become president at a difficult time. Japanese game industry software shipments kept falling from 1997 to 2004. The graph was startling. I wondered how long it would take for the business to get back on its feet. (Iwata)

Iwata thought that if more people did not play games, the game industry would have no future, and no matter how much game console technologies advanced, it would not be possible to stem the flow away from games. Iwata felt there was a need to abandon experiences of past success, and go back to the beginning to provide profound games with wide appeal. Thus, he created a game console concept in which anybody could stand on the same starting line. Nintendo intended to create a game that anybody could enjoy, whether they be seasoned gamers, or people who had no relationship to games at all.

Iwata said the following about the DS and Wii developments:

> Speaking without fear of misunderstanding, Nintendo has not made next-generation machines. "Next-generation" means an extension of a technological innovation. The market wouldn't grow if we continued along such a path – if we had, we may have found ourselves in a pinch. To increase the number of people who enjoy games we have to add new charm. Operating games has become difficult and unapproachable for people who aren't used to them. A person who has no experience with games will not feel like playing a game just by seeing someone else play. That's the reality. That's why we wanted to make a user interface that anybody would like to try. Normally, anybody would get cold feet about throwing out everything that they had become accustomed to, but when Nintendo created the 2-screen DS, there were more people questioning what we had done than those who praised us for the device. Nevertheless, the market ended up accepting DS. We were able to demonstrate that it's possible to acquire a new market by changing the user interface. Through that experience, I felt that there were increasing numbers of people who looked favorably upon the Wii controller also.

Nintendo specifically aimed to innovate the user interface (UI) and make people who do not normally play games feel like they too could operate the game. In DS, which was developed based on this product concept, two touch screens were introduced, operation was simplified and a completely different feeling of operations to the conventional was achieved. Since its release, 60 million DS units were sold around the world, with more than 20 million units sold in Japan alone. As well as that, a different product architecture to the conventional stationary game consoles was adopted for Wii, which entailed technological innovation to make a controller (the Wii remote) with an excellent low-power, lightweight and compact UI for convenient and simple game operation.

2.   ACHIEVING DESTRUCTIVE ARCHITECTURE

2.1   The Semiconductor Scaling Law Trap

In the past, video games had been advancing in one direction only. According to Moore's Law, in semiconductor large-scale integration (LSI),[1] the line width has been falling for several years, processing capability has increased and more electronic circuits can be packed onto a semiconductor chip. This has resulted in better performance, higher speed and resolution of screen expressiveness and hence greater levels of game user satisfaction, and also enabled the evolution of high product functionality leading to the Famicon (Nintendo Entertainment System (NES), "family computer"), Super Famicon, Nintendo 64, PlayStation, PlayStation 2 and Nintendo's GameCube.

In the previous generation game console market, SCE had surpassed other game console manufacturers with the PlayStation series which had the features of a high-performance computer and media player. SCE's product strategy was to develop semiconductors with amazing performance and recoup hardware development costs through synergies with profits from software sales to make a profit over the long term. The strength of this product strategy was its hardware supported by high-performance semiconductor chips. With the aim of increasing game console profitability, SCE made a huge investment in this development with a technology strategy of developing high-performance semiconductors, and thus developed the high-performance semiconductor "Cell" processor for PlayStation 3 (PS3).

Following these semiconductor scaling rules has been a common-sense, straight-forward technology strategy in the gaming industry. However, Nintendo decided to take a different direction and began talking to the game industry and game users about its specific vision for the future of game consoles. Notably with the Wii development, one of the major objectives of the company was to deviate from the trend of enhancing hardware in line with the semiconductor scaling rules. For this reason, Iwata had to explain the background product concept both inside and outside the company. He had to explain why Nintendo was going to deviate from the game console technology roadmap it had followed. There was a major difference between hardware enhancement trends that followed semiconductor scaling rules and the new game console concept and future market that the company was aiming for. In Nintendo, this difference induced new boundaries vision, described as follows.

Iwata said the following about the software development:

> On the other hand, as a result of the more elaborate and complicated path so far taken, development costs per game software have increased, and the development period has become longer. In the Famikon era, I completed games in two months in two-person teams. As young university graduates around 1983, we were allowed to do that. But now, you can't make a game unless you serve as a member of a team of 50 for at least three years. As well as that, the overall image of games has changed into a world that is completely unknown (with the increasing scale of software). I felt it would be very dangerous keep going in the same direction. Obviously, the game industry needs players who are aiming in different directions. We needed to get away from luxury and complexity.

2.2 Horizontal Thinking on Mature Technology

The two causes of the shrinking domestic game market and rising development costs due to larger development scales (hardware and software) had become the biggest challenges facing the Japanese game industry. To address these issues, Wii was designed with product architecture using mature technology. In the past, Nintendo originally had such a product architecture concept. The late Game Boy developer Gunpei Yokoi (former head of the development department 1 in the Nintendo Manufacturing Division, developed hit products such as the Famikon and Game Boy and died in 1997, aged 56) coined the phrase "horizontal thinking with mature technology". Yokoi asserted that using mature technology to compete with ideas was a core competence of Nintendo. Shigeru Miyamoto, who is currently a senior managing director at Nintendo, and who is famous worldwide for developing the arcade game machine Donkey Kong and the Super Mario Bros. software for the family computer and so on, was taught directly by Yokoi and has continued that idea.

"Mature technology" means technology that has already been widely used and its advantages and disadvantages have been clarified, which means using such technology can keep development costs low. "Horizontal thinking" means thinking up brand-new ways to use things. As long as games are made to be interesting, they don't require high-tech. Conversely, expensive high-tech can have adverse effects on product developments. For this reason, horizontal thinking is a concept of bringing about hit products by using very common or popularized technology for new and different purposes.

Both SCE and Microsoft improved their performance in line with the semiconductor scaling rules (the Nintendo 64 and its successor GameCube were game consoles on a similar path). Hence, the performance difference of game consoles based on horizontal thinking with mature technology became clear. It was difficult to get understanding of differentiation with ideas. Thus, Nintendo took on a significant risk with its decision, because the company decided to go down an unproven path that those in the industry and users did not really understand. For example, when Nintendo announced that it was going to release a 2-screened game console, some people wondered what had happened to Nintendo. Iwata said "When I said 'Nintendo does not just simply seek high performance. The company is not interested in just raising the performance of semiconductor chips', some people asked whether Nintendo had fallen out of the competition".

However, Nintendo felt it had to be good to its word and present the future. Nintendo's biggest goal of its product strategy is to make steady step-by-step progress while talking about and making visible what the company is trying to do so that users can understand it. A characteristic of the Wii product design was the development of semiconductor chips that were outside the technology roadmap. Nintendo decided it did not have to think rigidly because it was trying to avoid following the technology roadmap. The company recognized the folly of following the conventional technical route and updating platforms for such reasons as the semiconductor scaling rule had progressed or from the desire to sell new hardware in the near future. Nevertheless, Nintendo's objective was to surprise users. Improving product performance by enhancing game console processing and graphics in the same way as SCE's PS3 was one product strategy, but in contrast, Nintendo put most of its focus on being able to provide game consoles that included key factors that would surprise users. Key factors are not just hardware. Hardware is one kind – creating a brand-new type of user interface (UI) might lead to surprise. However, Nintendo thought more deeply about other key factors of surprise. Such differences with SCE's game console concepts inspired new boundaries vision at Nintendo.

For example, even as semiconductor processes became more refined, the scale of semiconductor chips was controlled. This runs counter to the common knowledge about semiconductor scaling. With each generation of semiconductor process, the chip scale doubles, which is an iron rule of semiconductor scaling. From the perspective of semiconductor technology, the Wii was quite exceptional, with its greatest point being the design of its semiconductor chips that were outside the technology roadmap. This is because fundamental to Nintendo's concept was the strategic objective of increasing users that would play games by increasing the population of gamers, and there was no other way to achieve this objective with hardware design other than to deviate from the technology roadmap. For example, the selection of thermal hardware design made it possible to take investment in UI development to another level. Increasing the area of semiconductor chips requires investment in development costs which means less money to invest in UI and low-power consumption development as a portion of overall development costs. In contrast, in the Wii development, more money was invested in developing the UI and low power consumption.

2.3   The Low Power Consumption Challenge

In the 90 nm process, power consumption becomes a critical issue leading to difficulties with semiconductor chip design. To address this, one of Nintendo's solutions was to keep the Wii semiconductor chip architecture simple and lower power consumption. In that sense, Wii's hardware design philosophy was very clear and unique. Especially at the 90 nm process or below, leakage current[2] becomes proportionally very large, meaning the power consumption will not decrease as the process line width is narrowed, which means a large noisy fan will be required in the casing. Nintendo's technology strategy was to use the same 90 nm semiconductor process, but without scaling up the semiconductor chip to match the process, and instead manufacturing with a mature chip architecture to control power consumption. This is Nintendo's technical DNA of horizontal thinking with mature technology, and also can be called "disruptive architecture" to achieve disruptive innovation (Christensen, 1997). Such "strategic transformation knowledge" to "destructive architecture" can also be called boundaries knowledge inspired by new boundaries vision as perception and recognition of the differences between the gamer and non-gamer markets. Thus, Nintendo bridged the boundaries between the gamer and non-gamer markets, and turned its strategy toward the concept of planning game products that could be enjoyed by everyone (gamers and non-gamers alike).

Nintendo used a silicon-on-insulator (SOI)[3] process to reduce power consumption and leakage current. Although one direction was to aim for ultimate racing-car-like speed like the PS3, the Wii was more like a high-tech hybrid car with really good fuel efficiency that could be interpreted as technical innovation in a different dimension. The development objective of Wii was to make a device in a compact casing that would run fanless when on standby, and when active could be sufficiently cooled without much fan speed. This was to prevent the device from bothering users (especially mothers in the home) even if it was running all the time. Additionally, the concept was for a machine that would be accepted in the home without resistance, and that could run 24 hours a day to download contents and so forth, meaning the main issues clearly were low noise and a housing with low space requirements.

2.4 Reversing Product Architecture Thinking: Technology Orientation from the Market Perspective

Iwata instructed his hardware developers to create the Wii case to be the size of two or three DVD cases. Normally, the design of a semiconductor chip determines the thermal design (the thermal design power consumption), which in turn determines the size of the housing. When the thermal design is finalized, the image of a suitably sized housing is derived. If the case is small, the temperature inside the case tends to rise, so the thermal budget (temperature margin for cooling the chips) is limited. As well as that, the fan speed has to be lowered to keep the unit quiet. Keeping the fan quiet means lower airflow, which is problematic unless the power consumption is substantially lowered. Raising the airflow but maintaining quiet raises the cost of the cooling system. When trying to ensure airflow, increasing the number of inlets makes it difficult to keep Electro Magnetic Interference (EMI) within the standard. Considering the trade-off between heat, EMI and quietness, creating a slim and quiet Wii at low cost was a considerable challenge for the Nintendo hardware developers.

Regarding the Wii controller development, Iwata used the following words to describe "creative disruption":

> The standard form of the controllers of today has been decided by Nintendo. Historically it was Nintendo that proposed the controller be held in both hands and controlled with a plus sign-shaped button, which was accepted by users and became an industry standard. Destroying a standard we had

established by ourselves drew opposition even within the company. Would it be okay? Nevertheless, 13 months before release, I got my hands on a prototype when it was completed, and operated an actual demo game. We got responses that the game was pretty good. Confident that we could get understanding just by holding the device, I declared at E3 (Electronic Entertainment Expo) that this innovative human interface will change games going forward.

Looking back on the history of the game consoles in the past, the transition from the Famicon to Super Famicon, and further to PS/PS2/PS3 and Nintendo 64/GameCube, was "sustainable innovation" based on semiconductor scaling rules (see Figure 8.1). However, from the user's point of view, the meaning of technical innovation as next-generation technology through innovating semiconductors as stated by game console manufacturers has actually become difficult to understand. The "Let's make something more amazing" appeal of game console manufacturers has become difficult to communicate to users just by extending the past. In other words, game console manufacturers faced an "innovation dilemma" (Christensen, 1997).

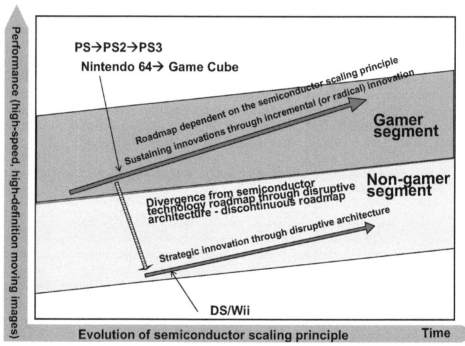

Note: Wii is the successor model to the GameCube but Nintendo diverged from continuing innovation that relies on the evolution of the semiconductor roadmap and adopted disruptive architecture. DS is the successor model to Game Boy Advance which adopted disruptive architecture.

Figure 8.1   Strategic innovation through disruptive architecture

The approaches taken to product development by SCE and Nintendo to support the home video game market were completely different. With its PS series, SCE tried to evolve game consoles into home-use, high-performance computers with dramatically higher computing performance and display capability than current models, while Nintendo's product strategy was to offer a unique UI completely different from the conventional to get users to enjoy its game consoles as far as was possible. In other words, Nintendo deviated from the semiconductor technology roadmap that was adopted by SCE and adopted a product architecture for its own products that entailed disruptive technology, and made the decision to assign development resources to UI and low-power consumption technologies. Thus, Nintendo aimed for innovation to achieve a product concept on a different and discontinuous roadmap to the historical game console development technology roadmap (see Figure 8.1).

For SCE, with its focus on performance level and image resolution, the design philosophy for its PS series was to race performance with each generation and target existing gamers like the shift from 2D graphics → 3D graphics, and CD-ROM → DVD → and Blu-ray disc. Game console performance can be demonstrated at its maximum in terms of speed and resolution with some game software that handles intensity of movement. On the other hand, without focusing on numeric specifications for operating functions, etc., Nintendo's strategy for Wii was to develop a game console (achieving an excellent UI and low power consumption, etc.) that could use a wide range of game software so that even more users would use it (particularly by targeting "nongame users" – people who normally had no interest in games). Again taking the example of automobile development, Nintendo's concept was similar to the proposition that "if there are automakers making F1 cars, then there should also be automakers making hybrids".

In this way, DS and Wii achieved great success in the direction of pioneering new users and are examples of boundaries knowledge utilizing mature technology with ideas through "inverted architecture thinking", equivalent to knowledge for strategy transformation in game console development. Iwata, who had succeeded with this game innovation, said the following:

> I was confident that there was a new market there, but frankly I didn't know how much time it would take to create that market. Because no one has ever traveled that road, when you pioneer a market, there is no way to know how many buds will appear and how many flowers will bloom when you prepare the soil, add fertilizer, sow some seeds and add water. I didn't know if it could be done right away, or whether it would take half a year, one year, three years or more than five years and the shareholders would want me fired. Nevertheless, there was a very strong belief that we could create the new market. So even before we got lots of results, I was able to say that I thought this was the way. And that is why I was able to feel the signs relatively early on.

Fundamental to the Wii development concept was the idea of a game that everybody could enjoy, and thus could be marketed to include the gamer layer, instead of only targeting the non-gamer layer.

3. INNOVATION BY NINTENDO'S UNIQUE DEVELOPMENT SYSTEM

3.1 Combining Hardware and Software Developments

Up to this point, Nintendo had engaged in projects to develop new UIs. About three years before the Wii went on sale, the company had begun researching elemental technology, and had formed a development team task force (TF). Even though Nintendo has software and hardware development organizations in its headquarters, developers regularly share information and repeatedly engage in discussions, hold weekly meetings with each other and continue dialogue about the way things should be. This philosophy of interactive organic cooperation in development between the hardware and software developments is Nintendo's unique developmental superiority, and is different from other game console manufacturers who do not have software developers.

The late Iwata, who became president in 2002, reformed Nintendo's official organizations in 2004. Nintendo's in-house software development team was divided into Information Development Headquarters (supervised by Miyamoto), and the Development Planning Department (Iwata's additional post) that engaged in software development in collaboration with external partners. Hardware development was divided into the General Development Division (supervised by Takeda) that develops stationary games such as Wii, and the Development Technology Headquarters that develops portable games such as DS. Prior to Iwata's organizational system, there were few exchanges between the hardware and software development departments, and several barriers existed between the organizations. Hence, there were barriers between the software in-house development departments and the software development department collaborating with external partners, between the hardware departments developing stationary and portable games, and between the software and hardware departments, therefore Nintendo could not integrate these departments and bring out synergies throughout Nintendo. By bridging the boundaries between people and organizations in-house, Nintendo generated boundaries knowledge as convergence capabilities.

After Iwata's organizational reforms, in-house collaboration in the software and hardware development departments proceeded at a pace, which drove mutual interaction between the software and hardware development departments, leading to the building of organizational systems to optimize both software and hardware development. As a result, numerous cross-functional teams (CFT), task forces (TF) and working groups (WG) were formed within and across the software and hardware development departments. For example, flexible teams were born such as the "user layer expansion PT" as a software development project for DS that included the sales department, the "unit function team" as a new service idea project for the Wii bringing together 25 elites from within the company, formed from various departments and all layers of management including top, middle and lower (these CFT, TF and WG are boundary teams, and equivalent to strategic communities (SC)). These multilayered SC formations around the software, hardware, sales, administrative and manufacturing departments were for Nintendo the source of its "knowledge roadmap" formations, discussed below.

3.2   Nintendo's "Knowledge Roadmaps"

In the field of home entertainment, Nintendo has continued to produce unique combination software and hardware leisure products driven by the company's software. Nintendo's basic strategy is to expand the game-playing population. To achieve this, the company strives daily to get as many people around the world to enjoy their video game entertainment regardless of age, gender, language and cultural differences, and regardless of whether users have game experience. Although Nintendo is a unique company that has not had an explicitly defined corporate vision, corporate motto or corporate morals, Iwata said Nintendo is "a company that creates smiling faces" based on its unique and flexible corporate culture.

In 2007, Nintendo set down its own unique corporate social responsibilities (CSR). In this context, as "a company that creates smiling faces", Nintendo takes up the challenge of achieving the objectives of developing products that match players and skill levels by pursuing the wonderful possibilities of leisure with video games that bring smiles to people who interact with Nintendo. Thus, by achieving one product that will satisfy all users, "a game for everybody" in the true sense, Nintendo declares that it will continue to take initiatives to increase the game population going forward.

The point that should be focused on with Nintendo is the regular questioning of how the company should be in the future, not only by the top management layer represented by Iwata (the "leader team"), but by all management layers. This enables the company to set new strategic targets to realize its (not explicitly expressed) vision of bringing smiles to people who interact with Nintendo. Nintendo aims to create "game culture" by asking questions for the future and getting users to accept and enjoy videogame entertainment, which leads to the company's specific strategic objective of increasing the game-playing population as the company continues this challenge.

In the development of products such as DS and Wii, employees in individual organizations such as the software and hardware development, sales, administrative and manufacturing departments staff reassess the basic value of the company while implementing specific strategies, which entailed strong will and determination to create a future toward the specific strategic objective. This enables Nintendo to reflect on its past and unite the past with the future to inspire staff to think about what Nintendo should do in the present to connect practical activities. As well as that, as Nintendo makes efforts to achieve its strategic objectives, the basic philosophy of "connecting everyone who is involved with Nintendo to a smile" led to the right form of management.

On the past–present–future time axis, Nintendo aims to win out in the competitive environment of the game market, and at the same time create new game-related markets, which entails realizing its "knowledge roadmap" – a knowledge creation process to continually bring about new knowledge. The knowledge roadmap is also a strategic map for creating a future. Therefore, where do Nintendo's organizations get the energy to continually create knowledge and achieve the knowledge roadmap?

At Nintendo, it is collections of humans embracing their visions, beliefs and thoughts that are the source of knowledge creation, which is rooted in the human capabilities of Nintendo's staff to subjectively bring about new knowledge and the human network that enables those capabilities. These human networks are organizational platforms for generating new knowledge, such as the "strategic communities (SC)" mentioned in Chapter 1. Thus, the organizational platforms required for creating, sharing and using knowledge and generating new value are multilayered SC. So, how do these practitioners form SC and create new business concepts?

Simon (1996) identified the limits of human knowledge capabilities, and how humans had established a management world of multilayered and separated job functions to overcome those limits. The limitations of knowledge was Herbert Simon's chief concept, and expressed the limitations of human knowledge and information processing capabilities. Simon developed this concept in the field of organizational theory. Why do humans build organizations? Firstly, humans need to reduce the complexity of the world because of these knowledge limitations. The social device to achieve that end is "the organization". By forming the multilayered structures of organizations, the complexity of making decisions can be divided into subsystems (so-called "modularization"). Simon argued that this enables advanced decision-making that would not be possible by individuals alone.

Certainly, corporate activity consists of a wide range of business processes (basic research through to applied research, marketing, product development, manufacture, sales, distribution and after services, etc.), and there are many diverse contexts in which businesses operate. There really is not any one person who has all basic skills needed to perform every task from developing new products and services through to sales. Clearly, from the analysis of Nintendo's development system, multilayered SC are indispensable for creating excellent business concepts and putting them into effect. SC are organizational mechanisms that transcend the boundaries of organizations and enable staff in core product development areas such as software and hardware development, sales, administration and manufacturing, and staff with game business ideas who are not involved directly in game console development to create and share dynamic contexts. These multilayered SC enable Nintendo's staff to generate and practice new knowledge (business concepts for products such as DS and Wii, and new services using these). The formation of such SC enables the discovery of differences between members of dissimilar departments, triggers boundaries vision in staff, and is a source of generating new boundaries knowledge.

Human beings have a diverse range of world views and value systems – individual lives are rooted in the paradigms of thinking and behavioral patterns that stem from the past experiences of the individual. Practitioners in the various departments at Nintendo are no different – they are also individuals with diverse world views and value systems. Fundamental to the individual's way of life are certain paradigms of thinking and behavioral patterns based on past experiences (drawn from jobs in various departments such as software and hardware development).

Staff involved in software development, product planning and sales unceasingly create new recognition such as "We have to plan products that will provide users with new value" or "How should we grasp latent user needs to plan new products?" through dialectical synthesis by synergies of their own subjective perspectives (to grasp latent demands by assuming the user position) and objective perspectives (analysis of competing products and user data). However, that does not mean they have absolutely no technical perspective. These practitioners are always keeping an eye on technical trends both in and outside of their companies, and making efforts to verify concepts of latent usage that users themselves would probably not even notice, while always bearing in mind that although there are many uncertainties, if they can bring about a particular technology, or use an existing technology, they will be able to provide users with new functions and services. These people demonstrate capabilities to drive boundaries vision by understanding and recognizing differences that respectively exist in the subjective and objective perspectives.

For example, with the Wii product development, it was software developers Iwata and Miyamoto who dared to deviate from the conventional semiconductor roadmap, and proposed the concept of unique product architecture incorporating the new development element of a low-power consumption and compact UI. With their familiarity with the trends and details of hardware technologies, they were able to propose a new disruptive architecture, which is an example of boundaries knowledge.

Former Nintendo president, the late Yamauchi said the following:

> Our business is a business integrating software and hardware. So, you can't talk about software if you don't know hardware. Once you know, where do you put the focus? For example, Sony follows a path on which hardware leads and software follows. At Nintendo, it's the reverse. Software leads and hardware follows. Nevertheless, Nintendo understands hardware. I'm sure this won't change.

Through dialectical synthesis by synergies of their own subjective perspectives (belief and passion that I would like to develop this) and objective perspectives (concentration and selection based on analysis and assessment of technical trends), staff involved in hardware development unceasingly bring about new recognition that they have to develop technologies that will satisfy users, and they must develop core technologies that cannot be copied by competitors. However, that does not mean that hardware developers have no idea about markets. Certainly, hardware developers make unique proposals to the market side from seed-oriented concepts about what can be achieved. For example, the Wii controller with its intuitive operation concept was the gift of the trial and error efforts of Takeda's development team, and was a killer application that infused entire families of users with the "game culture".

In this way, staff in all departments proactively formed multilayered SC in-house and brought about new energy from the clear vision of paradigms as their respective subjectivities clashed in the contexts and perspectives of software (markets) and hardware (technologies) to form new contexts at a higher dimension. Staff come to understand each other's diverse world views and values, and bring about mutually approved organizational rules and discipline through creative learning enabled by creative dialogue (or dialectical dialogue) between dissimilar organizations. However, as staff come to mutually understand and share the thoughts and feelings of others, they combine both assertiveness and humility, and they intentionally ask questions about the meaning of creating new knowledge.

These people demonstrate capabilities to bring about valuable boundaries knowledge by driving boundaries vision to understanding and recognizing differences that respectively exist in the subjective and objective perspectives. This enables staff to develop concepts and thinking with higher dimensions for the creation of new innovations. Thus, the creation and realization of business concepts as transcendent hypotheses are enabled through the synthesis of the market (software) and technological (hardware) roadmaps through abduction.

In this way, Nintendo has embedded a unique organizational culture in which staff transcend the boundaries between the hardware and software development departments by forming SC in which they are united and can collaborate together. Thus, staff in development departments (hardware and software) demonstrate boundaries vision and trial the boundaries knowledge brought about in their cooperative work to verify hypotheses and discover new problems and issues. By repeating this practical process through abduction, the dissimilar paradigms of the market (software) and technologies (hardware) are synthesized to come closer to the achievement of new creations (new products) as Nintendo's objective knowledge roadmap (see Figure 8.2).

Abduction is the concept of enabling the search for the unknown. This methodology is based on a practice in transcendent thinking that is neither deduction nor induction. Abduction was advocated by Charles Sanders Peirce (1839–1914), an American who founded pragmatism (Misak, 2004). In short, abduction is a knowledge methodology that entails: (i) organizationally grasping latent factors or mechanisms to bring about new value opportunities through

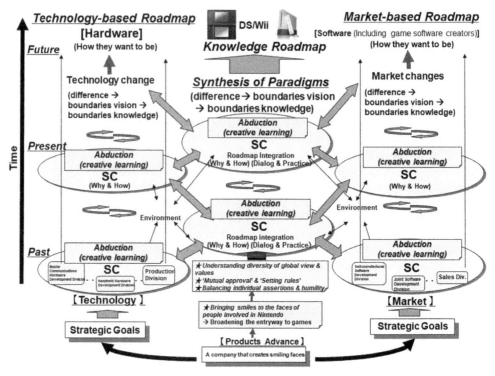

Figure 8.2   Nintendo's knowledge roadmap

sharing tacit knowledge with the market (or environment), (ii) creating specific models (explicit knowledge) that lead to prospects and execution in shareable markets, and (iii) verifying and correcting hypothesis in those processes, and achieving justification and theorizing of knowledge to solve problems when they are faced.

3.3   Achieving Concept Creation by Image and Entity Combination: The Knowledge Creation Spiral

As mentioned, fundamental to Nintendo's concept was the strategic objective of increasing users that would play games by increasing the population of gamers, and there was no way to achieve this objective with hardware design other than to deviate from the existing technology roadmap. The company had to take up the challenge of developing a game console product that would bridge the gamer and non-gamer layers in the market so that everybody could enjoy it. Thus, Nintendo itself had to recognize and become aware of the differences between the world views and values of gamers and non-gamers, and drive boundaries vision to promote sharing, empathy and resonance of values of the members of the in-house teams.

For Nintendo, the discovery of boundaries knowledge, knowledge for strategic transformation from conventional game consoles that corresponded with the technical roadmap to Nintendo's objective game consoles, was important under its fundamental concept of giving richer enjoyment to people all over the world with games as part of their lifestyles. Thus, in pursuit of the objectives of creating a user interface that anybody can use, and a game concept that would not make people feel the conventional image of a game console, the company dynamically transformed tacit and explicit knowledge, as discussed in detail in Chapter 2.

3.3.1   The Socialization area (tacit knowledge → tacit knowledge: knowledge integration process)

As shown in the socialization area of Figure 8.3, practitioners in product planning and marketing (game creators and product planning directors in the Nintendo case) have to experience and perceive social contexts where trends in market structures or latent needs of customers cannot be clarified as explicit knowledge in the life world domain. In such cases, marketers themselves must perceive and recognize knowledge differences of the target product image and real social contexts at the macro and micro levels. On the other hand, through direct experience in the workplace or through close dialogue with marketers, practitioners in engineering and development fields (software and hardware developers in the Nintendo case) have to perceive and recognize new knowledge differences as macro (overall) and micro (partial) technical contexts (for example, "reading" as an engineer whether it is possible to cover the product image within the scope expected from the tacit knowledge built up through time) that comply with (adapt to) tacit social contexts (the images and experiences of target products, etc.) at the macro (overall) and micro (partial) levels.

In the [Socialization] area, the abstract space (life world) in Figure 8.3, diverse tacit knowledge is interacted, exchanged and shared within oneself or with others through the spiraling synergies (abduction process) between social and technological contexts (and between contexts at the macro and micro levels). By leaving behind its experiences of past success, and going back to the beginning, Nintendo embraced an awareness of the issues of how to provide a profound game with a wide frontage, and how the game should be so that anybody could stand on the same start line, shared these contexts, and engaged in trial and error.

Through this abduction process of hypothesis setting and verification through trial and error by creative learning, practitioners perceive and recognize knowledge differences between the new intended hypothesis setting and test results at the macro and micro levels, and create new boundaries knowledge through adaptive (or intentional) processes.

In particular for practitioners, to achieve target (intended) tacit knowledge, it is important that the knowledge differences are correctly recognized for the knowledge integration process to integrate diverse tacit knowledge as tacit knowledge → tacit knowledge based on the accumulated experience and know-how, and boundaries knowledge is brought about. In other words, boundaries knowledge is a factor that drives new (tacit) knowledge integration processes. This newly generated boundaries knowledge is embedded in newly set hypotheses, and leads to the discovery and generation of new tacit knowledge through the reconfiguration and reintegration of diverse tacit knowledge aimed at dramatic refinement and renewal of hypotheses (see Figure 8.3).

For the tacit knowledge integration cited by Polanyi (1962), the generation of new meaning through the creation of boundaries knowledge by recognizing knowledge differences is crucial. Then, the generation of boundaries knowledge enables the integration of diverse tacit knowledge (tacit knowledge → tacit knowledge) and thus plays the role of new tacit knowledge creation (see "Socialization" in Figure 8.3).

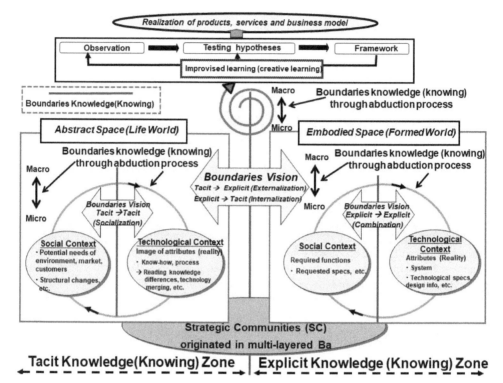

Figure 8.3   *The knowledge creation process through boundaries vision and boundaries knowledge*

Such capabilities to discover, sense, recognize and create new boundaries knowledge from the spiraling synergies through abduction between these social and technological contexts (moreover, between contexts at the macro and micro levels) is also "boundaries vision" (Kodama and Shibata, 2016) (see Figure 8.3). Through their direct experiences in abstract space (in the life world domain), observations such as "This is the image of the product exactly what the customers want", "It's different from what was originally sensed", and "Doing things in a certain way will go well?" and creative dialectic dialogue (Kodama, 2007) are made by marketers and engineers (sometimes customers as well), and in the time and space abstracted as the image, practitioners' beliefs and thoughts clash. Nintendo's intuitive strategic contexts derived through this process of trial and error were the result of the company's beliefs of breaking off from the track of semiconductor scaling laws.

3.3.2   Externalization area (tacit knowledge → explicit knowledge: knowledge transformation process)

Subject to the social contexts of customer requirements obtained through dialectic dialogue with engineers in the life world domain, marketers have to bring about more specific explicit knowledge. For this reason, practitioners must plunge into giving substance to the image as tacit knowledge in the abstract space between marketers and engineers. This is the embodied space (the formed world domain), in which images are converted into explicit knowledge (putting latent customer needs and requirements clearly into words) for analysis and design through the media of metaphors and analogies (see Figure 8.3).

An often-used method for generating concepts is a combination of deduction and induction. For example, this could entail a deductive approach to generating concepts from such things as business philosophy or strategy, or an inductive approach to inductively derive concepts from target customers or market research, etc. However, there are cases in which it is not possible to generate appropriate concepts from deductive or inductive approaches, and so a non-analytical approach is required, which could involve metaphors or analogies.

Metaphors have been described as a method of sensing another thing or intuitive understanding by painting a picture in the mind as a symbol of a thing. Using metaphors, people create new interpretations of experiences by appealing to listeners to see a thing as something different. Essentially, a metaphor is understanding and experiencing something by relating it to something else (Lakoff and Johnson, 1980). In this way, a metaphor is a communication mechanism that functions to harmonize mismatches in meaning (Donnellon et al., 1986). Using metaphors effectively enables thinking about similarities between concepts, and awareness of knowledge differences such as contradictions and imbalances between concepts, which contributes to the generation of new meaning. Association through metaphors is more intuitive and image-based, and leads to the discovery of the relationship to the object.

On the other hand, using analogies enables focus on common points between different objects, and enables reduction of parts that cannot be understood. Association by analogy is done with logical thinking, and enables clarification of knowledge differences by focusing on similarities of the structure and form of the object. Practitioners, through the aforementioned abduction and the use of non-analytical metaphors and analogies, are able to generate boundaries knowledge from knowledge differences, and effectively generate explicit knowledge as explicit concepts from tacit knowledge.

Using metaphors and analogies prompts practitioners to become aware and discover, and at the same time forces them to recognize knowledge differences. Then, by generating new meaning from these knowledge differences, practitioners bring about boundaries knowledge through the abduction process of setting and verifying hypotheses through trial and error. In particular, to achieve target (intended) explicit knowledge, it is important that the knowledge differences are correctly recognized for the knowledge transformation process as tacit knowledge → explicit knowledge based on experiential knowledge such as the accumulated experience and know-how, and that boundaries knowledge is brought about. In other words, boundaries knowledge born from "reading" the target technical potential, which is explicit knowledge (for example, differences from product development processes to date; also knowledge differences – in the case of Wii, these were the differences between disruptive architecture and the conventional technological roadmap architecture), is a factor that drives new knowledge transformation processes (see Externalization in Figure 8.3).

Practically, in the Externalization phase, there are demands to complete product planning and basic design documentation, etc. in-house. With high-tech products, engineers are required to "read" the potential of whether a new product can be technically achieved (differences from product development processes to date: grasping the knowledge differences). There are many cases of innovation where commercialization has proven difficult using only the accumulated path-dependent technologies of the engineers themselves. To establish explicit knowledge as content with planning and design documentation for the objective, engineers themselves must understand knowledge differences between their own technical capabilities and the target technical development, and conceptualize the technical development process.

In the aforementioned socialization phase and this externalization phase, interaction as "dialectical dialogue" gives practitioners recognition of knowledge differences for awareness and discovery in hypothesis setting and verification, and plays the role of promoting the creation of boundaries knowledge to supplement and raise the level of completion of the target knowledge integration process or knowledge transformation process.

Described in the context of Nintendo's product development, this externalization area is as follows: in the life world domain, games software creators and software developers have to experience and perceive social contexts as trends in market structures or latent needs of users that cannot be clarified as explicit knowledge. On the other hand, through direct experience in the workplace or through close dialogue with software developers, hardware developers have to create technical contexts (for example, reading as an engineer whether it is possible to cover the product image within the scope expected from latent user needs) that comply with tacit social contexts (images and experiences of target products, etc.).

In the knowledge transformation process, shifting from the abstract space (the life world domain) to the embodied space (formed world domain) (tacit knowledge → explicit knowledge), the aforementioned boundaries vision is the capability that enables discovery, sensing and recognition of new knowledge differences and boundaries knowledge through the abduction process from the spiraling synergies between social and technical contexts. Through their experience in abstract space (in the life world domain), questions such as whether a product or service with certain features can be achieved are asked, and creative dialogue and creative learning are made by software developers including game software creators and hardware developers, and in the time and space abstracted as the image, staff beliefs and thoughts clash.

However, it is not possible to achieve concrete concepts and prototypes while closed off in abstract space. In order to achieve this, the image that software developers, including game software creators and hardware developers, have in the abstract space, must be incorporated into the substance at hand. These are embodied spaces (the form world domain), where metaphors and analogies are the media through which images are converted into explicit knowledge (putting latent user needs and requirements clearly into words) for analysis and design. Software developers, including game software creators, have to engage with specific descriptions that more realistically describe the social contexts, obtained through creative dialogue with engineers in the life world domain, as latent user needs or customer requirements. Correspondingly, hardware engineers analyze specifications required by the product planning side including game software creators and software developers, etc., create specifications for functions, and create basic technical contexts including general system concepts design, etc. Also, in embodied spaces, creative learning happens through creative dialogue between software developers including game software creators and hardware developers.

However, it is not enough to simply shift once with the knowledge transformation process (tacit knowledge → explicit knowledge) from the abstract space (life world domain) to the embodied space (form world domain), for in real business activities this process recursively occurs over and over again through the process of abduction (improvised learning through trial and error, or hypothesis verification processes through creative learning) recursively between micro and macro contexts until the image and reality become one. Finally, explicit knowledge comes to completion as actual concepts and prototypes. The quality of knowledge differences and boundaries knowledge brought about through the macro and micro recursion in social and technological contexts determines the quality of the creativity of concepts.

A concept platform is a stage on which new knowledge is created from insights into latent market demands through the synthesis of abstract space (life world domain) and embodied space (form world domain). Ideas and concepts about new products and services do not suddenly appear out of the thinking of developers including game software creators; rather, the secret to success is not only empirical knowledge gained through actual experience, but also the sharing of tacit knowledge with users and absorption of dissimilar knowledge in addition to the extent of precision tuning of market demands through repeated trialing, prototyping and verification of ideas.

In its processes of achieving product concepts, Nintendo engages in repeated prototyping of products, and practices processes of trial and error until satisfaction is achieved without developers having to compromise. This resulted in the birth of the groundbreaking conceptual products of Wii and DS. The unification of software and hardware developments through the spiral synergies of these abstract (life world domain) and embodied (form world domain) spaces repeatedly rubbed together market and technical thinking, and was the source of the realization of new hit products (see Figure 8.3).

In particular, in the game console UI world, the point is to understand how a console feels to the user, and many parts cannot be understood without actually trying out the device, which is not the same as pursuing technical specifications. In the Wii controller development, Nintendo's developmental team created many prototypes and repeated the process of abduction while asking themselves questions such as "we have this technical element, but can we apply it?" or, "we've tried to make this thing, but can it be used?" Destroying existing ideas and raising new ones is not easy, which is why the spiral, dynamic circulation of tacit and explicit knowledge through trial and error, is indispensable.

3.3.3 The Combination area (explicit knowledge → explicit knowledge: the knowledge integration process)

Combination is the process of creating one type of knowledge system by combining concepts that are fragmented pieces of explicit knowledge. This process is also the process of creating new explicit knowledge by combining dissimilar explicit knowledge by fully using high-tech technologies such as IT and digital. For this, engineers in hardware and software development require "systems thinking" (e.g., Jackson, 2003). Systems thinking gives rise to boundaries knowledge to design boundaries.

Using systems thinking entails analyzing product development and design specifications, creating detailed specifications for functions, and designing systems for prototyping and the achievement of products (a whole range of design and analysis methods including total and subsystem design, function and structure design, integral and modular, open or closed, hardware and software coordination, total and partial optimization) to bring about technical contexts as detailed explicit knowledge. Marketers and engineers engage in dialectical dialogue and creative learning in embodied space to raise the level of completion of explicit knowledge.

The capability to recognize knowledge differences and create boundaries knowledge to accurately uncover new developmental factors in the combination area are related to the "common knowledge" (e.g., Carlile, 2002; Cramton, 2001; Star, 1989) of engineers. Common knowledge is required for engineers to acquire the unique knowledge of each area required to develop the target new product. Common knowledge drives knowledge sharing and knowledge inspiration among engineers with differing specialties (Kodama, 2007), raises the ability to recognize knowledge differences among engineers, and is a factor that efficiently and effectively brings about boundaries knowledge.

Discovering and creating boundaries knowledge enables the integration of diverse explicit knowledge. Combination happens when boundaries knowledge is incorporated into the integration process of diverse accumulated explicit knowledge. Integration of explicit knowledge does not only shift to a generalized knowledge system, but also leads to the generation of new knowledge or new concepts through the combination of diverse explicit knowledge. Game console development design through disruptive architecture with horizontal thinking with mature technology is achieved both objectively and rationally through this explicit knowledge integration process.

3.3.4   The Internalization area (explicit knowledge → tacit knowledge: knowledge transformation process)

Internalization is the process of individuals acquiring new tacit knowledge from explicit knowledge. Specific behaviors are required for these processes. In other words, it is necessary to consciously get acquainted with the theoretically understood explicit knowledge as tacit knowledge through actions. Internalization is not just simply practice, but an important perspective on practicing with awareness. The internalization phase is one in which practitioners turn explicit knowledge into skills and know-how as corporeal and empirical knowledge by conscious and introspective practice and behaviors. The thoughts and skills of individuals are crystallized as products, technologies and services, and when put onto the market trigger new synergies with customers, competitors, suppliers and localities, etc. through that medium, which further enriches the tacit knowledge of not only the individuals, but of organizations and corporations.

However, reflective practice through abduction processes is important for accumulating high-quality tacit knowledge in individuals and organizations. Behaviors that involve objectively looking at one's thinking and actions and correcting them have been described as "metacognitive ability" (e.g., Haynie et al., 2012) that enable corporeal intake and embedding of logically observed explicit knowledge as corporeal knowledge. This metacognitive ability prompts practitioners to become aware and discover, and at the same time forces them to recognize knowledge differences. Then, by generating new meaning from these knowledge differences, practitioners bring about boundaries knowledge through the abduction process of setting and verifying hypotheses through trial and error.

Knowledge differences and boundaries knowledge born through the reflective practice in the Internalization phrase drive the knowledge transformation process as practitioners accumulate high-quality tacit knowledge in themselves as a source of differentiation (see Internalization in Figure 8.3). Boundaries knowledge from new meaning generated from these knowledge differences is a factor that brings about high-quality tacit knowledge as a source of differentiation.

The various market responses resulting from the launch of Wii and DS were fed back introspectively to Nintendo staff for the formulation of future product development strategies. At one stage, sales of Wii stagnated, but Nintendo staff recognized and became aware of knowledge differences with the various tacit knowledge acquired from this introspective feedback. After that, Nintendo staff demonstrated boundaries vision, and from the boundaries knowledge drawn from the new meanings generated, generated high-quality tacit knowledge as a source of differentiation for later successful products. With the release of the Nintendo Switch, a later product, staff uncovered boundaries vision and boundaries knowledge between the different user interfaces and the usage forms of stationary and portable type products, and were able to promote the new idea of anybody, anytime and anywhere enjoying games, to customers all over the world.

4.   CONCLUSION

This chapter has observed and analyzed a new concept and framework of knowledge creation through boundaries vision and boundaries knowledge from an in-depth case study. In the acquisition of creativity through the framework of knowledge creation through boundaries vision and boundaries knowledge, in the knowledge economy, diverse human knowledge (of which technology is one element) is the source of valuable products, services and business models that can give a company new competitiveness. New value chains are formed as new strategic models by merging diverse technologies and different industries to bring about new products, services and business models that transcend various boundaries. Accordingly, a company must refresh its perspectives on management spanning the boundaries between the knowledge of individuals, groups and organizations, bring about boundaries knowledge through boundaries vision to create knowledge as new business.

NOTES

1. Intel CEO Gordon Moore accurately predicted that the gate scale and performance would quadruple every three years, a trend that is ongoing even now in the semiconductor industry.
2. Leakage current is a problem that occurs with electronic circuits, in which current "leaks" out like water at a place where it should not flow. Higher leakage current means more power is consumed and more heat is generated. For this reason, technology to reduce leakage current will be indispensable in the future to improve semiconductor integration and performance.
3. SOI is a semiconductor technology and semiconductor based on single crystal silicon formed on an insulating film. It was developed by IBM. SOI technology can reduce the charge flowing out from the transistor layer on the processor substrate across the insulating layer by 45 percent. Thus, chips that adopt SOI show performance improvements up to 30 percent, and power consumption reduced to half when compared to chips with similar clock speeds.

REFERENCES

Carlile, P. (2002). A pragmatic view of knowledge and boundaries: Boundary objects in new product development. *Organization Science*, *13*(4), 442–455.
Christensen, C. M. (1997). *The Innovator's Dilemma: When New Technologies Cause Great Firms to Fail*. Boston, MA: Harvard Business School Press.
Cramton, C. D. (2001). The mutual knowledge problem and its consequences for dispersed collaboration. *Organization Science*, *12*(3), 346–371.
Donnellon, A., Gray, B., & Bougon, M. G. (1986). Communication, meaning, and organized action. *Administrative Science Quarterly*, *31*(1), 43–55.

Haynie, J. M., Shepherd, D. A., & Patzelt, H. (2012). Cognitive adaptability and an entrepreneurial task: The role of metacognitive ability and feedback. *Entrepreneurship Theory and Practice, 36*(2), 237–265.

Jackson, M. C. (2003). *Systems Thinking: Creative Holism for Managers* (p. 378). Chichester: Wiley.

Kodama, M. (2007). *The Strategic Community-Based Firm*. Basingstoke, UK: Palgrave Macmillan.

Kodama, M., & Shibata, T. (2016). Developing knowledge convergence through a boundaries vision–a case study of Fujifilm in Japan. *Knowledge and Process Management, 23*(4), 274–292.

Lakoff, G., & Johnson, M. (1980). The metaphorical structure of the human conceptual system. *Cognitive Science, 4*(2), 195–208.

Misak, C. (2004). Charles Sanders Peirce (1839–1914). , in Misak, C. (ed.), *The Cambridge Companion to Peirce* (pp. 1–26). New York: Cambridge University Press.

Polanyi, M. (1962). Tacit knowing: Its bearing on some problems of philosophy. *Reviews of Modern Physics, 34*(4), 601–616.

Simon, H. A. (1996). *The Science of the Artificial*, 3rd edn. Cambridge, MA: MIT Press.

Star, S.L. (1989). The structure of ill-structured solutions: Boundary objects and heterogeneous distributed problem solving, in Huhns, M. and Gasser, I.L. (eds), *Readings in Distributed Artificial Intelligence*. Menlo Park, CA: Morgan Kaufman, pp. 37–54.

9. Boundaries knowledge through boundaries vision creation: driving dynamic capabilities and the SECI process

Mitsuru Kodama

1. KNOWLEDGE GAINED FROM CASE STUDIES, ETC. AND INDIVIDUAL CHAPTERS

As is common knowledge drawn from four case studies (Chapters 3, 4, 6, 7, 8) and one empirical study (Chapter 5), to integrate knowledge by external knowledge convergence capabilities through the demonstration of boundaries vision, it is indispensible to have creative learning and collaboration among practitioners through the formation of human networks in and between organizations (and between companies), as discussed in Chapter 1. The organizational platforms required to form these networks to bring about creative learning are "strategic communities (SC)" (see Box 1.2 in Chapter 1).

As mentioned in Chapter 1, practitioners must make use of their external knowledge convergence capabilities through boundaries vision to build SC that have boundaries knowledge (that inevitably exist) in and out of the company. Boundaries vision, which is the foresight of practitioners to achieve the asset orchestration process, is also the capability to obtain new insights from the multiple and diverse boundaries that exist both within and outside of companies and organizations. As mentioned in Chapter 2, boundaries vision creates boundaries knowledge through external knowledge convergence capabilities, and through the execution of the SECI process, creates new assets (knowledge) (knowledge transformation of tacit and explicit knowledge).

The SECI process has a mutual relationship with the DC framework (sensing, seizing, transforming (Nonaka et al., 2016) discussed later), and as mentioned in Chapter 1, the construction and practice of SC and networked SC are necessary as basic elements of asset orchestration architecture and asset orchestration dynamics, which are subsystems of seizing and transforming. It is the formation of SC and networked SC with dynamically changing boundaries knowledge by practitioners that enable the building of dynamic asset orchestration architecture in and out of companies, across boundaries within companies (between people, organizations and different specializations, etc.), and boundaries external to companies (between companies, between companies and customers, and between different industries, etc.) and the practice of asset orchestration dynamics. Both vertical integration architecture and horizontal integration architecture exist in asset orchestration architecture (see Figures 1.8 and 1.9 in Chapter 1). While linking asset orchestration architecture and asset orchestration dynamics, companies drive not only the incremental innovation of existing business, but also radical innovation to bring about new products and business models by newly redefining their corporate boundaries.

Firstly, this chapter reviews the relationship between the DC framework and the SECI model, and presents the relationship of the SECI model with boundaries vision, asset orchestration architecture and asset orchestration dynamics, which are subsystems of the sensing, seizing and transforming presented in Figure 1.3 in Chapter 1. The chapter also shows that the formation of strategic communities (SC) and their networks (networked SC) brings about the creation of boundaries knowledge and accelerates boundaries innovation through knowledge convergence (knowledge creation).

2.   THE RELATIONSHIP BETWEEN THE SECI MODEL AND THE DC FRAMEWORK

Although knowledge can be broadly defined as either tacit knowledge or explicit knowledge, these are not completely separate but in a mutual complementary relationship. Explicit knowledge is accumulated, and knowledge is used by combining it and associating it with other knowledge. Tacit knowledge is accumulated in individuals or in organizations in activities through the creation and usage of knowledge. Then, tacit knowledge is conceptualized, systemized and extracted as new explicit knowledge. This mutual cycling of tacit and explicit knowledge is the SECI model.

Such knowledge transformation activities do not necessarily take place within a single person, but within social processes between humans. When recognizing things, it is difficult to be completely isolated from social interactions, hence, knowledge transformation, the mutual cycling between tacit knowledge and explicit knowledge, takes place with the social processes between humans as the main stage. Knowledge transformation in social processes enables effective increase of tacit knowledge, both qualitatively and quantitatively.

As mentioned in Chapter 2, the SECI model consists of the four knowledge transformation modes of (1) "Socialization" that entails creation of group tacit knowledge from individual tacit knowledge, (2) "Externalization" that entails creation of explicit knowledge from tacit knowledge, (3) "Combination" that entails creation of systemized explicit knowledge from individual pieces of explicit knowledge, and (4) "Internalization" that entails the creation of tacit knowledge from explicit knowledge.

Socialization is the process of creating tacit knowledge such as mental models or skills by sharing experiences. In this activity, words may not necessarily be required – the important aspect is shared experience, like learning skills through observation, imitation and practice, etc. in on-the-job training used in corporate training and so forth. The tacit knowledge of individuals is gradually shared through such shared experiences. The origin of the idea of the mobile phone with built-in camera presented in Chapter 4 was the acquisition and sharing of tacit knowledge in the field.

Strategic communities (SC) originating in the formation of "ba" play a major role in innovation-oriented experience sharing that includes elements of pragmatic boundaries. The formation of SC for sharing tacit knowledge is a trigger in the process of socialization. Within SC, the socialization process is promoted as members share their experiences and mental models. Nonaka et al. (2016) associates such socialization processes with the sensing of the DC framework. In such shared experience, "tacit knowledge integration" (the integration or convergence of different tacit knowledge) is realized by the process of boundaries knowledge through boundaries vision (see Figure 9.1).

Externalization is the process of expressing tacit knowledge as clear concepts. In this step, tacit knowledge to be conveyed to multiple people is converted into explicit knowledge. As discussed in Chapter 1, in the externalization process, creative learning based on meaningful creative dialogue and learning is the trigger. Since it is difficult to create explicit knowledge purely with an analytical approach, it is possible to conceptualize tacit knowledge that is difficult to convey using metaphors and analogies. Tacit knowledge is made into concepts through dialogue and learning using metaphors, analogies, concepts, hypotheses and models, etc. to give it form.

The abduction process is an important method that is often used to generate concepts through a combination of deduction and induction. For example, this could mean taking a deductive approach to generating concepts from such things as business philosophy or strategy, or inductively being guided by target customers or market research, etc. However, there are cases in which it is not possible to generate appropriate concepts from deductive or inductive approaches, and so a non-analytical approach is required. This could be the use of metaphors or analogies.

Metaphors have been described as a method of sensing something different or intuitive understanding by painting a picture in the mind as a symbol of a thing. Donnellon et al. (1986) point out that metaphors generate new interpretations of experiences by urging whoever is listening to see things differently, and hence they are a communication mechanism that has the function of harmonizing mismatches in meaning. Using metaphors effectively enables thinking about similarities between concepts, and enables awareness of contradictions and imbalances between concepts. This can contribute to the generation of new meaning. In this way, the function of boundaries vision includes the use of metaphors.

In addition, analogies enable reduction of parts that cannot be understood by focusing on commonalities of different objects. Although metaphors and analogies are often confused, association by metaphor uses images and is more intuitive, but is not something that will reveal knowledge differences between individual specific objects. In contrast, association by analogy is done with logical thinking, and enables clarification of knowledge differences by focusing on similarities of the structure and function of the objects. Thus, using the analytical, deductive approach, the functional approach and non-analytic metaphors and analogies is an effective way of deriving explicit concepts from tacit knowledge. This way, the use of metaphors and analogies is involved in driving the process of boundaries knowledge through boundaries vision.

Combination is a process for creating knowledge systems by combining concepts, and is also the process of creating new explicit knowledge by combining dissimilar explicit knowledge (explicit knowledge integration). Through externalization, tacit knowledge is transformed into explicit knowledge, and systematization is enabled which makes knowledge transmission and sharing easier, and leads to rapid accumulation of explicit knowledge. Combination involves combining accumulated explicit knowledge. In fact, combination is contact with explicit knowledge through documentation, meetings, telephone calls or the Internet, and combining that explicit knowledge to reassemble it as a relation of explicit knowledge. Also, it entails putting knowledge into words, accumulating it in a database, or turning it into a theoretical model, etc., so that anybody can use it. The processing, modification and search of explicit knowledge can be promoted more effectively by using the advanced ICT of recent years that utilizes the AI, IoT and big data. These are also typical processes used in workplaces for education and training, etc.

Combination of explicit knowledge is not only a matter of arriving at a single summarized knowledge system, but also entails generation of new concepts and new knowledge. Often seen in the combination process is the introduction of business and product concepts into specific forms in middle management. On the other hand, when combination is used in top management, it creates a new meaning with company-wide concepts such as corporate strategy and vision in combination with medium-range concepts such as those handled by middle management. As mentioned in Chapter 2, the process of "boundaries knowledge through boundaries vision" is key, even in such explicit knowledge integration.

Nonaka et al. (2016) associate the externalization and combination stages to the seizing function of the DC framework. On the other hand, externalization and combination are equivalent to the building processes of asset orchestration architecture as shown in Figure 1.3 of Chapter 1 (see Figures 1.8 and 1.9 in Chapter 1), insofar as they entail the formation of specific theories (or frameworks), prototypes or business models from concepts (see Figure 9.1).

Finally, internalization is the process in which individuals acquire new tacit knowledge from explicit knowledge. Organizations or individuals must behave in specific ways in this process. Thus, by such behaviors, they gain experience and internalize explicit knowledge to make it their own tacit knowledge. Up to this point, practitioners come into contact with the tacit knowledge of others through accumulated dialogue, extract explicit knowledge from tacit knowledge, and create documentation and prototypes, etc. for the combination of such knowledge in the processes of collaboration, externalization and combination. Then, practitioners are able to internalize such knowledge by viewing documentation or actual prototyped items and their actual use.

Having shared experiences with others and follow-up experiences and knowing explicit knowledge leads the individual to convert what he or she knows to his or her own tacit knowledge, which triggers the sharing of values and leads back to socialization once again. The important thing with internalization is expanding the scope of experience, which entails efficiently acquiring and sharing the tacit knowledge of individuals and organizations by forming SC that span in and out of organizations (and between companies), and that have their origins in many diverse ba. For example, this does not mean just driving existing business through existing organizations, but also promoting wide-ranging experiences that transcend specialized job functions to bring about diverse tacit knowledge in individuals, teams and organizations by building new business development organizations, cross-functional teams and transformation (or innovation) teams. Expanding the scope of experience (e.g., new business development for radical innovation) is extremely effective for internalization. For example, this could mean practicing exploitation and exploration to combine existing business and new business. Here, "learning by doing" is the trigger – this process is "asset orchestration dynamics", which is the transforming function of the DC framework.

Put differently, the internalization stage is equivalent to practicing asset orchestration architecture built through trial and error in the externalization and combination stages, through asset orchestration dynamics. Through this practice, boundaries knowledge through boundaries vision born of the gaps between the acquired introspection and reality serves to expand the scope of experience and transform it, and internalize explicit knowledge. Nonaka et al.

(2016) associate this process with the transforming function of the DC framework. In terms of learning through specific practice and transformation, the internalization stage is equivalent to the execution of asset orchestration dynamics (see Figure 9.1).

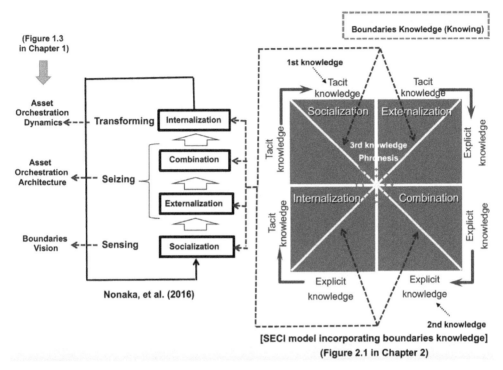

Figure 9.1   The relationship between the DC framework and the SECI model

3.   CREATING BOUNDARIES KNOWLEDGE AND DRIVING THE SECI PROCESS IN STRATEGIC COMMUNITIES (SC)

This section presents the relationship between knowledge differences, boundaries vision and boundaries knowledge shown in Figure 2.2 of Chapter 2, and strategic communities (SC). Practitioners recognize a wide range of boundaries in their daily business activities. "Boundaries" means the following.

First are the organizational boundaries between formal organizations in companies. These include organizational boundaries between formal organizations corresponding to those between business units or different job functions such as research, development, manufacturing or sales. Based on the authority they have been granted and the positions they hold, practitioners go about their daily business while complying with the rules of their individual job functions. Organizational boundaries between formal organizations determine the job territories of practitioners. Thus, individual formal organizations create "communities of practice" for their particular job functions and positions.

Second are boundaries related to the specializations of practitioners involved in research, design, manufacture, sales, etc., which are also related to job functions described in the first definition. These are called knowledge boundaries (Brown and Duguid, 2001). Knowledge boundaries form the individual "thought-worlds" (Dougherty, 1992) and mental models (Spender, 1996; Grinyer and McKiernan, 1994) of practitioners, and serve to solidify uniform perspectives on matters and job territories.

Third, and related to formal organizations described in the first definition, are the boundaries related to authority that comes with job positions in organizational hierarchy. The position and authority of individual practitioners create power (e.g., Pfeffer and Salancik, 1978) within an organization, and the power of individual practitioners forms boundaries as hierarchies. Other than organizational boundaries and knowledge boundaries within a company, there are also boundaries between practitioners within companies that include boundaries between practitioners rooted in individual corporate cultures, and boundaries rooted in the strategic intentions of individual companies.

Carlile (2004) characterized knowledge on boundaries in three ways, as deference, dependency and novelty (Carlile and Rebentisch, 2003), and asserted that the correlating characteristics of these three kinds of knowledge can be expressed as an image of boundaries described as vectors between two or more actors. Generally, the characteristics of these boundaries consist of three layers (Shannon and Weaver, 1949; Jantsch, 1980; Carlile, 2002, 2004) (see Figure 9.2).

In mass production models where business environments are stable and efficiency is promoted, these boundaries function effectively for practitioners who hold particular positions of authority so they can perform routine business in individual formal organizations. In hierarchical organizations, boundaries between practitioners are clearly defined in advance, and it is important that managers execute deliberate strategies with top-down leadership. In hierarchical organizations under the mass production model, the main operational objective is routines as predetermined business processes or commercialization of products through established development and production methods that require thorough efficiency. On individual boundaries (organizational, knowledge or hierarchical), practitioners mainly carry out business processes between organizations or convey business information. On the boundaries within corporations, importance is placed on discipline, internal procedure and rules such as determined business and management manuals with the objective of more efficient and productive processes. On such boundaries, as shown in Figure 2.2 in Chapter 2, practitioners must transfer information and knowledge accurately between themselves. These are syntactic boundaries (or information processing boundaries) (Shannon and Weaver, 1949; Jantsch, 1980; Carlile, 2002, 2004).

The information processing model explains the development of new products and the efficiency of business processes by coordinating communication and collaboration between formal organizations in companies, or between the practitioners of other companies. For example, existing research such as "differentiation and integration" by Lawrence and Lorsch (1967), "adequate information processing capacity" by Galbraith (1973) and "coordination theory" by Malone and Crowston (1994) provide a possible explanation of the optimization of information processing on the syntactic boundaries within and between organizations. In the transfer stage on such syntactic boundaries, the knowledge differences between practitioners are small (or almost nonexistent), and boundaries knowledge through boundaries vision rarely occurs (see Figure 9.2).

On the other hand, in communities of practice (CoP) responding to changes to ongoing improvements from the structural model of the hierarchical formal organization, boundaries with properties different from the syntactic boundaries mentioned above occur among practitioners. Here, practitioners form boundaries to engage in activities to generate new meaning, and interpret (translate) new knowledge. These are called semantic boundaries (or interpretive boundaries) (Shannon and Weaver, 1949; Jantsch, 1980; Carlile, 2002, 2004). Semantic boundaries entail practitioner activities to incrementally (gradually) upgrade and improve existing business processes, and development and production methods. On semantic boundaries in a company and between practitioners, importance is also placed on the discipline of the syntactic boundaries and the rules such as company procedures, but these boundaries are also used to promote best company practice and chains of organizational learning such as TQM to improve and upgrade business (see Figure 9.2).

The concept of the community of practice (Wenger and Snyder, 2000) described above entails creating and sharing new meanings among practitioners on semantic boundaries (e.g., Dougherty, 1992), and promotes organizational learning and best practices. In communities of practice rooted in resonance of values (Kodama, 2001), mutual learning is promoted on semantic boundaries through the understanding of mutual contexts among practitioners, and empathy and resonance of values to continually bring about new knowledge. On semantic boundaries, practitioner membership focused on activities is also gradually established, and practitioners create new contexts and promote organizational learning for target missions. Semantic boundaries that promote organizational learning are the first foundation for the formation of strategic communities (SC) (e.g., Kodama, 2007a, b). In the translation stage which occurs on these semantic boundaries, the knowledge differences between the practitioners is larger than that on the syntactic boundaries, and boundaries knowledge through boundaries vision is born.

On the other hand, as described in Chapter 1, on boundaries where there are high levels of novelty and uncertainty with innovation (e.g., to develop new products, services and new business models etc.) arises, new meaning must be generated, new knowledge that transcends organizational learning must be created, and existing knowledge must be transformed by context sharing in SC based on the creation of ba (see Box 1.2 in Chapter 1). These are called pragmatic boundaries (Shannon and Weaver, 1949; Jantsch, 1980; Carlile, 2002, 2004). On pragmatic boundaries, various problems and issues are raised, and practitioners must take up the challenge of solving such problems and issues and generating new knowledge. On pragmatic boundaries, practitioners are required to engage in creative conflict (e.g., Leonard-Barton, 1992) at a more practical level, and even participate in political negotiations (e.g., Brown and Duguid, 2001). To deal with new issues that have never existed and achieve objectives, practitioners have to work through conflict and friction, and even use political power in their activities to transform existing knowledge (see Figure 9.2).

Specifically, these issues and objectives correspond to the achievement of completely new and unheard-of business concepts (new product and service developments to achieve new business models, new technical architecture or component developments, or big changes to rules as new development and production methods). There is a high probability that new knowledge, the source of innovation, will be born on these pragmatic boundaries. SC are

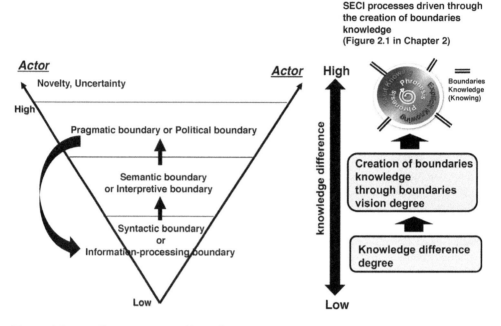

Figure 9.2   Characteristics of boundaries and their relationships with knowledge differences and boundaries knowledge

teams formed from various formal organizations and practitioners with various knowledge, are centered on boundaries with pragmatic boundary characteristics, and are founded on semantic boundary characteristics for the aforementioned organizational learning. In the transformation stage which occurs on these pragmatic boundaries, the knowledge differences between the practitioners are larger than those on semantic boundaries, and even more complex boundaries knowledge through boundaries vision is born.

As pragmatic boundaries, in SC, which are also a trigger for innovation, various conflicts, frictions and contradictions occur between practitioners. SC contain contexts that negate the existing mental models and experiences of practitioners, and hence various arguments and battles unfold. Also, in SC with specific customers, customers present various requests, issues and problems, and so the SC also changes to have pragmatic boundaries. However, achieving innovation starts with practitioners engaging in creative friction and constructive dialogue (Kodama, 2005).

However, the boundaries in these three layers are interdependent, and their characteristics change dramatically with changes in the environment (customer needs, the competition, etc.), or according to the thoughts and interests of actors (syntactic boundary → semantic boundary → pragmatic boundary). In achieving innovation or corporate reform in particular, the boundaries among actors shift towards the pragmatic (syntactic boundary → semantic boundary → pragmatic boundary) when there are strong changes in circumstances or movements in the intentions of actors.

The vector of the syntactic boundary → semantic boundary → pragmatic boundary shifts beginning at the origin where deference and dependency are known, and as novelty increases, deference and dependency also increase, hence the amount of effort required to manage boundaries and increasing complexity also grows. When related deference and dependency are known, they have positive effects on the practical use of common knowledge (or mutual knowledge) (e.g., Kodama, 2007c) and have advantages for knowledge path dependency (March, 1972; Carlile, 2004). However, there are many cases where the common knowledge of the past cannot express the novelty being currently faced (Carlile and Rebentisch, 2003), thus, as novelty increases, knowledge path dependency has increasingly negative effects (Hargadon and Sutton, 1997).

In Figure 9.2, there are clearly defined lines between the types of boundaries. However, in actual practice, it is not easy for the actors involved (main players and partners) to consciously (or unconsciously) distinguish where one boundary finishes and another starts. As well as that, the purpose of the hierarchy in Figure 9.2 is to express the necessity for actor capabilities on even more complex boundaries (e.g., pragmatic boundary) with expanding complexity (expanding novelty) to have capabilities on the subordinate boundaries (e.g., semantic and syntactic boundaries). For example, this means the existence of common language and common meaning is necessary to transform knowledge effectively.

Carlile (2004) states that multiple iterations are required between the three types of boundaries. It is impossible to achieve results in one go on pragmatic boundaries. In other words, to solve problems, actors must engage in repeated processes of mutual sharing and evaluation of knowledge, forming of new agreements and making changes where required. Thus, as actors engage in these repetition stages, it becomes easier to recognize (although skill is required) important deference and dependency on boundaries, and more easily find suitable common language and common meaning, reach integrated understanding and methods of taking action. Capabilities to engage in repetition gives actors the ability to transform the characteristics of path-dependent knowledge.

Problematic scenarios often found in corporations occur due to the use of path-dependent knowledge (or common knowledge) by administrators in positions of power that constrains new knowledge of other managers from expressing the novelty that they are facing. Such mismatches on boundaries result from putting managers with power in even more powerful positions where they demonstrate their unique knowledge of the fields in which they are involved. As a result, important knowledge differences are not noticed, which makes it impossible to create boundaries knowledge (knowing) through boundaries vision.

For example, in often-faced cases pragmatic boundaries or semantic boundaries are truly necessary, but practical processes and boundaries are only transfer and syntactic boundaries. These scenarios include, for example, actors failing to notice disruptive innovation (Christensen, 1997) – the most strategically dangerous situation. When actors fail to recognize and resolve disruptive innovation, it is because boundary vision, a sub-function of sensing does not function, and the novelty of the disruptive innovation becomes extremely serious with the passing of time.

The communications theory of Shannon and Weaver (1949) and Carlile's (2004) 3T model, which expands on that organizational theory, were reported as analytical frameworks in case studies of product innovation or corporate reform, etc. For example, existing research reports on the Matsushita Electronics (Panasonic) corporate reform model (Kodama, 2007d), new product development between corporations (Kodama, 2007e), knowledge-sharing processes between customers and suppliers in product development (Le Dain and Merminod, 2014), and project management among stakeholders (van Offenbeek and Vos, 2016). As described above, along with the increase in novelty and uncertainty of transfer (syntactic boundaries) → translation (semantic boundaries) → transformation (pragmatic boundaries), practitioners in SC perceive increasing knowledge differences and generate new knowledge through the dynamic SECI processes by the process of creating boundaries knowledge through boundaries vision (see Figure 9.2). This is also an example of the DC framework for asset orchestration discussed in Chapter 1. The following section analyzes how asset orchestration within and between different SC results in the asset orchestration architecture and asset orchestration dynamics mentioned in Chapter 1.

4.   CREATING BOUNDARIES KNOWLEDGE IN SC AND NETWORKED SC

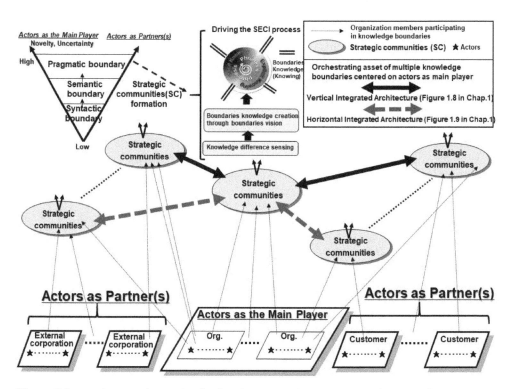

Figure 9.3   Asset orchestration by forming strategic communities between the main player and partner(s)

SC that bring about great innovations are not single units, but are multiple in companies (between departments, between business divisions and between all management levels) and outside of companies (with partners and customers), and practitioners integrate these multiple SC. The more complex a newly proposed business model is, the more SC practitioners must form and network together. Specifically, asset orchestration architecture (Figures 1.8 and 1.9 in Chapter 1) entails forming business models with vertical integration architecture and horizontal integration architecture. The author has shown that the new knowledge that comes about in the various SC that exist both inside and outside of companies is a source of dynamic capabilities (DC) (Kodama, 2018a). In particular, it is the thinking and actions of practitioners that integrate new knowledge via boundaries knowledge through boundaries vision that occurs from knowledge differences within and between various SC in and out of companies, including partners. In addition the SECI process (in other words, integrating SC inside and outside of companies) is a source of innovation, which also comes back to dynamic capabilities (DC) to bring about sustainable competitiveness. Networked SC are examples of multiple SC on the many pragmatic boundaries within and between companies that have been linked, bridged and integrated internally and between each other by practitioners (see Figure 9.3). Figure 9.3 shows a network system with vertical integrated architecture (vertical value chain and multi-layered models) (see Figure 1.8 in Chapter 1) and horizontal integrated architecture (horizontal value chain and complementary models) (see Figure 1.9 in Chapter 1) between the main player and partners including multiple customers, for executing asset orchestration architecture, a seizing function (see Figure 1.3 in Chapter 1).

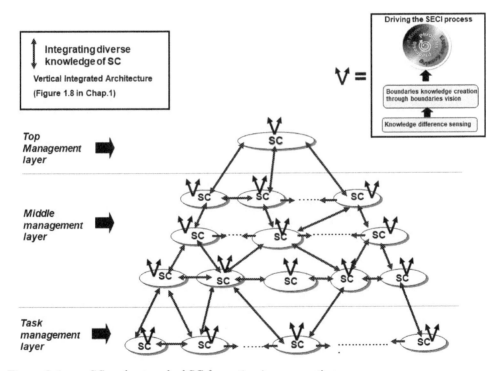

Figure 9.4   SC and networked SC formation in corporations

SC and networked SC in real organizations are not as simple as the SC and networked SC in Figure 9.3. For example, taking the multi-layered model (see Figure 1.8 in Chapter 1) as an example, the SC in the main player (the corporation) in Figure 9.4 exist in multiple layers across management layers in formal organizations, and are networked. The larger the company, the more complex the layers of the SC and networked SC formations become. Here, the author would like to show one example of SC and networked SC formation.

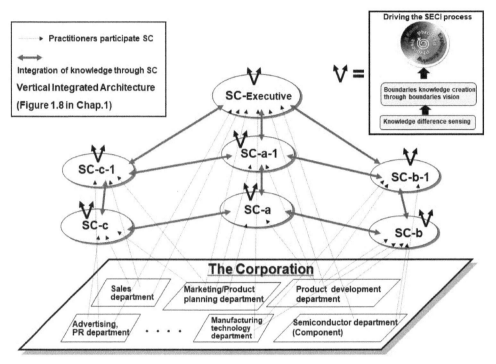

Figure 9.5   *SC and networked SC formation in product development in corporations*

Figure 9.5 describes the business processes from new product development through to sales in the five formal organizations of the marketing/product planning, product development and design, parts development, production/manufacturing and sales departments. This case targets companies with vertical integration-type value chains as their vertical boundaries.

First, to bring about new products, an SC (SC-a) was formed between the marketing/product planning and product development/design departments, and discussions were held on the realization of new products from different specialty perspectives. After that (or nearly concurrently), an SC (SC-b) was formed between the product development/design, parts development and production/manufacturing departments, and discussions were held from the viewpoint of design and production technologies. In SC-b, product development and design department practitioners participating in discussions in the SC-a presented technical issues and problems based on the new product concept (mainly product specifications and completion date), while several action items and division of roles were determined among the practitioners as well as specific scheduling for product development.

Meanwhile, practitioners in the marketing and product planning departments formed an SC (SC-c), which included the sales and PR/advertising departments, and developed sales plans, sales systems and advertising strategies for new product releases. For example, many of the challenges often encountered in new product development are technical in aspect. In particular, in cases involving new parts development (hardware and software modules), joint development or new parts procurement involving SC formation with external development partners, changes in the development schedule often affect plans for product releases and sales. Therefore, problems and issues that arise in SC-b will also be shared on the SC-a, SC-b and SC-c network through practitioners in the product development and design departments. Boundary knowledge through boundaries vision is created from the knowledge differences within each of the SC (SC-a, SC-b and SC-c) and between these SC (on the network), which drives the SECI process.

In product development systems in large companies, the networking of these SC exists in multiple layers with organizational hierarchy. Supposing the SC-a, SC-b, and SC-c mentioned above are staff-level teams that carry out the work, then manager-class SC also exist for each SC (SC-a-1, SC-b-1, SC-c-1). These SC (SC-a-1, SC-b-1, SC-c-1) are individually networked with the subordinate staff SC (SC-a, SC-b, SC-c), and in addition to sharing product development information, they also promote coordination and collaboration for problem-solving.

In the upper layers of the manager class SC (SC-a-1, SC-b-1, SC-c-1), the top management class SC (including persons responsible for formal organizations including the CEO and the director of headquarters) (SC-Executive) exists and is responsible for decision-making for product development (business judgments). Boundary knowledge through boundaries vision is created from the knowledge differences within each of the SC, SC-a-1, SC-b-1, SC-c-1, and SC-Executive, and the network between these SC, which similarly drives the SECI process.

The formation of such SC and networked SC differs from company to company, but according to the author's survey, these formations contain around 3–5 levels for large companies and around 1–2 levels for small-class companies and ventures. As SC, three types, SC-a, SC-b and SC-c, have been described. In reality, however, there are SC formations, such as PR/advertising, parts procurement, logistics and after support departments, that exist multitudinously and in complicated networks.

5.   ASSET ORCHESTRATION ARCHITECTURE AND ASSET ORCHESTRATION DYNAMICS THROUGH THE CREATION OF BOUNDARIES KNOWLEDGE

As mentioned above, the construction of asset orchestration architecture as seizing drives the SECI process from the boundaries knowledge generated from boundaries vision, which is sensing, and acts as a blueprint for the future in the building of new business by orchestrating various assets. In particular, to generate new assets by co-specialization (Kodama, 2018a, 2018b), an integration mechanism unique to the company (difficult to imitate by other companies) is required. This is also asset orchestration architecture.

For example, within Toyota Motor Corporation, SC with vertical integrated architecture (vertical value chain model and multi-layered model) are formed in multiple layers as cross-functional task teams at all management levels (group, section, department, division, executive levels). Task teams at group and section levels regularly engage in finding solutions to chronic and technical problems, while task management teams at the section or department director level work to generate general solutions that can be universally applied, rather than only solutions to individual problems. Total task management teams at the executive level engage in activities related to initiatives for new global manufacturing systems, raising the level of linkages between departments, and the creation of advanced technologies. The company also has joint total task management teams that include suppliers in Japan and around the world (keiretsu/non-keiretsu) and SC formed for activities to ensure the high reliability of products. Amasaka (2004) named Toyota's multi-layered task teams as "strategic stratified task teams".

Toyota does not only link SC among its technology departments. In-service departments such as sales, development and design, and manufacture (13 departments in all) are linked to enable the company to continually provide even better motor vehicles to its customers. Moreover, these are connected and layered with vertically integrated architecture (vertical value chain model and multilayered model) between administrative departments (technical, production, procurement and sales management, information technology, quality assurance), and the company's business and back-office departments (general planning, TQN promotion, advertising and PR, safety and health, environment, external affairs, finance and accounting, overseas businesses, personnel and general affairs), which the company combines for partial and total optimization by organic layering and invigoration resources and capabilities in the company. Decisions are made in the SC, which consists of management leaders (managers with positions at each level of management), and strategic goals and priority issues are immediately executed at each business division and group company. Thus, SC with vertical integrated architecture (vertical value chain model and multi-layered model) exist at various management levels within Toyota.

Furthermore, to expand the new businesses called Mobility as a Service (MaaS) of recent years, instead of only engaging in bureaucracies of layered SC with vertically integrated architecture, the company has also established horizontal networks with horizontal integrated architecture (networked SC) by establishing strategic alliances with and corporate ventures with dissimilar and similar business types, and integrating the vertical bureaucratic and horizontal network characteristics of both horizontally and vertically integrated SC.

Canon is a company that is highly selective about its internal technical developments, and drives its manufacturing with unity between development and design, production technologies and manufacturing. At Canon, the vertical integrated architecture (vertical value chain model and multi-layered model) that integrates the product planning, product development, production technology and manufacturing groups, is formed on multiple layers within the company. These SC are layered at each management level to pursue Canon's overall optimum management. For new growth, the company has also taken up the challenge of major strategic transformation by leaping into four new businesses: commercial printing, network cameras, and medical and industrial equipment. The company's organizational behavior promotes the establishment of horizontal networks (networked SC) that expand horizontal boundaries using horizontal integrated architecture. Similarities exist in Samsung and LG Electronics, companies which promote digital product manufacturing strategies through the formation of networked SC that expand the vertical and horizontal boundaries.

SC with pragmatic boundary characteristics ensure creativity and flexibility when the company vision is externalized in particular businesses or when solutions to new problems need to be found. In addition, SC layering ensures efficiency, speed and quick decisions to enable businesses to respond to changes in the environment. To adapt to environmental uncertainties, the seizing function of the asset orchestration architecture (see Figure 1.3 in Chapter 1) of vertical integrated architecture (vertical value chain and multi-layered models) (see Figure 1.8 in Chapter 1) and horizontal integrated architecture (horizontal value chain and complementary models) (see Figure 1.9 in Chapter 1) changes the vertical and horizontal boundaries, and properly uses the SC hierarchical bureaucracy with vertical integrated architecture and the horizontal network (networked SC) with horizontal network architecture to bring about the greatest synergies of the characteristics of both, depending on the situation.

The key is the execution of the strategy-making process through "asset orchestration dynamics", which is the DC function of transforming to flexibly and improvisationally change the networked SC with its vertical integrated architecture and horizontal integrated architecture. As sensing, boundaries vision is a company's capability to gain insight to design optimal vertical and horizontal boundaries through asset orchestration architecture, architecture thinking as seizing, which not only dynamically changes a company's boundaries in response to changes in environments (markets), but also dynamically changes the company's boundaries to create new environments (markets) and bring about new boundaries innovation (Kodama, 2009, 2014), and is thus a thinking system and executional capability that both corporate leaders and many of their managers should acquire.

Moreover, asset orchestration dynamics, which continually and dynamically execute transformation and innovation by using boundaries vision and building asset orchestration architecture, which is architecture thinking, at the same time as driving the SECI process, is a function of "transforming". As mentioned in Chapter 1, asset orchestration dynamics promote the balance between the growth of existing businesses (exploitation activities) through vertical integrated architecture and the development of new businesses (exploration activities) through horizontal integrated architecture.

In network SC, thorough understanding of problems and issues is promoted by creative learning through creative dialogue among practitioners across different organizations and the areas of specialization, which enables practitioners to mutually recognize each other's roles and value through mutual coordination and collaboration. As a result, this enables practitioners to turn the various conflicts that emerge among themselves into constructive conflicts. In this process, on a mission to pursue a goal, practitioners require a pattern of thinking and action that entails asking themselves the question "what actions should I take, with what strategies and tactics, and how will I contribute to the company innovation by doing so?", which requires creative learning combining both self-assertiveness and humility. Meanwhile, the CEO, as the leader and the final decision-maker, must at times demonstrate top-down leadership while simultaneously reinforcing linkages for close collaboration between company heads and management leaders by intentionally creating opportunities for creative learning in SC and networked SC to maximize the coherence of the leadership of all management leaders.

6.   CREATING BOUNDARIES KNOWLEDGE: ACCELERATING THE DYNAMIC RANGE OF KNOWLEDGE BOUNDARIES

Practitioners possess their own unique thought worlds and mental models. Not only do businesspersons both mentally and physically have unique world views born from personal experiences of society, but as practitioners, businesspeople also have practical knowledge rooted in tacit knowledge deeply embedded within themselves, born through professional experience across a range of job functions. Depending on the level of novelty and uncertainty in the target strategy, in other words the higher the level of knowledge difference, the easier it is for friction and conflict to occur due to the mutual diversity and differences among the knowledge of practitioners.

In boundaries innovation for new products and new business development that is completely different from conventional concepts and straddles different areas of specialization, practitioners must transform their existing knowledge. However, like the innovator's dilemma, knowledge embedded deeply in individual practitioners can conversely become a hindrance when it comes to taking action to face a challenge. To successfully develop new business, practitioners creating SC based on ba first need to create new meaning through deep creative dialogue among themselves, and creative learning (see Chapter 1) and mutual understanding for the creation of new meaning.

Creative dialogue and creative learning are enablers that promote sharing and understanding of the meaning of a new challenge among practitioners. However, "we have general agreement, but there are problems with the details!" or "this lacks any concrete theory!" can often be heard in discussions among practitioners in the business workplace. In addition, specific separate discussions such as "we know what needs to be done now, but specifically who is going to do it and when, and how is it supposed to be done?", or "do we have the resources?" or "which other companies should we engage?" emerge. This kind of friction and discord between organizations is unavoidable. However, the friction and discord that arises in facing the challenge of new issues or current problems are also opportunities for innovation. Therefore, management at all levels, including those at the top, must proactively and diligently engage in deep dialogue that asks "where is the friction and discord?", "what are the problems, and what are the solutions?" It is no good to try reaching easy compromises against friction and discord including relationships with external partners either. This will nip new business growth in the bud. Former Panasonic Chairman Kunio Nakamura said that fear of friction in a company is not conducive to transformation.

To turn friction and discord into growth drivers for a corporation, practitioners must acquire common and mutual perspectives by establishing common interests (e.g., advantages common to their organizations) among themselves (Kodama, 2007c), motivating partners and building win–win relationships with all stakeholders, sharing strategic objectives and clarifying specific action plans, etc. In the internal context of a company, clarification of decision-making processes and rules regarding important questions such as what are the priorities now and in the future? what must be done now? what are the hurdles to R&D and commercialization? and what investments need to be made for the future? are important and must be disclosed fairly to all members of staff. If these issues are not addressed, trust and unity will not arise through creative dialogue and creative learning among practitioners.

The formation of SC enables practitioners to establish mutual trust among themselves by finding common ground (Bechky, 2003) such as common interests, and transforming mutual friction and conflict into creative abrasion (Leonard-Barton, 1995) and productive friction (Hagel and Brown, 2005), and promoting communications and collaboration on the boundaries of the dissimilar knowledge between practitioners. It is important to see confrontation as a source of creative encouragement, rather than something that invites confusion and is thus to be avoided (Kanter, 1983). These behaviors are a factor in accelerating the creation of boundaries knowledge through boundaries vision.

As shown in Figure 9.6, increasing diversity of contexts and knowledge raises the level of knowledge differences and boundaries knowledge. In contrast, as uncertainty and novelty increase, creative dialogue and creative learning to form common ground raises boundaries vision, practitioners' knowledge capability for dissimilar contexts and knowledge, and at the same time promotes collaboration between different departments and different areas of specialization to create boundaries knowledge. Promoting creative dialogue and creative learning expands practitioners' dynamic range for the changing of knowledge boundaries back and forth between formal organizations and SC (called the "dynamic range of knowledge boundaries"). Thus, practitioners maximize the functioning of their boundaries vision and expand the dynamic range of their thinking and actions to create boundaries knowledge between dissimilar knowledge. As well as that, practitioners' dynamic range of knowledge boundaries simultaneously raises their capabilities to recognize similar knowledge by sharing knowledge in formal organizations that execute daily business – their business territories (see Figure 9.6).

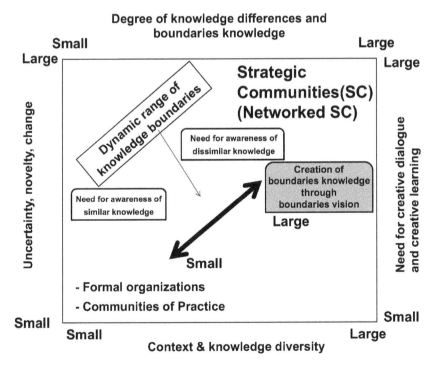

Figure 9.6   *Knowledge boundaries and organizational systems*

For boundaries innovation to succeed through the creation of boundaries knowledge through boundaries vision, new organizational structures that can bring about congruence with strategy and new knowledge convergence (knowledge creation) are critical. One factor is the creation of new organizational culture that does not exist in existing traditional organizations. This means creating SC consisting of practitioners with backgrounds in dissimilar specializations or a variety of different capabilities (projects, cross-functional teams, small-scale independent organizations, venture teams within companies, etc.). It is also important to bring in personnel with different ideas from both within and outside of companies. These teams and organizations formed from members with dissimilar backgrounds or specializations invigorate existing traditional organizations, and stimulate and inspire many practitioners as they work towards strategic objectives to achieve breakthroughs, transformation, creativity and boundaries innovation (and of course it involves conflict and friction).

The creation of boundaries knowledge through boundaries vision occurs on the multilayered networks of SC (and networked SC) originating in ba in which practitioners from dissimilar cultures and areas of specialization interact. At the intersections of new ideas born in SC (Johansson, 2004), practitioners must have the courage to overcome and transcend the knowledge boundaries between themselves to discover boundaries knowledge. Thus, the formation of SC further tempers and strengthens the boundaries vision of practitioners. The key to this is creative learning and the creation and maintenance of organizational environments that promote close-knit collaboration through creative dialogue between SC and existing organizations, and the continued support from top management.

7.   CONCLUSION

In the knowledge economy, diverse human knowledge is important for bringing about valuable products, services and business models to give a company new competitiveness. This chapter has described how the creation of boundaries knowledge through boundaries vision through the formation of the organizational platforms of strategic communities (SC) and networked SC drives corporate (organizational) dynamic capabilities and the SECI process.

Boundaries knowledge (knowing) drives the transcendence of various boundaries by merging diverse technologies and different industries, brings about new products, services and business models that contain new meaning, and forms value chains as new strategic models. To achieve boundaries innovation, corporations (organizations and industries) need to expand the dynamic range of knowledge boundaries, and bring about boundaries knowledge through boundaries vision. To do so, this chapter has identified the fact that management and industrial policy that transcend the boundaries between the knowledge of people, groups, organizations, corporations and industries must be re-recognized.

REFERENCES

Amasaka, K. (2004). 'Applying new JIT: A management technology strategy model at Toyota: Strategic QCD studies with affiliated and non-affiliated suppliers', *Proceedings of the Production and Operations Management Society*, Cancun, Mexico, 1–11.
Bechky, B. A. (2003). 'Sharing meaning across occupational communities: The transformation of understanding on a production floor', *Organization Science*, 14(3), 312–330.

Brown, J. S., & Duguid, P. (2001). 'Knowledge and organization: A social-practice perspective', *Organization Science*, 12(2), 198–213.

Carlile, P. (2002). 'A pragmatic view of knowledge and boundaries: Boundary objects in new product development', *Organization Science*, 13(4), 442–455.

Carlile, P. (2004). 'Transferring, translating, and transforming: An integrative framework for managing knowledge across boundaries', *Organization Science*, 15(5), 555–568.

Carlile, P. R., & Rebentisch, E. S. (2003). 'Into the black box: The knowledge transformation cycle', *Management Science*, 49(9), 1180–1195.

Christensen, C. M. (1997). *The Innovator's Dilemma: When New Technologies Cause Great Firms to Fail*, Boston, MA: Harvard Business School Press.

Donnellon, A., Gray, B., & Bougon, M. G. (1986). 'Communication, meaning, and organized action', *Administrative Science Quarterly*, 31(1), 43–55.

Dougherty, D. (1992). 'Interpretive barriers to successful product innovation in large firms', *Organization Science*, 3(2), 179–202.

Galbraith, J. (1973). *Designing Complex Organizations*, Reading, MA: Addison-Wesley.

Grinyer, P., & McKiernan, P. (1994). 'Triggering major and sustained changes in stagnating companies', in Daems, H. & Thomas, H. (eds), *Strategic Groups, Strategic Moves and Performance* (pp. 173-195), New York: Pergamon.

Hagel III, J. and Brown, J. S. (2005). 'Productive friction', *Harvard Business Review*, 83(2), 139–145.

Hargadon, A., & Sutton, R. I. (1997). 'Technology brokering and innovation in a product development firm', *Administrative Science Quarterly*, 42, 716–749.

Jantsch, E. (1980). *The Self-Organizing Universe*, Oxford, UK: Pergamon Press.

Johansson, F. (2004). *The Medici Effect*, Boston, MA: Harvard Business School Press.

Kanter, R.M. (1983). *The Change Masters*, New York: Simon & Schuster.

Kodama, M. (2001). 'Creating new business through strategic community management: Case study of a multimedia business', *International Journal of Human Resource Management*, 12(6), 1062–1084.

Kodama, M. (2005). 'Knowledge creation through networked strategic communities: Case studies on new product development in Japanese companies', *Long Range Planning*, 38(1), 27–49.

Kodama, M. (2007a). *The Strategic Community-Based Firm*, Basingstoke, UK: Palgrave Macmillan.

Kodama, M. (2007b). *Knowledge Innovation: Strategic Management as Practice*, Cheltenham, UK and Northampton, MA, USA: Edward Elgar Publishing.

Kodama, M. (2007c). *Project-Based Organization in the Knowledge-Based Society*, London, UK: Imperial College Press.

Kodama, M. (2007d). 'Innovation through boundary management: A case study in reforms at Matsushita electric', *Technovation*, 27(1), 15–29.

Kodama, M. (2007e). 'Innovation and knowledge creation through leadership-based strategic community: Case study on high-tech company in Japan', *Technovation*, 27(3), 115–132.

Kodama, M. (2009). 'Boundaries innovation and knowledge integration in the Japanese firm', *Long Range Planning*, 42(4), 463–494.

Kodama, M. (2014). *Winning Through Boundaries Innovation: Communities of Boundaries Generate Convergence*, Oxford, UK: Peter Lang.

Kodama, M. (2018a). *Sustainable Growth Through Strategic Innovation: Driving Congruence in Capabilities*, Cheltenham, UK and Northampton, MA, USA: Edward Elgar Publishing.

Kodama, M. (Ed.) (2018b). *Collaborative Dynamic Capabilities for Service Innovation*, Basingstoke, Palgrave Macmillan.

Lawrence, P., and Lorsch, J. (1967), *Organization and Environments: Managing Differentiation and Integration*, Cambridge, MA: Harvard Business School Press.

Le Dain, M. A., & Merminod, V. (2014). 'A knowledge sharing framework for black, grey and white box supplier configurations in new product development', *Technovation*, 34(11), 688–701.

Leonard-Barton, D. (1992). 'Core capabilities and core rigidities: A paradox in managing new product development', *Strategic Management Journal*, 13(2), 111–125.

Leonard-Barton, D. (1995). *Wellsprings of Knowledge: Building and Sustaining the Source of Innovation*, Cambridge, MA: Harvard Business School Press.

Malone, T., and Crowston, K. (1994). 'The interdisciplinary study of coordination', *ACM Computer Surveys*, 26, March, 87–119.

March, J. G. (1972). 'Model bias in social action', *Review of Educational Research*, 42(4), 413–429.

Nonaka, I., Hirose, A., & Takeda, Y. (2016). '"Meso"-foundations of dynamic capabilities: Team-level synthesis and distributed leadership as the source of dynamic creativity', *Global Strategy Journal*, 6(3), 168–182.

Pfeffer, J., and Salancik, G. (1978). *The External Control of Organizations: A Resource-dependence Perspective*, New York: Harper & Row.

Shannon, C. E., & Weaver, W. (1949). *The Mathematical Theory of Information*, Urbana, IL: University of Illinois Press.

Spender, J. C. (1996). 'Making knowledge the basis of a dynamic theory of the firm', *Strategic Management Journal*, 17(S2), 45–62.

van Offenbeek, M. A., & Vos, J. F. (2016). 'An integrative framework for managing project issues across stakeholder groups', *International Journal of Project Management*, 34(1), 44–57.

Wenger, E. C., & Snyder, W. M. (2000). 'Communities of practice: The organizational frontier', *Harvard Business Review*, 78(1), 139–146.

10. Implications and conclusion

Mitsuru Kodama

1. KNOWLEDGE CONVERGENCE

The core leading technologies in the cutting-edge technology fields of ICT, energy, automobiles, electronics, semiconductors, biotechnology, pharmaceuticals and materials science, etc. have become dispersed among companies and organizations across the globe. Boundaries innovation across the boundaries between these dissimilar core technologies is a source from which new products and services originate (Kodama, 2011, 2014).

One of the strategic objectives of high-tech companies in the past was to advance and develop products by sustaining innovation with individual technologies. However, not only are there demands for products with high functionality and performance in recent years, but also demands for low-cost products, wide-ranging product lineups, and drastically shortened product development life cycles. In addition to that, new user needs have emerged through new product value creation caused by the diversification of customer needs and changes in value systems typical of disruptive technology (Christensen, 1997).

Looking at markets around the world, global companies are facing the pressing challenges of new marketing and creative product strategies due to the maturing of their domestic markets and emerging markets in developing countries. Thus, as new product development policy to bring about differentiation from other companies, global high-tech corporations face an increasing need to develop new products and services based on new technologies brought about through the convergence of dissimilar technologies and services. This is because there are now many never-before-seen cases of new and imaginative product and service developments achieved through the merging of technologies from one field with those of another. Thus, the business strategies required to deal with convergence – products and service developments by merging and integrating dissimilar technologies and services, or across differing industries, and the configuring of those business models – have become of particular importance.

The advance of ICT has also shrunk space–time in business processes and supply chains across all kinds of industries, raised business efficiency, raised the speed at which decisions can be made, and brought about new business models through the merging and spanning of dissimilar industries. The achievement of a variety of e-businesses and the emergence of new content industries are not only due to the technological aspects of ICT development, but are also the result of boundaries innovation creating new markets through convergence of the knowledge of the variety of players involved. These product and service innovations have driven co-creation and co-evolution across the entire ICT industry, and have formed dynamic "business ecosystems" as new value chains. Internet businesses using smartphones, social networking services and social games, etc. have their origins in the dynamic structures of business ecosystems through co-creation and co-evolution (e.g., Kodama, 2009a, b).

Knowledge convergence of dissimilar technologies and industries is advancing at a rapid pace in a wide range of high-tech areas such as smartphones, smart houses, smart cities, smart agriculture, the smart grid, solar power generation, vehicle computerization, eco-vehicle developments and semiconductors. The rapid advance of ICT coupled with diversification and technical advances are complicating the business models that companies should provide. The environments that modern companies find themselves in, with such rapid technological innovations, shortening product lifestyles, mature markets in developed countries, expanding markets in developing countries, the search for new business models with the progress of ICT and so forth, mean that companies must struggle to develop new technologies and services and configure new business models. This means they must pursue boundaries innovation to provide customers with new value by driving convergence of dissimilar technologies and services and driving the creation of ICT businesses across dissimilar industries. Thus, not only is the necessity to fuse and integrate dissimilar specialist knowledge within themselves a challenge facing companies, they also face the challenge of converging dissimilar knowledge that spans between themselves and other companies.

Boundaries knowledge between dissimilar knowledge must be created for corporate activity to adapt to (or create) the knowledge convergence world view, which means corporations must build new "relationship platforms". The corporate and organizational platforms that support knowledge convergence through the building of these relationship platforms are the formation of ma (discussed later), and strategic communities (SC) that originate in the ba that have been discussed so far (see Figure 10.1).

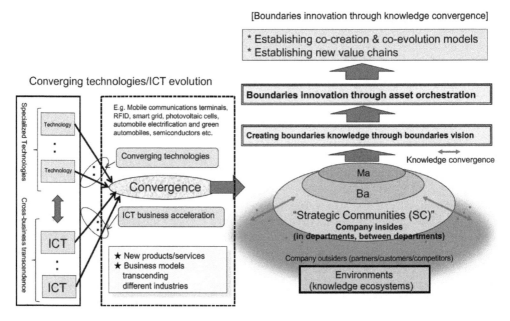

Figure 10.1   Boundaries knowledge through ma, ba and SC formation

In a corporation, to promote knowledge convergence, the most important issue is to build global knowledge networks (or asset networks) with leading partner companies around the world, uncover the boundaries knowledge that exists between knowledge within a company and leading knowledge dispersed around the world through the use of boundaries vision, and converge dissimilar knowledge. Responding to this challenge entails building relationship platforms with the ma, ba and SC elements to speed up the asset orchestration process in and out of companies for boundaries innovation (see Figure 10.1).

Forming high-quality ma, ba and SC that span within and between companies promotes the creation of boundaries knowledge through boundaries vision. Building the relationship platforms of ma, ba and SC leads to the proactive searching out of the best knowledge around the world and the creation of boundaries knowledge between the core knowledge inside and outside of companies, and at the same time integrate (or converge) this dissimilar knowledge with the core knowledge of one's own company.

2. POWER OF HARMONY AND KNOWLEDGE CONVERGENCE

To converge knowledge, "the power of harmony" is required. As discussed in Chapter 4, regarding the development of the mobile phone with built-in camera, former Sharp chairman Machida had the following to say about his company's realization of a number of hit products through technological innovation with the creation of unique technologies and black boxing.

I believe Sharp is a company that runs on the "power of harmony." This is something that is very important to us. "Harmony" suggests technological convergence. By successfully fusing different devices, we created mobile phones with cameras and "sha-mail" (e-mail with photographs). Nokia and Motorola only had communications technology. We combined communications, video, word processor technologies, and the information processing technology of "Zaurus". The camera phone and sha-mail were created by mixing these things up. I think new products are born by a similar principle to that of causing a chemical reaction to create crystals.

How do you make such a "chemical reaction" happen? The special power of harmony that Japanese people have is important. For example, if someone that has been in charge of advanced semiconductor technology was assigned to supervise a consumer appliance, he or she would ordinarily quit. However, at Sharp, we believe that it's possible to find harmony through introducing unfamiliar things. That's because we have set up conditions that make it easy to cause "chemicals to react" and create "crystals." To enable these "chemical reactions", I don't use the ordinary company system. The old-fashioned company system does not enable convergence. As technology deepens, there are limitations to how much a single engineer can think about it. In this era, ideas about assembling combinations to make different products are becoming increasingly important.

Machida also had the following to say regarding his "chemical reaction" analogy.

It is important that engineers expand the scope of a technology as they deepen their understanding of it. Into the future, bringing about new products through the convergence of different technological functions will become increasingly necessary. This is analogous to a chemical reaction, for example reacting hydrogen with oxygen to produce water. It's important to fuse dissimilar technical functions to bring about products with characteristics that are completely different to their sources. If you think you want to pioneer new demand, you need to create new products converged from completely different technologies.

The mobile phone with built-in camera, AQUOS mobile phone, large-screen LCD television and so forth are creative products that have been brought about through Sharp's processes of inducing "chemical reactions". Sharp is a company that has a well-established corporate culture of dynamically forming SC to bring about boundaries knowledge through boundaries vision for practicing its "chemical reaction" processes.

To instigate the asset orchestration process in a company, the active "chemical reactions" by the creation of boundaries knowledge through boundaries vision, what sort of mechanisms are required? What should top and middle management do? One solution is to build a "culture of harmony" within the company, which can be described as Machida's "power of harmony" discussed earlier. Staff come together in pursuit of unique technology, maintain their culturally important idea of harmony and pool together each others' wisdom to work as a team. This management style is the basis of the creation of boundaries knowledge through boundaries vision.

For example, the source of "harmony" at Sharp is the company's commitment to its management creed of "sincerity and creativity". At Sharp, sincerity and creativity means the following:

> Sincerity is a virtue fundamental to humanity, always be sincere. Harmony brings strength … trust each other and work together. Politeness is a merit … always be courteous and respectful. Creativity promotes progress … remain constantly aware of the need to innovate and improve. Courage is the basis of a rewarding life … accept every challenge with a positive attitude.

As DNA-level values, sincerity and creativity are infused into every member of staff, promote empathy and resonance of values, and trigger the "chemical reactions" through teamwork between different organizations within the company, which enables Sharp to bring about its one-of-a-kind technologies, products and businesses.

In the next section, the author would like to look at managerial factors that bring about a "culture of harmony" to generate the "power of harmony".

3.   CULTURE OF HARMONY TO INSTIGATE "CHEMICAL REACTIONS" WITH KNOWLEDGE

The tendency for existing business to become overreliant on customs accumulated over long years and experiential knowledge, and the accompanying inability to deal with changes in circumstances (markets and technologies) has been variously clarified in a wide range of existing research as "competency traps" (e.g., Levitt and March, 1988; Martines and Kambil, 1999), "core rigidities" (Leonard-Barton, 1992, 1995), and as the "innovator's dilemma". It is impossible to predict whether a company can maintain its competitiveness over the long term, even if it is currently making a profit.

Therefore, top and middle management in companies must have an awareness of a dynamic view of strategy (e.g., Chakravarthy, 1997; Markides, 1997, 1999; Eisenhardt and Sull, 2001) to acquire the new strategic positioning needed to create the businesses of the future, without ever becoming overly contented with their current core businesses. Companies have to simultaneously execute radical innovation to create new and highly uncertain businesses (environment creation strategies) and incremental innovation to reinforce core businesses to expand markets (environment adaptive strategies). In particular, companies aiming for radical innovation to bring about breakthroughs in existing business need to inject new and dissimilar knowledge from both inside and outside of the company into existing knowledge to make such "knowledge chemical reactions" happen. Large-scale knowledge chemical reactions both in and out of companies enable the creation of new business models that span different industries. This means it is necessary to demonstrate boundaries vision to uncover the boundaries knowledge that exists between dissimilar kinds of knowledge.

Crucial for the "knowledge chemical reactions" process in companies is top management's allowance of climates that encourage and drive conflict and friction between dissimilar SC and existing organizations at all management levels. Frank and thorough dialogue and discussions between businesspeople are an integral part of productive and constructive problem solving. However, as a precaution against conflict becoming hostile, the context of discussions between businesspersons should be thoroughly understood by top management and upper level administration. For this reason, the creation of a culture of harmony within organizations is crucial.

Nevertheless, in creating and executing specific measures with radical innovation, large companies in particular will face a number of problems. These kinds of problems include such issues as "it's hard to get understanding and cooperation in the company to make specific new business plans and execute them", or "there are thick partitions between our company organizations that prevent good communications" or "various business divisions are all battling (or cannibalizing) for new business proposals, and competitive relationships have sprung up inside the company". The root causes of these problems – organizational barriers – are actually problems of mental barriers between businesspeople. The knowledge boundaries that result from these mental barriers are the things that form the unique thought worlds and mental models of businesspeople in different fields of specialization and different job functions. Businesspeople come to be dominated by certain fixed values that are closed off by these various individual boundaries, and they form organizational cultures with the practice of routines in their daily business as systems and structures.

If these mental barriers are not eliminated, it is impossible to form a culture of harmony. As long as mental barriers between businesspeople are not swept away when mixing divisions or forming new organizations, those active business "chemical reactions" will not occur in a company. It is important that approaches to innovation activities through the formation of SC and network SC will form such "creative reaction" mechanisms inside and outside of the company.

Thus, to make these "chemical reactions" occur, what kind of mechanisms are required in a company? What should top and middle management do? One practical method is to build new SC originating in ba from dissimilar human resources in the company and promote deep sharing of company visions and organizational culture. Companies also have to stir up traditional organizational culture from time to time (e.g., Kodama, 2003). Companies aiming for radical innovation to bring about breakthroughs in existing business need to inject new and dissimilar knowledge from both inside and outside of the company into existing knowledge to create boundaries knowledge through boundaries vision and make such "knowledge chemical reactions" happen. Large-scale knowledge chemical reactions both in and out of major companies significantly raise the level of the evolution of technical innovation within companies, and enable the creation of new business models that span different industries.

For example, as shown in the cases of "culture of harmony" through value-based management in Sharp and Nintendo in Chapter 4, values-based management rooted in values such as the thoughts of top management, business philosophies, corporate visions and mission are deeply infused throughout those companies to form a unique organizational culture. Sharp's and Nintendo's unique corporate cultures, infused into top management through to management leaders in all layers and staff working on the extremities of the companies, have brought about the power of harmony and a culture of harmony, which are factors in the formation of SC as organizational platforms for sustainably realizing technical innovation.

The power and culture of harmony at Sharp and Nintendo form SC across and between diverse organizations and people to create new boundaries knowledge on the boundaries between dissimilar knowledge, which brings about convergence knowledge as "chemical reactions". In other words, creating the power of harmony and cultures of harmony in organizations are important factors in bringing about boundaries innovation. The following section looks at the factors for bringing about such power and cultures of harmony.

4. "PSYCHOLOGICAL MA" FOR BRINGING ABOUT THE POWER AND CULTURE OF HARMONY

Japan is a country that has a culture of "ma", and the Japanese people have a unique type of ma culture. Ma can be found in the exquisite sensitivities, imagery, colors and meanings, etc. that are expressed in traditional Japanese culture and arts. In no small measure has such unique and refined ma influenced the sensibilities of the Japanese people and brought about the special aspects of their culture and crafts.

Many Japanese cultural anthropologists and researchers have publicized research and discussions about ma. For example, they highlight the differences in the way the physical spaces are arranged in rooms by comparing Japanese and Western dwellings. Rooms in Western houses are separated by walls and completely compartmentalized. In contrast, rooms in Japanese houses are separated by Japanese-style sliding doors or paper-covered shoji screens which allow a spatial ma to exist. Thus, the boundaries between rooms are somewhat ambiguous. Examples of ma can be found in traditional Japanese buildings, such as "madori" (the traditional floorplan), "cha no ma" (Japanese-style living room), "toko no ma" (Japanese-style alcove), "kyaku no ma" (a space for receiving guests) and "suki-ma" (gap). Traditional Japanese dwellings do not have many walls. Instead, walls are delineated by sliding fusuma doors or paper shoji screens. These can be removed to create a wide-open and well-ventilated space if required.

Japanese people also give importance to ma in music and dance. Here, ma refers to the sensation of space–time, and is in contrast to the unceasing sound of Western symphonies, concertos or quartets – the sound of orchestral performances can be particularly boisterous. In contrast, there is ma in Japanese music. Generally Japanese musical instruments do not make a continuous sound like the drawing of a bow across strings. Instead, the sounds from Japanese taiko drums, hand drums, koto and shamisen come from striking or plucking, giving them ma. The same is true for dance – there is an obvious difference in ma when comparing Western ballet and Japanese dance.

And, the same can also be said about works of art. The canvases in Western art are often thickly covered with colors, a fact visible in the mosaics of the Middle Ages, the paintings of the Renaissance and in the 19th-century impressionist works. In Western art work, blank usually means incomplete, whereas in Japanese artwork empty space plays an important role. Perhaps it could be said that Western paintings can feel hot and somewhat crowded (of course this depends on the subjectivity of the individual), whereas Japanese art (if limited to pre-modern works) has a certain coolness.

Meanwhile, there is also research into ma mainly in architecture and the arts in countries other than Japan. According to Giedion (1967), the influence of the discovery of the three-point perspective in the renaissance, the period in which science began, led to the development of models combining space and time in European arts and architecture. In architecture also, Giedion emphasized the critical role of ma as media for expression using spatial perception, and in particular linking the passing of time with space. After Giedion, a range of research into Japanese culture and ma clearly defined the spatial concepts of ma used in architecture, which led to a variety of other research (e.g., Nitschke, 1988; Kwinter, 2008; Isozaki and Oshima, 2009; Kodama, 2017).

French geographer Augustin Berque's *Vivre l'espace au Japon* (1982) is a discussion on Japanese culture that presents both the uniqueness found in Japanese customs and language and their differences with Judaeo-Christian culture. Berque's writings offer a uniform view in which he multilaterally verifies the existence and organic spatial aspects of Japanese cultural-specific ma such as the way the Japanese language is structured, the mindset of the Japanese, organizational principles behind Japanese families and corporations and so forth, the layout of cities and usage of land.

Inspired by Junichiro Tanizaki's "In Praise of Shadows" the Japanese haiku poet Hasegawa (2009) developed unique Japanese cultural theories that focus on the characteristics of ma and the "coexistence of dissimilars" in Japanese culture. Hasegawa offers a fascinating hypothesis that the source of new creativity by harmonizing dissimilars and allowing them to coexist is "the power of harmony" discussed in the previous section, and the existence of ma is the foundation on which this "harmony" is born. According to Hasegawa, Japan has created its own unique culture by absorbing many aspects of international culture and allowed them to coexist with highly refined ma.

Although research focusing on the concept of ma has developed ideas about culture, architecture, arts and linguistics, there has been almost no research into its relevance to research on human beings and organizations engaging in economic and social activities on a daily basis, or on the field of economics. Just as Hasegawa (2009) identified ma as an enabler of the "coexistence of dissimilars", this book identifies the formation of ma as a crucial element in bringing about boundaries knowledge through boundaries vision as a base for convergence of dissimilar knowledge in organizations and corporations.

Based on the concept of ma, case studies on Apple, a company that succeeds with product development, and Shuji Nakamura (Professor, University of California, Santa Barbara), who won the Nobel Prize in Physics for invention and practical application of blue light emitting diodes, have been reported (Kodama, 2018b). In addition, Dr. Akira Yoshino from Asahi Kasei in Japan, who won the Nobel Prize in Chemistry for the invention and commercialization of lithium-ion batteries in 2019, discovered a new carbon fiber that is an organic material with a special crystalline structure through much trial and error with various materials. By experimenting using carbon fiber as a negative electrode instead of polyacetylene, he successfully obtained compatibility with lithium cobalt oxide, which is an inorganic material used as the positive electrode. This became the lithium-ion battery of today. The combination of inorganic and organic materials with different characteristics (different areas of expertise) made Dr. Yoshino aware of new boundaries knowledge as a "psychological ma".

The existence of psychological ma that binds together dissimilar specialized knowledge has major effects on the activities of companies and organizations. For example, Dyson is a company that places importance on thinking about design and engineering simultaneously – the company's designers participate in testing, and its engineers similarly participate in creating concepts. Dyson does not have the traditional barriers (in other words boundaries) between the specialized knowledge of designing the external appearance of a product and engineering the structural design of products, as often seen in other companies. Everyone in a particular department can work on any kind of issue. In this way, all employees are able to understand what they and others are doing, and by finding boundaries knowledge between dissimilar areas of specialization, their freedom increases for new creativity and imagination. This is the freedom of creativity which make Dyson's product development processes particularly innovative.

Founder and former CEO James Dyson put considerable importance on raising the conceptual and creative capabilities of all his staff. It is certainly true that many of the ideas originate in the department responsible for Research Design & Development (RDD),[1] but it might not always be like that. For example, Dyson is the only company that had the idea of making products with the customer service telephone number on the handle, which was suggested by staff in the company's service desk department. In this way, Dyson improves products using ideas from people in other departments, which also raises the thinking and imaginative capabilities of the company staff, which is a factor that drives new asset orchestration processes at the company. In this way, Dyson incorporates psychological ma for binding together dissimilar areas of knowledge into the consciousness of staff and embed them into the company's organizational culture.

5.   THE RELATIONSHIP PLATFORMS (MA, BA AND SC) AS MACRO AND MICRO LINKAGES, AND BOUNDARIES KNOWLEDGE

Knowledge platforms to achieve the boundaries knowledge creation required for knowledge convergence are the aforementioned relationship platforms of ma, ba and SC, whose construction is enabled by the boundaries vision demonstrated by leading practitioners.

The relationship platforms of ma, ba and SC dynamically bring about new contexts for practitioners (relationships between people in time and space), enable these contexts to be shared, and bring about new boundaries knowledge. These relationship platforms enable practitioners to coexist with external environments including others, and to share contexts with others through the synergies therein. By changing these contexts, they become generative and transformational space–time. Rather than just places for sharing tacit knowledge, these relationship platforms are the space–time for engaging in creative dialogue and the practical processes of strategy.

Organizations and individuals are in dialectical relationships. Thus, practitioners create relationship platforms as the space–time of the here and now, and transform organizations by recursively relating dynamic practical awareness through their human capabilities and broad perspectives with organizations. As discussed in the case studies in this book, practitioners have the practical power to transform organizations and environments with their own behaviors, while accepting the limitations of the organizations and environments that they themselves have brought about (Giddens, 1984; Giddens and Pierson, 1998). Sharp, Nintendo, Apple and Fujifilm (Kodama, 2018a) are good examples of companies that have succeeded at product development or achieved strategy transformation.

In short, relationship platforms are space–time where leading practitioners consolidate their boundaries vision and uncover boundaries knowledge to practice strategic activities both inside and outside their own companies. These relationship platforms bridge practitioners and organizations (and companies and industries). Practitioners use these relationship platforms to share the contexts that are unceasingly and dynamically created in daily events and episodes on the relationship platforms. Thus, through official and unofficial practical processes, practitioners achieve boundaries innovation as convergence through the creation of boundaries and convergence knowledge. Moreover, through the configuration and reconfiguration of these relationship platforms, the strategic activities of practitioners at the micro level affect the macroscopic structures of organizations, companies, industries and society as a whole.

These relationship platforms do not just play an important role in the micro–macro linkages in the structure of social networks. As practitioners create and reconfigure these relationship platforms between themselves, organizations, companies, industries, countries and the whole world, they influence the performance of companies and knowledge ecosystems through the generation and accumulation of social capital (e.g., Cohen and Prusak, 2000). Conversely, from the perspective of how practitioners themselves are influenced, relationship platforms are an important analytical unit.

Additionally, from the point of view of knowledge management, social capital that has value as knowledge capital and knowledge ecosystems come about mainly on these relationship platforms. Furthermore, by clarifying the asset orchestration process from the micro perspective, the process of generating wide-ranging boundaries knowledge through these relationship platforms opens up a new proposition. These processes are generated and amplified by practitioners as they work subjectively to influence other people in environments (knowledge ecosystems) or inside and outside of organizations and companies.

Thus, in future, a theory of the architecture (design thinking) of these relationship platforms will become increasingly important, due to their deep involvement with new business models brought about through knowledge convergence as boundaries innovation. For practitioners also, the concept of the architecture thinking of these relationship platforms is also of practical significance from the perspective on how to bring about new knowledge through the creation and reconfiguration of these relationship platforms. Thus, in this business society of ever-increasing complexity, the author anticipates even deeper quests to clarify both the theoretical and practical perspectives on these relationship platforms.

6.   CONCLUSION

Forming high-quality ma, ba and SC that spans within and between companies promotes the creation of boundaries knowledge through boundaries vision. Building the relationship platforms of ma, ba and SC leads to the proactive searching out of the best knowledge around the world and the creation of boundaries knowledge between the core knowledge inside and outside of companies, and at the same time integrates (or converges) this dissimilar knowledge with the core knowledge of one's own company. Thus, in future, theorization of the architecture (design thinking) of these relationship platforms and a practical framework of these will become increasingly important, due to their deep relationship with the new business models brought about through knowledge convergence as boundaries innovation.

NOTE

1. Research Design & Development (RDD), located at Dyson's UK headquarters, is divided into departments by process. The department that produces ideas that could become new products is called New Product Innovation (NPI). When there is a possibility of a new product, the item so judged by the person responsible moves to New Product Development (NPD). Finally, when it is decided to create the product, RDD in Malaysia takes over. Teams start out with two to three people, but as the project increases in size, the number of staff also increase. RDD is a department usually called R&D, but at Dyson this department combines design work with development, hence its name.

REFERENCES

Berque, A. (1982). *Vivre l'espace au Japon*. Paris, France: Presses Universitaires de France.
Chakravarthy, B. (1997). 'A new strategy framework for coping with turbulence', *Sloan Management Review*, 38(2), 69–82.
Christensen, C.M. (1997). *The Innovator's Dilemma: When New Technologies Cause Great Firms to Fail*. Boston, MA: Harvard Business School Press.
Cohen, D. and Prusak, L. (2000). *In Good Company: How Social Capital Makes Organizations Work*. Boston, MA: Harvard Business School Press.
Eisenhardt, K.M. and Sull, D.N. (2001). 'Strategy as simple rules', *Harvard Business Review*, 79, 106–116.
Giddens, A. (1984). *The Constitution of Society. Outline of the Theory of Structuration*. Cambridge: Polity Press.
Giddens, A. and Pierson, C. (1998). *Conversation with Anthony Giddens: Making Sense of Modernity*. Oxford: Blackwell Publishers Ltd.
Giedion, S. (1967). *Space Time and Architecture: The Growth of a New Tradition*. Boston, MA: Harvard University Press.
Hasegawa, K. (2009). *Thoughts of Wa* (in Japanese). Tokyo, Japan: Tyuo Kouron Publishing.
Isozaki, A. and Oshima, T. (2009). *Arata Isozaki*. London, UK: Phaidon Press.
Kodama, M. (2003). 'Strategic innovation in traditional big business: Case studies of two Japanese companies', *Organization Studies*, 24(2), 235–268.
Kodama, M. (2009a). 'Boundaries innovation and knowledge integration in the Japanese firm', *Long Range Planning*, 42(4), 463–494.
Kodama, M. (2009b). *Innovation Networks in Knowledge-Based Firms: Developing ICT-Based Integrative Competences*. Cheltenham, UK and Northampton, MA, USA: Edward Elgar Publishing.
Kodama, M. (2011). *Knowledge Integration Dynamics: Developing Strategic Innovation Capability*. Singapore: World Scientific Publishing.
Kodama, M. (2014). *Winning Through Boundaries Innovation: Communities of Boundaries Generate Convergence*. Oxford, UK: Peter Lang.
Kodama, M. (2017). *Developing Holistic Leadership: A Source of Business Innovation*. Bingley, UK: Emerald.
Kodama, M. (2018a). *Sustainable Growth Through Strategic Innovation: Driving Congruence in Capabilities*. Cheltenham, UK and Northampton, MA, USA: Edward Elgar Publishing.
Kodama, M. (2018b). 'Managing innovation through ma thinking', *Systems Research and Behavioral Science*, 35(2), 155–177.
Kwinter, S. (2008). *Far from Equilibrium: Essays on Technology and Design Culture*. New York, Barcelona: Actar.

Leonard-Barton, D. (1992). 'Core capabilities and core rigidities: A paradox in managing new product development', *Strategic Management Journal*, 13(1), 111–125.

Leonard-Barton, D. (1995). *Wellsprings of Knowledge: Building and Sustaining the Sources of Innovation*. Boston, MA: Harvard Business School Press.

Levitt, B. and March, J.B. (1988). 'Organization learning', in Scott, W.R. and Blake, J. (eds), *Annual Review of Sociology*, Annual Reviews, 14, 319–340.

Markides, C. (1997). 'Strategic innovation', *Sloan Management Review*, 38(2), 9–23.

Markides, C. (1999). *All the Right Moves: A Guide to Crafting Breakthrough Strategy*. Boston, MA: Harvard Business School Publishing.

Martines, L. and Kambil, A. (1999). 'Looking back and thinking ahead: Effects of prior success on managers' interpretations of new information technologies', *Academy of Management Journal*, 42, 652–661.

Nitschke, G. (1988). *From Shinto to Ando. Essay: Ma: Place, Space and Void*. London: Academy Editions.

Index